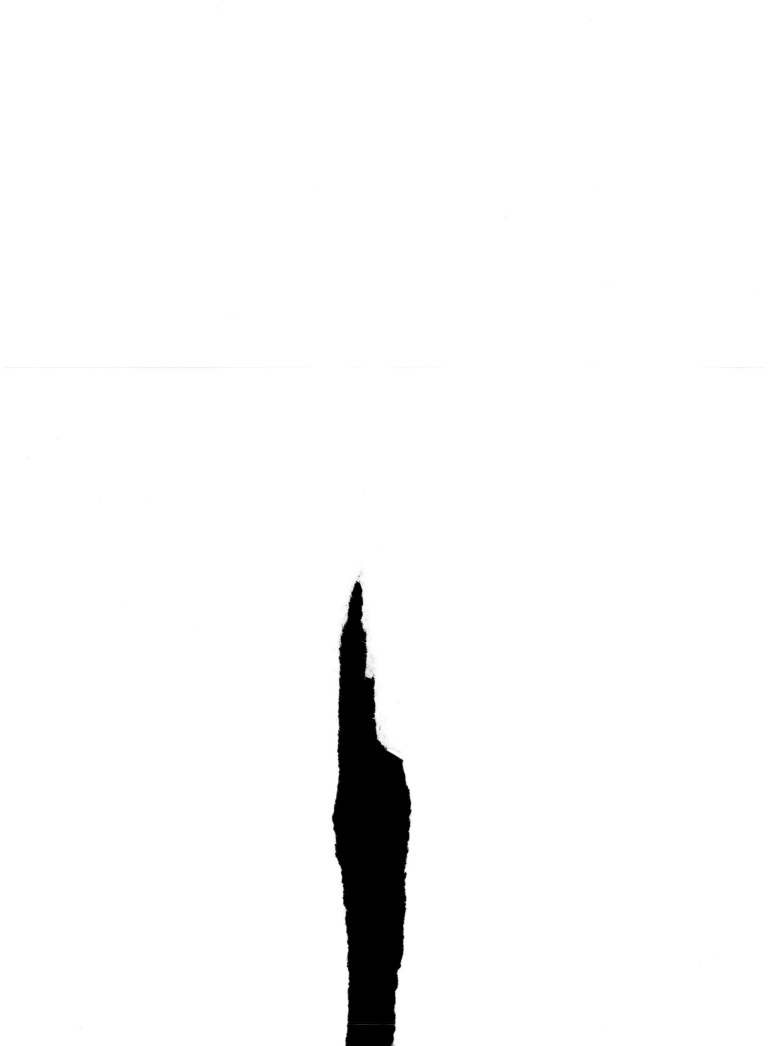

Between Continents/Between Seas:
Precolumbian Art of Costa Rica

Text by
Suzanne Abel–Vidor/ Ronald L. Bishop/ Warwick Bray/ Elizabeth Kennedy Easby
Luis Ferrero A./ Oscar Fonseca Zamora/ Héctor Gamboa Paniagua
Luis Diego Gómez Pignataro/ Mark M. Graham/ Frederick W. Lange
Michael J. Snarskis/ Lambertus van Zelst

Photographs by Dirk Bakker

Harry N. Abrams, Inc., *Publishers,* New York
in association with The Detroit Institute of Arts/1981

Library of Congress Cataloging in Publication Data
Main entry under title:

Between continents/between seas.

Bibliography: p.
1. Indians of Central America—Costa Rica—Art—
Exhibitions. 2. Indians of Central America—Costa Rica
—Antiquities—Exhibitions. 3. Costa Rica—Antiquities—
Exhibitions. I. Abel-Vidor, Suzanne. II. Bakker, Dirk.
III. Detroit Institute of Arts.
F1545.3.A7B47   709′.7286′074013   81-10862
ISBN 0-8109-0729-1 (H.N.A.)   AACR2
ISBN 0-89558-088-8 (D.I.A.)

Catalogue Coordinator: Julie Jones
Editor: Elizabeth P. Benson
Designer: Judith Michael

Photographs not taken by Dirk Bakker were provided by the following people
and institutions: Museo Nacional de Costa Rica (figs. 2, 35); Juan Vicente
Guerrero (MNCR) (figs. 3, 20); Frederick W. Lange (fig. 4); Brian D. Dillon,
UCLA Institute of Archaeology (figs. 7—9); Henry D. Wallace (fig. 10); Michael
J. Snarskis (figs. 11, 16, 18, 21, 27, 31); Maritza Gutiérrez (MNCR) (fig. 14);
C. Enrique Herra (MNCR) (figs. 15, 17, 22, 28); Ricardo Vázquez (MNCR) (figs.
23a-b); R. Drolet (fig. 32); Luis Ferrero A. (fig. 34); Ricardo Luna (figs. 37—39);
Oscar Fonseca Zamora (fig. 40); Ronald L. Bishop (figs. 43—45).

Front cover and half-title page: Anthropomorphic-effigy vessel, Guanacaste–Nicoya zone, ceramic (cat. no. 83).
Back cover and title page: Pendant, costumed figure, Palmar Sur, Diquís, gold (cat. no. 283).
Frontispiece: Two alligator–effigy beads, Atlantic Watershed zone, jade (cat. no. 158).

Printed and bound in Japan.

Contributors to the catalogue:

Suzanne Abel–Vidor/ *Brown University*

Ronald L. Bishop/ *Research Laboratory, Boston Museum of Fine Arts*

Warwick Bray/ *Institute of Archaeology, University of London*

Elizabeth Kennedy Easby/ *The University Museum, University of Pennsylvania*

Luis Ferrero A./ *Museo Nacional de Costa Rica*

Oscar Fonseca Zamora/ *Department of Anthropology, Universidad de Costa Rica*

Héctor Gamboa Paniagua/ *Museo Nacional de Costa Rica*

Luis Diego Gómez Pignataro/ *Museo Nacional de Costa Rica*

Mark M. Graham/ *Department of Art, University of California, Los Angeles*

Frederick W. Lange/ *Department of Sociology, Anthropology and Social Work, Illinois State University*

Michael J. Snarskis/ *Museo Nacional de Costa Rica*

Lambertus van Zelst/ *Research Laboratory, Boston Museum of Fine Arts*

This book is published in conjunction with a major loan exhibition of objects from the following institutions and private collections in Costa Rica:

Banco Nacional de Costa Rica
Caja Costarricense del Seguro Social
Instituto Nacional de Seguros
Museo de Oro del Banco Central de
   Costa Rica
Museo Nacional de Costa Rica
Collection Alfonso Jiménez–Alvarado
Collection Carmen de Gillen

Collection Dr. Hernán Paéz U. and
   Dr. Carlos Roberto Paéz S.
Collection Juan and Ligia Dada
Collection María Eugenia de Roy
Collection Maritza Castro de Laurencich
Collection Molinos de Costa Rica
Collection Mr. and Mrs. Harry Mannil
Collection Oduber

The exhibition was organized by The Detroit Institute of Arts and made possible through a grant from the National Endowment for the Arts, a Federal agency; and the National Foundation on the Arts and Humanities, Arts and Artifacts Indemnity Act.

Scientific Committee:

Julie Jones, *Curator, Department of Primitive Art, The Metropolitan Museum of Art*
Michael Kan, *Deputy Director and Curator, Department of African, Oceanic, and New World Cultures, The Detroit Institute of Arts*
Michael J. Snarskis, *Director of Archaeological Research, Museo Nacional de Costa Rica*

CONTENTS

FOREWORD

"Between Continents/Between Seas: Precolumbian Art of Costa Rica" is the first comprehensive exhibition of Costa Rican art to tour the United States. Consisting of approximately 300 ceramic, gold, jade, and monumental stone objects, it brings together a rich and superb assemblage of ceremonial, utilitarian, and decorative works dating from the era before the arrival of Columbus. Recent systematic archaeological exploration is now making it possible to reconstruct scientifically the sequence of cultures and styles in Costa Rica. "Between Continents/Between Seas" was conceived to provide a rich survey of our knowledge to date, as well as to offer the viewer a visual survey of that country's abundant artistic heritage.

We would like to express our gratitude to the many individuals and institutions without whose participation and assistance this exhibition could not have been realized. In particular, we wish to mention the President and First Lady of Costa Rica, Lic. Rodrigo Carazo O. and Estrella de Carazo. We are grateful to U.S. Ambassador Francis J. McNeil. We would also like to thank Manuel Naranjo, Executive President, and Rodrigo Caamano R., Banco Central de Costa Rica; Oscar Rivera and Guaria Vargas Alipzar, Banco Nacional de Costa Rica; Cristóbal Zawadzki, Executive President, and Ricardo Monge O., Instituto Nacional de Seguros, as well as Zulay Soto de Andrade, Curator, Museo del Jade; Luis Diego Gómez Pignataro, Director, and Héctor Gamboa Paniagua, Museo Nacional de Costa Rica; and Enrique Odio S., Executive President, Robert Smith, and Carlos Longan, Instituto Costarricense de Turismo. We would also like to acknowledge our gratitude to the following individuals who have generously loaned works from their collections: Juan and Ligia Dada; Carmen de Gillen; Alfonso Jiménez–Alvarado; Maritza Castro de Laurencich; Mr. and Mrs. Harry Mannil; Daniel and Marjorie Oduber; Dr. Hernán Páez U. and Dr. Carlos Roberto Páez S.; María Eugenia de Roy; and Margarita de Ruenes.

In the United States, we wish to thank Philippe de Montebello, Director, The Metropolitan Museum of Art, for his cooperation in allowing his staff to work on this exhibition. Mark Leithauser, Charles Parkhurst, Gaillard Ravenel, and Dodge Thompson, National Gallery of Art, have been enormously helpful in all aspects of organization and installation, as has Charles Froom, New York. At the Detroit Institute of Arts, the following staff members have assisted in various ways: Robert Weston, Administrator and Secretary; Boris Sellers, Manager and Director of Development; Susan Weinberg, Registrar/Assistant Administrator; Abraham

Joel and Susan West, Conservation Services Laboratory; Vada Dunifer and Joann Accuso, Department of African, Oceanic, and New World Cultures, who assisted beyond their normal duties; Susan F. Rossen, formerly of the Publications Department; Andrea P. A. Belloli, Publications Department, who coordinated the catalogue in Detroit; Rollyn Krichbaum; and, finally, Dirk Bakker, Photography Department, who produced the stunning photographs that illustrate this catalogue. In conclusion, the members of the Scientific Committee—Julie Jones, Curator of Primitive Art, The Metropolitan Museum of Art; Michael Kan, Deputy Director and Curator of African, Oceanic, and New World Cultures, The Detroit Institute of Arts; and Michael J. Snarskis, Director of Archaeological Research, Department of Anthropology and History, Museo Nacional de Costa Rica—must be recognized for the outstanding work they have done in organizing this exhibition and assembling the catalogue. We would also like to thank Elizabeth P. Benson for her extremely able editing of the complex catalogue manuscript.

Important financial aid has been received from the National Endowment for the Arts. Without this assistance, both the exhibition and the catalogue that accompanies it would not have been possible.

Frederick J. Cummings
Director, The Detroit Institute of Arts

Kevin Consey
Director, San Antonio Museum of Art

Steven L. Brezzo
Director, San Diego Museum of Art

John Lane
Director, Carnegie Institute

J. Carter Brown
Director, National Gallery of Art

Earl A. Powell, III
Director, Los Angeles County Museum of Art

PREFACE

"**I**n the year of our salvation 1540, the Emperor made Diego Gutiérrez, native of Madrid, the Governor of New Cartago, a rich coast, a province rich beyond imagination..." Although this description, published by the European chronicler Girolamo Benzoni in 1565, reflected a soon–to–be disabused notion that the province then called New Cartago was immensely rich in gold, it was more accurate than he knew. Within that area—what is today called Costa Rica, a republic not quite equal in size to the state of Indiana—there exists a biological cornucopia, a diversity of flora and fauna unequaled in any other part of the Americas of comparable size. The meeting of two great climatic realms, the Nearctic and the Neotropical, has produced this phenomenon, and while Costa Rica has long been known to naturalists as a research paradise, archaeologists have been slow to abandon the idea that the country is a cultural backwater situated between the pinnacles of Precolumbian America: Mesoamerica and the Central Andes. To the north, Mesoamerica, including southern Mexico, Guatemala, Belize, and parts of Honduras and El Salvador, produced, over millenia, the cultures of the Olmec, the Maya, the people of Teotihuacan, the Toltec, and

9

the Aztec, among others. To the south, Colombia, Ecuador, Peru, and Bolivia achieved a long succession of high cultures. Increased interest in the nature of cultural frontier zones and a recent burst of investigative activity by the Museo Nacional de Costa Rica have brought into focus elements of Costa Rican prehistory only sketchily understood before. It now has become possible to demonstrate that the indigenous human animal was also a generator of remarkable cultural variability, for reasons often related directly to the general biological fecundity of the region.

The exhibition "Between Continents/Between Seas: Precolumbian Art of Costa Rica" was conceived to illustrate the development of Costa Rican prehistoric art as well as to explicate some of the causes behind its evolution, inasmuch as they are understood to date. In assembling information for the exhibition, a concerted effort was made to use materials that had been scientifically excavated by professional archaeologists. The catalogue text is based in large part on the comparative stylistic information provided by objects uncovered in controlled excavations. This is especially significant since past exhibitions of prehistoric Costa Rican art contained many objects of unknown date and provenance, objects which therefore had no developmental thread to link them in a comprehensible progression. Thus, while aesthetic considerations were of primary importance in the selection of pieces for the present exhibition, representativeness has also played a part. It has been our aim to present an assemblage of objects of didactic as well as artistic merit.

This catalogue consists of nine essays whose purpose is to present a comprehensive overview of the present state of Costa Rican art and archaeology. The first essay traces the evolution of Costa Rican prehistoric culture from the earliest known human presence after the end of the Pleistocene era to the time of the Spanish arrival in the 16th century. The next two essays present detailed studies of the ethnohistory and ethnography of Costa Rica's three archaeological zones: Guanacaste–Nicoya, the Central Highlands–Atlantic Watershed, and the Diquís area. These chapters are designed to provide a broad cultural panorama into which the reader can then place specific objects in the exhibition. Stone, jade, and gold objects are discussed—arranged by medium—in three chapters that follow an essay on the most important archaeological site in the Central Highlands, Guayabo de Turrialba. This large site, known since the late 19th century, has been excavated by the Universidad de Costa Rica since the late 1960s, and several objects uncovered almost a century ago at Guayabo are included in the exhibition. The catalogue also contains a technical appendix on Costa Rican jades. Its final section comprises entries that discuss each of the exhibited pieces. Together, these essays provide a multi–faceted view of the diversity and richness of Precolumbian Costa Rica, contact zone between two major traditions of indigenous culture in the Americas.

Michael J. Snarskis
Julie Jones
Michael Kan

NOTES ON THE HISTORY OF
THE MUSEO NACIONAL DE COSTA RICA

Luis Diego Gómez Pignataro
and Héctor Gamboa Paniagua

In the 1820s, the early years of independence, Costa Rica was not only poor but also lacked a cultural life of any significance. Far away from Guatemala, the political center of the region, Costa Rica's few intellectuals and artists mostly belonged to the clergy or to church-sponsored ateliers devoted to religious art and the study of Thomist texts and a few of the classics. For the vast majority of the recently freed *criollos*, nature was the foremost barrier to expansion of their settlements, something they had to fight and conquer in order to survive, and the remains of the Precolumbian cultures were to them only reminders of the paganism that had been eradicated by the Book or by the sword. Obviously, natural history and the study of aboriginal man could not prosper under such conditions. But then, unexpectedly, Europe decided it had to have a daily cup of coffee.

By the 1850s Costa Rica was heading full speed into the most remarkable and rapid transformation of its economic, socio–political, and cultural life. With each bag of the golden bean sent abroad, the public coffers grew, and so did the needs of the inhabitants, who shared in the profits and tried to catch a glimpse of the refined Old World in the quantities of imported European goods that began to

Figure 1. Photograph of the Troyo Collection, c. 1902. Photo: Museo Nacional de Costa Rica.

arrive—European goods *and* Europeans, that is, for the desire to get a glimpse was reciprocal. The difficult political and social conditions in Europe at the time triggered many visits by liberals who wanted to see for themselves the vast panoramas and romantically appealing ways of the New World, described in European salons and elsewhere by Humboldt, LaCondamine, and other savants. Central America was invaded by a peculiar brand of immigrant—the traveler–naturalist. Soon the dirt roads of San José were teaming with visitors who, finding the peaceful and friendly country much to their liking, established themselves as merchants, teachers, doctors, and so forth. At this time such books as *Die Republik Costa Rica*, by Wagner and Scherzer, appeared and attracted the attention of more and more itinerant observers. Writings in the Baedekers of the time or in the periodicals of learned societies contributed to another spectacular transformation—a change in attitude. Soon, nature became an instructive and recreational source of wonder, and the remains of Precolumbian cultures attained the status of "antiquities"; nature and Early Man became as important to the studious as Etruscan artifacts and paleotropical wildlife had been to the erudite cabinet–owners of England and Continental Europe.

By the end of the 19th century, Costa Rica, with hardly 100,000 inhabitants in the whole nation, was commercially buoyant and culturally interesting, if not exciting. San José was the third city in the world to have public electric lighting, one of the first to have public telephones, and certainly the first in the area to establish compulsory and free public education, and to allow women to attend high school. Because the changes happened fast and almost without transition, some enterprises sprouted in a rather whimsical fashion. Good examples are the National Theater, built in 1897, a reduced-scale replica of the Paris Opera, and the National Museum, created some ten years earlier. There was a neoliberal government, inspired by Comte, Spencer, and the French Revolution, economically Anglophile, but culturally French. Roads were unpaved but there were pianos in most of the well–to–do homes. Such figures as Hoffman, Frantzius, and Pittier, although not Costa Rican, had a great deal to do with the cultural movement, particularly in regard to the National Museum, the story of which—with its intricacies, cloak–and–dagger episodes, and the coming and going of great names in natural history, both local and international—would make a fine novel.

Started after Costa Rican participation in one of the first World Fairs, the National Museum soon received the donation of a large collection of archaelogical artifacts from the Troyo family (see fig. 1). This is the nucleus of the present-day Department of Anthropology and History. The museum was known as the National Museum and Plant and Animal Garden when it was given its first lodging in Laberinto, an old *hacienda* slightly out of town. In charge of geographical exploration and meteorological observations, it housed the Seismological Institute, the National Herbarium, an experimental garden, a zoo, the National Observatory, and exhibits of "natural wonders and antiquities." From Laberinto the museum was transferred to a more central location in a large adobe building with a square white tower (now the offices of the Costa Rican Social Security Administration), not including the Plant and Animal Garden due to neighborhood complaints about the roaring of the lions.

After the 1948 Civil War, the government, deciding to abolish all military installations of the past regime, gave the Bellavista Fortress, site of today's National Museum, to that institution's Board of Trustees. The Bellavista, a romantic conception of the Tinoco era, with bullet holes in its walls, appears to be old, but is not (it dates from 1917). It overlooks an ever-growing city, which will soon engulf the placid museum in a sea of tall, glass–and–concrete towers. But the museum will remain a resting place for mind and eye. Here, many a battle has been fought to reconstruct obsolete policies, create new directions, and strengthen research in natural history as well as in anthropology and archaeology. In the past ten years, the National Museum's output of new information on past Costa Rican cultures has been so disproportionate, when viewed in the perspective of the 90–some years of the institution, that it is almost impossible to assess its impact. Afflicted by low budgets (a chronic disease of museums) from its inception to the present day, it has nevertheless carried a message to generations of Costa Ricans and to wave after wave of visitors from abroad: "This was your past, this is your present; let us work together for your future."

Figure 2. Map of Costa Rica (C. Enrique Herra, Museo Nacional de Costa Rica).

THE ARCHAEOLOGY OF COSTA RICA

Michael J. Snarskis

In spite of its small size, Costa Rica can be divided into three general zones whose cultures produced artifacts of distinctly different styles, especially after c. 500 A.D. (fig. 2). Natural boundaries, like the Cordillera Central and the Talamanca mountain range, with the contrasting climatic regimes that they create, were of considerable importance in the development of this cultural diversity.

The northwest quarter of Costa Rica, on the Pacific side, forms a prehistoric cultural zone that will be referred to here as Guanacaste–Nicoya. Guanacaste is the name of the modern political province that includes long stretches of gently sloping inland plains that are today mostly divided into large cattle ranches, with some farming. The more mountainous, squared–off peninsula to the west is Nicoya. Both are part of what archaeologists call the Greater Nicoya Subarea, a Precolumbian cultural designation including part of western Nicaragua.

Guanacaste–Nicoya is set apart from the rest of Costa Rica by relative aridity and marked seasonality. Its original cover of tropical dry forest is today mostly destroyed by agriculture and conversion to pasture, an alteration that began in Precolumbian times. Only .5–1 meter of rain falls each year, usually between May and December; some years not a drop of rain falls for four or even five months. Many small streams dry up, some trees lose their leaves, and the man–made grasslands turn brown and sere. Strong, dustraising winds that buffer the countryside are responsible for this *verano*, or dry season, as they rush the moist air from the Caribbean side over the plain and out into the Pacific before rain clouds have a chance to form.

The broken Pacific coastline, with its numerous, small embayments and rocky headlands, also played a role in shaping Precolumbian cultures. Although only two bays (Santa Elena and Culebra) are large enough to shelter ocean–going craft from the gusty winds, they and the much larger Gulf of Nicoya provide myriad marine–estuary biotopes, environmental niches produced by reef formations, sand splits, and swampy, mangrove–filled backwaters, which are (or were, before overexploitation and pollution) hosts for an array of fresh and salt–water fauna, especially shellfish.

Plate 1. Globular jar, Guanacaste–Nicoya zone, ceramic (cat. no. 1).

15

The long and partially navigable Tempisque River has formed, with its tributaries, a large and fertile alluvial plain between the Nicoya Peninsula and the line of volcanoes that marks the beginning of the Pacific watershed in Guanacaste. This region, heavily settled in Precolumbian times, together with receptive sections of the coast, formed the primary backdrop for indigenous cultural development in Guanacaste–Nicoya.

By far the largest and most disparate of Costa Rica's archaeological zones, the Central Highlands–Atlantic Watershed is a composite of four or perhaps five geographic subzones, grouped here because the stylistic similarities of their artifacts suggest that they shared more or less common cultural traditions.

The largest and most characteristic part of this zone is made up of small to medium–sized valleys, with clear, rushing rivers, and the extensive, fertile lowland plains that make up the Atlantic Watershed of Costa Rica north and west of modern Port Limón. Below that city, the plains are abbreviated because the Talamanca range approaches the Caribbean. Here the Precolumbian cultural pattern seems to resemble more closely that of the Bocas del Toro region of Panama. The extreme northwest corner of the Atlantic Watershed seems to tend to Greater Nicoya affiliations. Neither subzone has been investigated systematically to date. Throughout most parts of the Atlantic Watershed, rainfall is heavy, generally from two to five meters per year, with no distinct dry season; less rain usually falls in March and April. The steeper eastern face of the Cordillera Central causes the moisture–laden easterlies to rise, cool, and release most of the resulting rain on the Caribbean side. The original vegetation in the zone was tropical rain forest, and it still remains in a few parts, although most of it has been cut down to make pasture lands and banana plantations, and to stock the strong market for tropical hardwoods. In spite of extreme weathering, soils are, for the most part, rich, dark, and of good drainage, although typical rain–forest laterites are sporadically present. Most rivers run with sparklingly clean white water in their upper reaches, where they are filled with rounded volcanic cobbles, and are partially navigable in the more sedate meandering stages near the Caribbean. Cyclical flooding is the rule, not the exception.

The Central Highlands can also be divided into two subzones, the temperate valley where the modern capital of San José and most of the country's population are located, and the central Pacific drainage, composed of parallel ranks of rugged mountains and steep valleys which terminate in a limited strip of coastal plains. Although a part of the Pacific drainage and subject to its sharp seasonality, the Central Valley is closely related to the Atlantic Watershed throughout the known prehistoric cultural sequence. The central Pacific drainage appears to follow the same pattern, but this subzone is, archaeologically, one of the least known in Costa Rica; its limits on the Pacific coast fall roughly between the modern towns of Quepos and Puntarenas. Like the Central Valley, it has a basically Pacific climatic regime.

The Diquís archaeological zone is also composed of topographically and climatically diverse subzones. While most of the Pacific coastal strip below Quepos and the broad upland valleys to the southwest of the Talamanca mountains have a severe, clearly demarcated dry season, a localized Pacific wind pattern causes parts of the Osa Peninsula and localities around the Golfo Dulce to experience the intense rainfall typical of much of the Atlantic Watershed, up to five meters a year, with no definite dry season. Although they support a plentiful and varied natural flora, large upland valleys like the General have mostly red,

Plate 2. Anthropomorphic–effigy vessel, Guanacaste–Nicoya zone, ceramic (cat. no. 13).

relatively infertile soils compared with those of the Central Valley and the Atlantic Watershed. Fundamentally, this is because the nonvolcanic Talamanca range has failed to provide the soil nutrients so generously bestowed on other parts of Costa Rica by the volcanoes running along the center of the country.

Of the three archaeological zones, Diquís, with the smallest number of controlled excavations, is the least understood. No radiocarbon (C-14) dates are yet available, and the regional sequence of archaelogical phases must be considered tentative. Culturally, Diquís is considered to form part of the larger subarea known as Greater Chiriquí, which includes the Panamanian province of Chiriquí, to the southeast.

In certain publications and textbooks, especially within Costa Rica, Guanacaste–Nicoya is referred to as the "Chorotega" cultural area, the Central Highlands–Atlantic Watershed as "Huetar," and Diquís as "Brunka." The use of these names stems from a misunderstanding of the Spanish chroniclers, later propagated by several historians (Ferrero 1977a: 56). The names were those of individual chieftains or of larger socio–cultural groups that dominated part (but not all) of the three respective archaeological zones of Costa Rica around the time of the Spanish arrival, or, in the case of the Chorotega, some centuries before. To use the names as descriptive of the whole prehistoric cultural tradition of a zone is as misleading as referring to all the occupants of Manhattan Island during the last 10,000 years as New Yorkers. Although the actual names of many different peoples occupying Costa Rica when the Spanish came are known (Ferrero, Abel–Vidor, this volume), we do not know, and probably never will know, what more ancient cultures called themselves. Costa Rica, unlike parts of Mesoamerica, has produced no evidence of a written, or hieroglyphic, record from Precolumbian times.

The Europeans who arrived in Costa Rica at the beginning of the 16th century observed indigenous cultures which in most cases have since been characterized by anthropologists as "chiefdoms," societal groupings intermediate between simple egalitarian bands and highly structured political states. More complex than groups formed by kinship alone, chiefdoms (which may be made up of several thousand people) are organized around a centralized, hereditary–status hierarchy with a theocratic orientation, but they lack the rigid social stratification and institutionalized means of forceful repression that are the products of civil law in a formal political state (Service 1975:14–16). The monumental architecture, writing systems, and calendrics that often characterize the state, or "civilization," are usually absent in the chiefdom. Instead, we see a succession of richly diverse styles in pottery, stone carving, lapidary work, and metallurgy, the preferred media changing through time. Craft traditions and religious symbolism are almost always highly developed, a result of the status–reinforcing needs of a "warrior–priest" chief and his coterie.

Archaeologists and *Huaqueros*

The treasure–hunters, amateur excavators and tomb–robbers (known from Costa Rica to Peru as *huaqueros*) are invariably earlier in the field than the archaeologists; and this rule—to which there are regretably few exceptions—is particularly well illustrated in Central America (Baudez 1970:25).

Claude Baudez, during the 1960s, was one of the first scientific archaeologists to speak out strongly on the devastations of looters in Costa Rica, remarking that the relatively primitive state of the discipline in Central America was due in large part to the utter destruction of countless archaeological sites by tomb–robbers. This unfortunate situation is poorly understood by the general public, who enjoys impressive collections of beautiful and exotic objects, but often does not understand that archaeologists, to interpret correctly the meaning or function of an object, must know the context of its recovery—how, where, and with what it was found. The materials that allow scholars to reconstruct the fascinating details of prehistoric life and the interacting processes that shaped its development are usually modest things like scraps of stone and pottery, bones, charcoal, and food remains, or even things invisible to the naked eye, like pollen grains. Looters destroy or disturb all these things and render their interpretative potential null. If the remains of past cultures are not recovered and analyzed in a controlled, scientific way, the door is left open to naive speculations and self–serving, sensationalized accounts that propagate falsehoods and stimulate further destruction.

Uncontrolled digging in Costa Rica is recorded as early as the beginning of the 19th century; it has continued apace ever since. Toward the end of that century, the first railway in the Atlantic Watershed (built by Minor C. Keith to haul out the bananas grown by the soon–to–be–formed United Fruit Company) was put through the middle of Las Mercedes, an important late architectural site, and crews of looters employed by Keith and others quickly assembled large collections of stone sculpture and other artifacts (Mason 1945).

Archaeological investigations in the modern sense may be said to have begun in Costa Rica with the work of Swedish archaeologist Carl V. Hartman in 1896 and 1897. Hartman worked at Las Mercedes, in the Atlantic lowlands, and at several other late sites in the Cartago valley (1901), as well as at the site of Las Huacas in Guanacaste (1907a). Although nonstratigraphic, Hartman's excavations were recorded carefully and comprehensively, and he set forth the first evidence for a sequence of archaeological cultures in Costa Rica (1907b). Hartman concentrated on burial grounds, and his meticulous recording of funerary constructions and associations remains unsurpassed today. While his methods were empirical and his goals old–fashioned (he ignored midden deposits, and one of his major duties was to obtain pieces for the Royal Natural History Museum in Sweden), Hartman accomplished the first clearing and mapping of habitational and cemetery features in Costa Rica, and his systematic recording of information allows modern archaeologists to ask different questions of the data.

Sadly, Hartman's admirable pioneering example was not followed up in Costa Rica for more than 50 years. Archaeological syntheses as recent as that of Gordon R. Willey (1971) continued to rely on the relative and very general two–part stylistic sequence for the Central Highlands–Atlantic Watershed regions (Curridabat–Stone Cist Ware, the latter coeval in part with the Spanish arrival, as shown by the presence of European glass beads in some tombs) established by Hartman at the turn of the century.

The next major publication dealing with Costa Rican archaeology was *Pottery of Costa Rica and Nicaragua* (1926) by Samuel K. Lothrop. This two–volume compendium sought to classify Costa Rican and some Nicaraguan Precolumbian ceramics through a stylistic analysis of pottery in private and museum collections in several countries. Since the material studied came from uncontrolled digging, stratigraphic and associational controls were lacking, and the resulting classification is purely descriptive, with no temporal significance. Lothrop was aware of the limitations imposed by his sample, and did not attempt unwarranted specula-

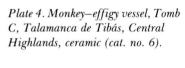

*Plate 3. Avian–effigy vessel,
Guanacaste–Nicoya zone, ceramic
(cat. no. 5).*

*Plate 4. Monkey–effigy vessel, Tomb
C, Talamanca de Tibás, Central
Highlands, ceramic (cat. no. 6).*

*Plate 5. Effigy axe–god pendant,
Vereh, Alta Talamanca, Atlantic
Watershed, jade (cat. no. 33).*

*Plate 6. Avian axe–god pendant,
Atlantic Watershed zone, jade (cat.
no. 23).*

tions about chronology. His work constituted the first comprehensive description of Costa Rican archaeological materials, including an excellent summary and interpretation of relevant Spanish historical chronicles.

Doris Stone, who served as President of the Board of Directors of the Museo Nacional de Costa Rica (MNCR) from 1949 to 1967, conducted brief excavations, mostly of tomb features, in many parts of the country during that time, but publications were few and informal. Her first summaries of Costa Rican archaeology (1948, 1958, 1966b) were primarily descriptive, following Lothrop's and Hartman's terminology in great part. In 1962, Stone published the first full–fledged ethnography of the surviving Talamancan Indian tribes, the Bribri and Cabecar. She also published two archaeological syntheses, one on Central America (1972) and one on Costa Rica (1977).

Scientific, goal–oriented archaeology got off the ground in the late 1950s, when Claude Baudez of the Musée de l'Homme and Michael D. Coe of Yale University conducted stratigraphic excavations in Guanacaste–Nicoya. Their careful work produced the first reliable archaeological sequence for that region (Coe and Baudez 1961; Baudez and Coe 1962; Baudez 1967), complete with radiocarbon dates and chronologically significant ceramic types. An almost identical sequence was published by Albert Norweb (1964) for the Rivas Peninsula of Nicaragua. The local periodization set up by these archaeologists is still in use.

Wolfgang Haberland, of the Museum für Völkerkunde, Hamburg, also worked in Costa Rica during the 1950s, in the Diquís zone. He identified and classified many of the ceramics published earlier by William H. Holmes (1888) and George G. MacCurdy (1911) for the adjacent Panamanian province of Chiriquí, and sought to establish a relative archaeological sequence for Diquís by comparing its ceramics to the dated material from Guanacaste–Nicoya (1969). At that time, Haberland excavated mostly cemetery sites, and did not publish any radiocarbon dates; most of his articles were short, descriptive site reports (1955, 1959, 1960, 1961a, 1961b).

In 1963, Lothrop published the results of rather extensive test excavations in the Diquís Delta. Although he dug some pits in one–foot levels, he was able to offer only very general observations on the relative ages of the pottery he found. He published no radiocarbon dates, typing his ceramics descriptively and seeking to associate them with dated material from other parts of the country.

During the 1960s, controlled archaeological excavations were carried out by Matthew W. Stirling of the National Geographic Society (1969) on the Línea Vieja lowlands, and by William J. Kennedy of Florida Atlantic University (1968, 1976) and Carlos Aguilar of the Universidad de Costa Rica (1972b) in the Reventazón River valley near Turrialba. These reports make up the first body of published data derived from stratigraphic digging in the Atlantic Watershed of Costa Rica, a method in use more than 50 years earlier in other parts of the Americas. Focusing primarily on tombs, Stirling dug at five sites between Siquirres and Guápiles, and published a series of C–14 dates ranging from 144 to 1470 A.D., establishing for the first time at least 1,400 years of time depth for the Precolumbian cultures in the region. Kennedy sought to correlate archaeological sites of different time periods with a series of nine environmental zones or biotopes (W. Holdridge 1947), finding that prehistoric man preferred, for the most part, those zones also occupied by the modern population. He published eight C–14 dates ranging from 420 to 1220 A.D., and observed a sequence of ceramic styles similar to that found by Stirling. Aguilar partially excavated the

Figure 3. Archaeologists from the Museo Nacional de Costa Rica performing salvage operations at the site of Barrial de Heredia in the Central Highlands. Photo: Juan Vicente Guerrero, Museo Nacional de Costa Rica.

"ceremonial center" of Guayabo de Turrialba (Fonseca Zamora, this volume). While Stirling, Kennedy, and Aguilar arranged much of the pottery first described by Lothrop in an approximate (but incomplete) chronological sequence for the Atlantic Watershed, lack of communication between them prevented the establishment of standardized ceramic types and archaeological periods.

From 1966 until the present, Frederick W. Lange (1971a, 1971b, 1975, 1976), now of Illinois State University, has excavated at many sites along the Nicoya coast, often in shell middens. His work has shed light on changing settlement patterns and subsistence activities, especially in relation to small–scale climate change and other natural phenomena, such as volcanic activity. Jeanne Sweeney (1975) has reanalyzed the ceramics, lithics, and faunal material excavated by M. Coe some 20 years earlier in Nicoya, and Paul Healy (1974) of Trent University has done likewise for Norweb's mostly unpublished material from Rivas.

Since the mid–1970s, there has been a quantum jump in scientific archaeology in Costa Rica. In 1974–75, the author, later assisted by Lange, established a comprehensive program for archaeological investigation, based in the MNCR, incorporating long–term and salvage projects (fig. 3), the training of Costa Rican students, and the publishing of a professional anthropological journal, *Vínculos*. Through a series of projects, knowledge of the settlement patterns and subsistence of past cultures has been greatly broadened, the classification of artifacts and other cultural features systematized, and the cultural sequence greatly lengthened (Snarskis 1975, 1976a, 1976b, 1977, 1978, 1979a; Lange 1975, 1976, 1977, 1978, 1980a, 1980b). In 1977, Ferrero (1977a) published a broad, up–to–date synthesis of the archaeology and ethnohistory of the country, the first of its kind in Spanish. Aguilar has continued work at sites in the Central Highlands (1974, 1975, 1976), and his student, Oscar Fonseca Zamora—who obtained a graduate degree at the University of Pittsburgh, where he published analyses of some of Hartman's material (Fonseca and Richardson 1978; Fonseca and Scaglion 1978)—has reopened and greatly broadened the excavation and restoration project at Guayabo de Turrialba (Fonseca 1979).

Many of Lange's former students on field projects in Guanacaste–Nicoya have begun to publish their work (Accola 1977, 1978, 1980; Lange and Accola 1979; Abel–Vidor, 1978, 1980a, 1980b; Ryder 1980; Bernstein 1980; Wallace and Accola 1980; Norr 1979; Creamer 1980; Moreau 1980), as has the first generation of *criollo*, or "home-grown," archaeologists, trained by the MNCR and the Universidad de Costa Rica (Snarskis and Blanco 1978; Guerrero 1980; Blanco and Salgado 1980; Snarskis and Herra 1980; Vázquez 1980; Vázquez and Weaver 1980; Acosta and Le Franc 1980).

In April 1980, a School of American Research Advanced Seminar on Central American Archaeology was held in Santa Fe, New Mexico. Organized by Lange and Stone, and chaired by Willey, additional participants were Haberland, Healy, the author, Robert Sharer (University of Pennsylvania), Payson D. Sheets (University of Colorado), Allison Paulsen, and Richard F. Cooke (Smithsonian Tropical Research Institute, Panama). Discussion focused on the complex processes that shaped all aspects of prehistoric cultures in Central America. A standardized six–part archaeological periodization was put forth for all of Central America, to replace the confusing variety of local schemes and to provide a general, broadly drawn frame on which to tie the many regional and local variants of a culturally diverse area. Central American and, specifically, Costa Rican archaeology have only recently begun to go beyond the Classificatory–Historical stage (Willey and Sabloff 1974: 88). We must now advance to another plane of analysis, not only in order to grasp the when and where of prehistory but to explain the how—the dynamic interaction of processes that stimulated the production of the artifacts that survive to fascinate us today.

The time–space framework used in this catalogue is as follows: the three archaeological zones are divided into subzones or localities, usually based on the amount of controlled archaeology done there. The principal time scale will be the new periodization established for Central America at the S.A.R. Seminar in 1980: Period I (?–8000 B.C.), Period II (8000–4000 B.C.), Period III (4000–1000 B.C.), Period IV (1000 B.C.–500 A.D.), Period V (500–1000 A.D.), Period VI (1000–1550 A.D.). This periodization avoids semantic problems by using Roman numerals instead of proper or descriptive names; nevertheless, its divisions correspond approximately to cultural thresholds important throughout Nuclear America.

Former regional periodizations, if they are established in the literature, will also be included in the chronological charts, as will cultural phases, in cases where they have been established by archaeologists. Phases signify prehistoric cultural differences over smaller ranges of space and time, as defined by changes in artifact styles, settlement patterns, subsistence systems, and the like. Their names are usually taken from geographic features, and in no way reflect what cultural groups called themselves.

Guanacaste–Nicoya

PERIODS I, II, AND III (?–1000 B.C.)

When the Americas were first populated by *Homo sapiens*, who came across the Bering Strait between 15,000 and 35,000 years ago, the Central American

Figure 4. View of Guanacaste near Buenavista. The Gulf of Nicoya and the Nicoyan Peninsula are visible in the background. Photo: Frederick W. Lange.

isthmus had to be crossed. C–14 dates from sites in Patagonia tell us that this occurred around 10,000 B.C. The only evidence of the presence of these migratory bands of hunters and gatherers in Guanacaste–Nicoya is a single fluted spear point, obtained by Hartman in the 1890s and not identified until 50 years later (Swauger and Mayer–Oakes 1952).

PERIOD IV (1000 B.C.–500 A.D.)

Although the first pottery in northwest Costa Rica probably appeared in Period III, our present knowledge of the ceramic sequence picks up between 1000 and 500 B.C. Through the controlled stratigraphic excavation of only a handful of potsherds from depths of nearly six meters at some coastal sites, archaeologists have been able to identify a few whole vessels in museum collections as products of early Period IV. Decoration usually consists of wide, round–bottomed, incised lines, sometimes traced around thickened vessel rims, or in parallel bands separating areas of red slip; two colors predominate, red and the natural buff or brown of the fired clay itself. "Zoned Bichrome" is the name given Period IV in the regional periodization. This pottery shows a general stylistic relationship to other contemporary ceramic traditions throughout Nuclear America, especially those of the Middle Preclassic in southern Mesoamerica.

Sedentary settlements are suggested by a circular oven at the Vidor site, which produced a C–14 date of c. 800 B.C. (Abel–Vidor 1980a). Early Period IV is known as the Loma B phase in the Bay of Culebra archaeological sequence, the longest sequence for Guanacaste–Nicoya (Lange 1980a).

A trend toward increasing size and complexity of sites began during middle to

Figure 5. Map of the Guanacaste–Nicoya archaeological zone (C. Enrique Herra, Museo Nacional de Costa Rica).

late Period IV (300 B.C.–300 A.D.). M. Coe and Baudez (1961) first described the archaeology of this time; their stratigraphic excavations also provided supporting radiocarbon dates. Like Lange and his students some years later, they noted extensive cemeteries with differential mortuary goods, implying rank–ordered social structure. Village size and layout and house forms are as yet unknown, but, so far, more sites of this period have been found inland, on the foothills of the central volcanic range, than near the coast. Interestingly, the occupants of Zoned Bichrome coastal sites did not utilize marine molluscs, a major resource in later periods (Lange 1980a). It is likely that hunting, gathering of wild fruits and nuts, and agriculture were all practiced.

High–ranking burials frequently contain *metates* (grinding tables) along with jade pendants. Some archaeologists, including Lange (1971a; in press), feel that the metates were "thrones" for high–status personages and not grinding tables. Their owners may sometimes have sat on these highly valued objects, but I do not believe this to have been their primary function, for several reasons: (1) the majority show considerable wear by grinding, even in sections of the upper surface that are decorated with low–relief carving; (2) the MNCR excavated two decorated examples of the period 300–500 A.D. at the Nacascolo site in 1980, each with heavy wear and a long "overhang" type of *mano*, or muller, in association; (3) the noticeable increases in population and social stratification during this period were almost certainly linked with more productive agricultural tech-

26

ARCHAEOLOGICAL PHASES

New Central American Periodization	Old Regional Periodization	Calendar Years	Bay of Salinas Santa Elena Peninsula	Bay of Culebra	Tempisque River Valley	Matapalo, Tamarindo, Nosara (Lower Nicoya Peninsula)	Calendar Years
		1600					1600
Period VI	Late Polychrome	1500	La Cruz A	Ruiz			1500
		1400				?	1400
		1300	La Cruz B	Iguanita	Bebedero		1300
		1200					1200
	Middle Polychrome	1100		Monte del Barco	Palo Blanco B		1100
		1000	Doscientos			Tamarindo	1000
Period V		900		Panamá	Palo Blanco A		900
		800					800
	Early Polychrome	700	Santa Elena				700
		600		Culebra	San Bosco	Matapalo	600
		500					500
	Linear Decorated	400	Murcielagos	Mata de Uva	Ciruelas	Las Minas	400
		300					300
Period IV	Zoned Bichrome	200					200
		100					100
		AD — BC	Chombo	Orso	Catalina	Monte Fresco	AD — BC
		100					100
		200					200
		300					300
	?	400					400
		500		Loma B			500
		600					600
		700					700
		800					800
		900					900
		1000					1000

Figure 6. Chronological chart of archaeological periods and phases for Guanacaste–Nicoya.

27

Plate 7. Ceremonial mace head, Nicoya Peninsula, stone (cat. no. 46).

Plate 8. Ceremonial mace head, Guanacaste–Nicoya zone, stone (cat. no. 43).

Plate 9. Ceremonial mace head, Línea Vieja, Atlantic Watershed, stone (cat. no. 49).

Plate 10. Mace head, Guanacaste–Nicoya zone, stone (cat. no. 51).

niques, and it is not surprising to find among the paraphernalia of the ruling elite articles symbolic of food preparation and its ceremonial redistribution, major sources of political power in chiefdom societies.

I would also link the other well–known high–status object of this period, the jade "axe–god" pendant, to the spread of full–scale—probably maize—agriculture (Snarskis, in press). Stone axes, or celts, were the standard forest–clearing tools in Nuclear America. Used for girdling and splitting tree trunks from late Preceramic times onward, they were especially numerous in agricultural societies. The axe-gods incorporate the celt form, usually with an avian effigy. These symbolic celts, the associated zoomorphic effigies, and the sometimes elaborately decorated ceremonial metates may have formed part of a politico–religious complex associated with the control of agricultural lands and the processing and redistribution of foodstuffs.

Behind most developed prehistoric subsistence systems was a mythological framework, the knowledge and perpetuation of which explained the origins of the system, usually in an allegorical fashion, and defined the rituals that formalized seasonal and other cyclical, necessary procedures. Priestly and administrative classes arose to handle the organization and sanctions required. Unfortunately, iconographic research in Costa Rican archaeology is scanty. Mark Graham (this volume) has taken the first steps toward interpreting the various effigies that appear on stone sculpture.

There are indications that Mesoamerican influence was important in northern Costa Rica during several centuries before and after Christ. Elizabeth Easby (1968: 81–97) has noted the importance of the celt form in both Olmec and Costa Rican lapidary work and has suggested that important gem–quality jade sources were located in Costa Rica, stimulating trade with Olmec centers like La Venta to the north. Recent physical analyses (Lange *et al.*, this volume) dispute this hypothesis, indicating that the highest quality jadeite may have been traded into Costa Rica from the north. In any case, there is increasingly better evidence (Sharer, in press) for well–established trade routes between northern Costa Rica and southern Mexico from late Olmec times (800–400 B.C.) on. Since, as Easby (this volume) notes, the stylistic links between the Olmec and Costa Rican Zoned Bichrome cultures are tantalizing yet incomplete, we cannot describe with certainty the nature of Olmec influence in Costa Rica. The few Olmec jades found here appear to have been heirlooms, associated with local objects hundreds of years younger. This suggests a "down–the–line" trading system (in which objects from point A reached point D through intermediaries at points B and C) rather than a direct Olmec–Costa Rica contact.

Ceramics from Guanacaste–Nicoya during the second half of Period IV (300 B.C.–500 A.D.) often display strong sculptural qualities and an elegance of line that strike sympathetic chords in modern aesthetic sensibilities. The human and zoomorphic effigy forms of the ceramic type archaeologists call Rosales Zoned Engraved (cat. nos. 4–6, 9, 10, 12, 13) are probably the most outstanding ceramic objects of this time. Some have been found in the Central Highlands–Atlantic Watershed zone, in contexts suggesting trade between elite groups. Many pieces, especially spouted forms, are reminiscent of formative styles in both Mesoamerica and the Andes. Like most prehistoric pottery from Costa Rica, these red, black, and brown or cream–colored vessels were made by a combination of molding and coiling, and were fired at relatively low temperatures in open hearths or rudimentary kilns. The potter's wheel was not used.

Mortuary evidence suggests that, in the last centuries of Period IV (200/300–500

A.D.), population and social stratification continued to increase. Many cemeteries of this time have been excavated in part, beginning with Hartman's (1907a) Las Huacas excavations. There, in what was obviously a high–status burial ground, decorated metates, ceremonial mace heads, and jade pendants were found in many tombs, with relatively little pottery. In the nearby Bolsón cemetery, Baudez (1967) found both secondary and primary burials with more modest grave goods, mostly ceramics. This pattern was also observed in the MNCR excavations of contemporary cemeteries at Mojica, near Bagaces, Guanacaste, and at the coastal site of Nacascolo on the Nicoya Peninsula, where culinary pottery, a few modeled and incised ceramic effigy vessels, and mostly undecorated metates were recovered from burials containing both articulated, flexed individuals and secondary interments (fig. 7). Archaeologists deduce from these differential mortuary patterns well–developed class or rank divisions, although enduring evidence, such as architecture, is absent.

Figure 7. Burial at Nacascolo, Bay of Culebra, Guanacaste, dating to 300–500 A.D. Note the flexed position of the skeleton. Photo: Brian D. Dillon, UCLA Institute of Archaeology.

The repertoire of ceramic decoration begins to enlarge importantly in the two or three centuries before 500 A.D. The early bichromes are now often trichromes, the black motifs usually outlined with white. Incised and appliqué techniques are more frequent, and motifs become increasingly angular and geometric. Linear, rather than sculptural, qualities are emphasized. Modeled and/or effigy vessels of Guinea Incised ware include many striking representations (cat. nos. 54–57), but they lack the subtle quality of line characteristic of earlier ceramic sculptures. Some Guinea vessels incorporate the image of one or more people reclining in a hammock, an object associated with southern tropical–forest peoples. Bat motifs (cat. nos. 58, 59) begin to appear with greater frequency; the large, modeled, and painted *ollas* of Tola Trichrome are often decorated with bat forms. Figurines, ocarinas, stamps, and other specialized ceramic objects were particularly abundant during this time (cat. nos. 59-63); they were perhaps indicative of a preoccupation with ritual required to bind together a society of increasing complexity.

The wider distribution of portable status objects like jades and ceremonial mace heads (cat. nos. 43–50) suggests that geographically dispersed upper classes may have possessed strong social or even hereditary ties, and that their status was produced and maintained, at least in part, by their access to foreign trade articles or peoples (Lange, in press). Regionally important chiefdoms had probably developed in many parts of Costa Rica before 500 A.D.

PERIOD V (500–1000A.D.)

The famous Guanacaste–Nicoya polychrome–pottery tradition and the beginning of a significant stylistic divergence between the material culture of this zone and that of the Central Highlands–Atlantic Watershed mark this period. Although the causes are far from understood, the rupture of old northern trade routes, combined with new political, commercial, and perhaps spiritual allegiances to the south, may have been of considerable importance. A trend toward greater marine exploitation (at least of molluscs) began c. 400–500 A.D., and it is possible that other ocean products like salt and purple dye from *Murex* Mollusca became increasingly valuable trade items.

Domestic features have been found at coastal sites like Vidor or Nacascolo: large, circular, rock–filled ovens or kilns; small, ellipsoidal, fired adobe hearths; fired adobe chunks with cane impressions, testifying to wattle–and–daub house constructions; floors; and postholes. The same sites had apparently differentiated burial grounds: at Vidor, more than 20 burials of females, children and infants (the last often in urns) were excavated in a vicinity of domestic activity and refuse, while Nacascolo yielded tombs of the same period, constructed entirely of natural basalt columns, overlain by a cap of fieldstone, and positioned along the contours of a steep natural slope. Grave goods were much more elaborate in the latter tomb type.

Carrillo Polychrome, with angular geometric patterns of red and black lines (often carelessly executed) on a buff or brown ground, is one of the most representative ceramic types of the period 500–800 A.D. (cat. no. 80). It begins at the end of Period IV as a variant of Tola Trichrome, and eventually grades into the striking Galo type. Most forms are bowls, jars, and *ollas*; motifs thought to be stylized alligators or bats occur. Chávez White on Red, characterized by zoomorphic effigies as well as by functional bowls, also has roots in earlier styles. This type probably spanned the Period IV–V transition. Some archaeologists find in it stylistic affiliations to certain Ecuadorian ceramics (Stone 1977: 56–57). Pelicans or similar water birds are often represented.

Perhaps the finest ceramics from the period c. 500–800 A.D. are Galo Polychrome (cat. nos. 83–88). Their mirror–bright burnished surfaces are technically unsurpassed by any Precolumbian pottery, and the yellows, reds, oranges, creams, maroons, and blacks of their polychrome decoration are impressively vivid. This ware is closely related to the Ulua Polychromes found in western Honduras and El Salvador. Galo, with cylindrical vessel forms and slab tripod feet, often looks very Mayoid. Guilloche and woven-mat patterns, seen on contemporary Maya pottery, where it is indicative of high rank, are also conspicuous. Galo has been found by looters in Nicoya with a fresco–painted vessel reminiscent of Teotihuacan pottery, and marble (alabaster) vessels from the Sula plain in Honduras. Galo was even found in the earlier Las Huacas cemetery and in Nicoya sites where Classic Maya glyph-incised jades have surfaced. The largest and most impressive ceramic figurines of prehistoric Costa Rica fall into the Galo

*Plate 11. Composite–effigy whistle,
San Juan de Santa Cruz,
Guanacaste, ceramic (cat. no. 58).*

*Plate 12. Effigy vessel, Canas,
Guanacaste, ceramic (cat. no. 69).*

category (cat. no. 86). They may be full human figures or effigy heads; the former usually have a pubic cover, and are painted with elaborate, busy representations of tattoos or body paint. Human faces are often exceptionally expressive. A striking and ornately modeled ceramic type of this same time is Potosí Appliqué or Modeled Alligator pottery. These vessels, which perhaps served as incense burners, often have a large, hemispherical base and a ventilated lid, elaborately decorated with a multicrested animal effigy, usually an alligator or crocodile (cat. nos. 89–92). Variants of this pottery type persist into Period VI.

The brilliant polychrome tradition that began in Guanacaste–Nicoya with Carrillo and Galo may represent an important new social dimension; when the northern trade network that brought jade, slate–backed pyrite mirrors, foreign ceramics, and other luxury goods broke down (c. 500 A.D., it seems), the Nicoyans responded by producing their own special–purpose pottery. Inspired by northern models, it also incorporated local and southern elements, forming a vigorous hybrid style that would be traded around Central America and southern Mesoamerica in the centuries to come.

Striking changes took place in almost all aspects of prehistoric life in Guanacaste–Nicoya from c. 800 A.D. on. Sites increased dramatically in both number and size. There seems to have been a marked shift of population concentration toward the coast, although inland zones some distance from the mountains apparently remained occupied. Lange (personal communication) has noted the presence of a thin volcanic–ash layer in coastal sites near the middle of Period V; volcanic activity may have driven people from the central piedmont toward the Pacific. While agriculture must have remained important, a much greater exploitation of marine protein sources began; most of the large and numerous Nicoyan shell middens began to accumulate after 800 A.D. (fig. 8).

External factors also functioned as agents of change in northwestern Costa Rica during the eighth and ninth centuries. The central Mexican empire of Teotihuacan had long since dissolved, and now the Classic Maya lowland centers had also suffered catastrophic collapses. When these basically theocratic empires were fragmented by more militaristic nations, the ceremonial context in which

Figure 8. Excavation of a stratigraphic trench in a shell midden some two meters in depth, part of a project at Nacascolo sponsored by the Museo Nacional de Costa Rica. Photo: Brian D. Dillon, UCLA Institute of Archaeology.

elite-associated artifacts played important roles was drastically altered. In Costa Rica, the symbolic importance of carved jades, ceremonial mace heads, and elaborate metates suddenly declined midway through Period V.

Today, archaeologists tend to play down the importance of actual migrations of peoples as causes of cultural change, preferring to see cultural history as a result of the interplay of social and environmental elements. Nevertheless, there is evidence (Abel–Vidor, this volume) for the arrival in Guanacaste–Nicoya during this period of Mesoamerican peoples of the Oto–Mangue language group, probably as a result of social disruptions in the north. No doubt these influxes changed the stylistic tenor or local material culture.

The time of greatest diversity and production of polychrome ceramics (Middle Polychrome) was 800–1200 A.D. The earliest varieties of Mora Polychrome, like the older Galo type, incorporate elements common in certain Late Classic Maya pottery—the seated figure with headdress, the mat pattern, and the Kan cross. Typical Mora painted decoration is mostly geometric, executed in red, black, and maroon on a buff-orange ground; vessel forms are usually simple hemispherical bowls. The other hallmark of the period is Papagayo Polychrome (cat. nos. 95, 96) with a cream–to–white slip and brilliant orange–red paint, usually paired with black, and sometimes gray, in later varieties. Motifs on Papagayo pottery range from simple bands to complex figural scenes, including humans, jaguars, and a version of the Mesoamerican plumed serpent. Papagayo's great range of forms includes bowls, jars, zoomorphic effigies, and effigy-head tripods; some forms resemble those of Mesoamerican Early Postclassic horizon types like Tohil Plumbate and X Fine Orange.

Papagayo brought renown to the "Nicoya Polychromes," but it is just one of several related white–slipped wares that began to be manufactured in Pacific Central America during this time. Baudez (1971:35) noticed that polychromes like Mora and Birmania are found with great frequency in the southern half of Greater Nicoya, while Papagayo tended to augment toward the north. There is increasing evidence for a system of local centers of production for each major polychrome type (Accola 1977, 1978); Abel–Vidor (Day and Abel–Vidor 1980) has postulated that almost all white–slipped pottery, beginning with Papagayo, was made at least as far north as Rivas, Nicaragua, and then traded to Guanacaste–Nicoya. Papagayo-like ceramics have been found as far north as the Toltec capital of Tula, in central Mexico.

There was a trend away from sculptural qualities toward painted ceramics in the second half of Period V; new effigy styles appeared, however, notably those of Guabal (cat. nos. 93, 94) and early Birmania Polychromes. The former emphasize broad-legged seated human figures, most with intricate painted clothing, tattooing, or body painting; an invariably flattened headdress and face suggest possible cranial deformation, and ear flares are prominent. Birmania, with technically inferior painting, generally takes zoomorphic effigy forms that incorporate a small bowl; felines, birds, and even sea turtles appear. Ocarinas, especially turtle and avian forms, also are seen in these types.

Potosi "alligator incensarios" persist through Period V, becoming less elaborate. Brown–slipped "Chocolate Ware" (Lothrop 1926: 227–234) begins in, and lasts through, this period and most of the next. Early types in the tradition, like Huerta Incised, are more skillfully executed, displaying motifs also seen in Galo Polychrome; later, the geometric painted designs of other polychrome types, especially Mora, are translated into incised decorative bands on mostly open bowls and dishes of the Belen Incised type.

Plate 13. Funerary mask, Playas de Sámara, Nicoya, ceramic (cat. no. 64).

PERIOD VI (1000–1550 A.D.)

The trends in settlement patterns that begin in mid–Period V generally continue throughout Period VI. Centers of population appear nearer the Pacific coast of the Nicoya Peninsula. The utilization of marine resources becomes increasingly important, while manos, metates, and similar ground–stone tools decrease dramatically. Archaeologists do not know if this indicates a drastic shift in agricultural systems and food–processing technology, if the associated tools began to be made mostly of wood (not preserved), or if they have simply not appeared in the small samples excavated so far.

Data on house forms and sizes are still scanty, but part of one house, dating 1000–1300 A.D., was recently excavated by the MNCR at La Guinea on the Tempisque River. This structure was apparently ellipsoidal or rectangular, and 30–50 square meters in area. An unusual feature was the use of fired adobe blocks at intervals along the perimeter of the house, apparently placed to chock wooden poles in much the same way that river cobbles or field stones were used in other parts of Precolumbian Costa Rica (fig. 9); natural stone is scarce in the Tempisque drainage around La Guinea. Along one edge of the house, a large fragment of cane–impressed fired adobe was found, showing that the house walls were made of upright canes, c. 2.5 centimeters in diameter, lashed together with vines or ropes, and covered with adobe to a height of at least 50 centimeters. In other parts of the site, compressed sandy clay floors, with post holes, were found. The stratigraphy in the trench walls illustrated many prehistoric flooding episodes and, unfortunately, our excavation was destroyed by a modern flood before it was completed.

During Period VI, simple primary interments and multiple secondary burials were practiced. At Nacascolo, La Guinea, and other sites, dental mutilation, also observed in southern Mesoamerica, has been noted. Tomb structures may consist of a single, naturally columnar stone slab (a vertical marker) or a group of stones placed above (or single stones within) a burial, or may be unmarked pits. Ceramic grave goods of variable quality are usual. Long, triangular celts of chipped or polished stone have also been found in tombs; the chipped forms are probably tree–felling tools (almost identical versions come from the Atlantic Watershed), but the elegant polished examples suggest a ceremonial role (cat. no. 110). Many elaborate burials of this period have been looted; only one (Wallace and Accola 1980) has been excavated by archaeologists. It contained the primary extended skeleton of a middle-aged male, surrounded by high–status polychrome pottery, a copper bell at his wrist, red ochre on the pelvis, and the skulls of six people of varying ages placed on his chest; their long bones rested nearby (fig. 10).

Early Period VI corresponds to the last half of Middle Polychrome. There is an increasing emphasis on white–slipped polychrome pottery; new types like Vallejo (cat. nos. 111, 112), using blue–gray paint, and Mombacho, with under-slip incising, incorporate Mexican–looking design elements. While the nature of this northern "influence" is not clear, there is reason to believe that the Postclassic Mixteca–Puebla expansion was instrumental in the dissemination of certain deity concepts and motifs. These and other white–slipped types concentrated in northern Greater Nicoya inspired somewhat inferior copies to the south, for example, Jicote Polychrome (cat. nos. 103, 104) apparently manufactured along the lower reaches of the Tempisque River (Day and Abel-Vidor 1980). Buff–orange–slipped polychrome types persist through at least the first half of Period VI.

36

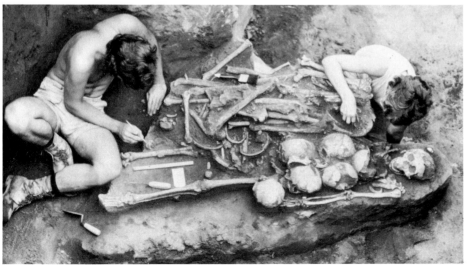

Figure 9. Circular oven and ellipsoidal hearths at Nacascolo. Note how the fired—adobe hearth system was made to accommodate several oblong vessels at a time. Photo: Brian D. Dillon, UCLA Institute of Archaeology.

Figure 10. Composite burial from Nacascolo dating to c. 1200 A.D. A primary extended individual has the skulls of six others on his chest, with their long bones piled nearby. Many Period VI Nicoya Polychrome vessels and a copper bell accompanied this burial. Photo: Henry D. Wallace.

After c. 1150–1250 A.D., Papagayo Polychrome grades into the striking black–and–red–on–white pottery called Pataky. This obviously elite–associated ceramic may have been manufactured as mortuary furniture. Its intricate, lacy black–on–white panels repeat unusual stylized jaguar motifs; the best–known vessels are modeled jaguar effigies, incorporating a pear–shaped container (cat. nos. 107, 108). The jaguar replaces the alligator (or crocodile) and the bat as the key animal figure in what are almost certainly mythologically symbolic contexts.

Two unusual ceramic types make their appearance rather late in Period VI. Murillo Appliqué (cat. no. 113) is a glossy black or red pottery that features only modeled decoration. It has few antecedents in the region, and has been thought to indicate a late, undefined South American (or, at least, Atlantic Watershed–Tropical Forest) influence (Lange 1971). Unfortunately, it cannot be associated with antecedent pottery traditions either to the south or to the east. An even greater enigma is posed by Luna Polychrome (cat. nos. 114, 115). Its varieties of painted decoration, from "minimalist" patterns—with large, open zones of cream slip—to busy, honeycomb designs, resemble the Late Polychrome pottery made on Marajó Island, at the mouth of the Amazon River in Brazil. Luna is seen more often in southern Nicaragua, and has been found along with Spanish iron artifacts in burials. Was there a trans–Caribbean trading network that extended along the navigable San Juan River that divides Costa Rica and Nicaragua? Such a concept is not to be discarded out of hand, for Columbus described 40–man trading boats of the coastal Yucatan Maya plying the Caribbean coast of Central America in the early 16th century.

Prismatic blades of obsidian, while not numerous, are found in many Period VI sites. These are almost certainly trade articles from at least as far north as Nicaragua or Guatemala, for Costa Rican obsidian deposits are unknown. A more complex pattern of trade and technological diffusion is provided by metallurgy, which first reached Costa Rica from the south c. 500 A.D. Cast gold or *tumbaga* (a gold–copper alloy) artifacts are rarely found in Guanacaste–Nicoya, and it was thought that they were trade articles from Diquís or the Atlantic Watershed. Recently, however, Lange surface–collected a small, gold frog pendant, as well as a clay mold for a virtually identical, but different, piece at two different sites around Culebra Bay. Perhaps at least some gold work was produced in Nicoya (Lange and Accola 1979). While copper artifacts were produced in the southern (Colombian–Panamanian) tradition, certain types of copper bells, occasionally found in northern and Central Costa Rica, are thought by some archaeologists to be products of the Mesoamerican trade network. One such bell (type IA3 in David Pendergast's classification; Wallace and Accola 1980) was found in the important Period VI burial at Nacascolo.

Crude, basin–shaped, stone metates have been found in a few sites of this period, but the ornate varieties seem to have declined or disappeared. Much of the columnar stone sculpture known from around Lake Nicaragua apparently can be placed in this time. Supposedly, similar sculptures were removed from the site of Nacascolo many years ago. Extremely crude versions of such statuary are still to be found there, and were also recovered by Baudez at the nearby site of Papagayo.

The first Spanish visitors to Greater Nicoya found large villages ordered around a kind of central plaza, which itself was bordered by residences and tombs of the ruling household. They recognized subsistence patterns (maize and beans), fragments of language, deity concepts, and even certain ritual activities (*voladores*, men suspended "flying" from a pole, and *patolli*, in which grains of

Plate 14. Anthropomorphic–effigy vessel, Bagaces, Guanacaste, ceramic (cat. no. 82).

38

maize were moved around a board according to throws of a die), similar to those previously observed to the north, in Mexico.

Central Highlands–Atlantic Watershed

PERIOD I (12,000?–8000 B.C.)

A workshop site from this period was recently discovered on the eastern slopes of the Cordillera Central. Called Turrialba (Snarskis 1979b), it shares with Madden Lake, another Paleo–Indian site near the Panama Canal, the distinction of having yielded two distinct types of chipped–stone spear points used by hunters of the Pleistocene megafauna 10,000–12,000 years ago. One is a variation of the Clovis–point type, known throughout North America, while the other, the so–called fishtail, or Magellan point, was typical of paleo–hunters in South America. Costa Rica and Panama seem to form the border between the spatial distributions of these two well–known classes of Paleo–Indian points. Even at that early date, this part of Central America functioned as a buffer or transitional zone between important cultural traditions on the two American continents.

PERIODS II (8000–4000 B.C.) AND III (4000–1000 B.C.)

No sites can yet be placed in these periods with certainty, although one site has chipped–stone tools and debris much like that found in certain Pacific Panamanian sites of the Tropical Forest Archaic (Period II; Linares and Ranere 1980).

PERIOD IV (1000 B.C.–500 A.D.)

The earliest securely radiocarbon–dated pottery known in Costa Rica is the La Montaña complex (fig. 14a), from a site of the same name in the Turrialba valley. Five C–14 dates from the site range from 1500 to 300 B.C., clustering around 500 B.C. La Montaña–phase pottery, almost entirely monochrome, is well made and has a fairly wide range of forms; it was almost certainly preceded by earlier ceramics. In general, it resembles pottery dating to 2000–1000 B.C. from northern South American sites like Barlovento, Colombia. This impression is strengthened by the presence of flat, rimmed griddles (*budares*), which are associated with the processing of bitter manioc or cassava in Colombian, Venezuelan, and Brazilian archaeological sites. Since they, and an unusual beveled type of mano, do not appear again in the Atlantic Watershed archaeological sequence, it is possible that La Montaña peoples were the last to rely on root and tree crops as food staples (a carbonized avocado seed was found with La Montaña deposits).

In 1977, the year La Montaña was discovered, a very different–looking pottery came to light in the San Carlos region of the northern lowland plains. Called the Chaparrón complex, it is a distinctly zoned bichrome pottery, characterized by a hard, glossy, red slip separated from the polished–brown or buff–clay surface by wide incised lines (fig. 14b). The Chaparrón complex is most like the Conchas–phase ceramics (Middle Preclassic) from the Pacific coast of Guatemala both in form—*tecomates*, or incurving, restricted–mouth bowls, predominate—and in decoration. Chaparrón form and decoration suggest that

Figure 11. Remnants of tropical rain forest in the Atlantic lowlands near Guacimo. Photo: Michael J. Snarskis.

40

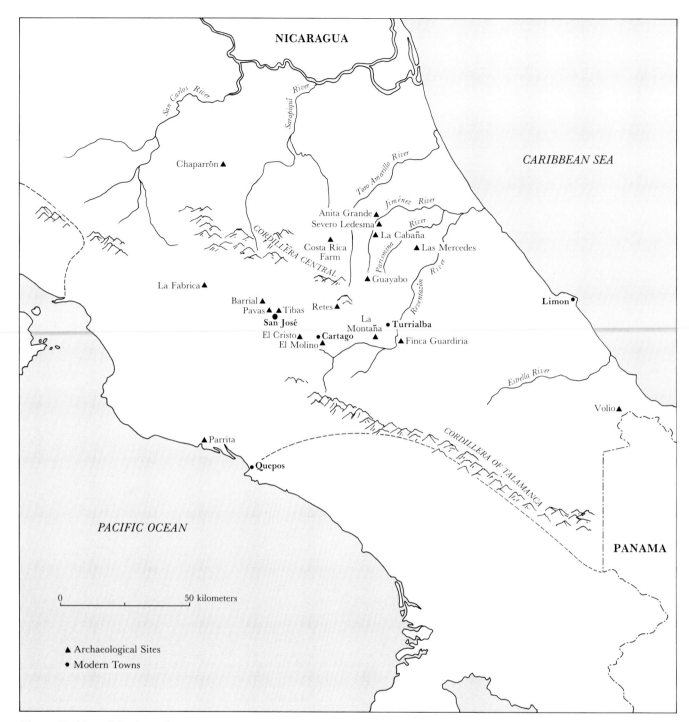

Figure 12. Map of the Central Highlands–Atlantic Watershed archaeological zone (C. Enrique Herra, Museo Nacional de Costa Rica).

it is nearly contemporaneous with La Montaña. If so, Chaparrón might represent a northern, Mesoamerican influence in Costa Rica, while La Montaña most closely resembles southern styles.

The period 500–100 B.C. is still poorly known, although pottery probably dating to this time has been found at several sites. From c. 100 B.C. to 200 A.D., there was a veritable explosion of sites (i.e., population) and a trend toward social stratification, evidenced by a new series of high–status artifacts—elaborate metates, ceremonial mace heads, carved jade or similar stone, flutes, rattles, and,

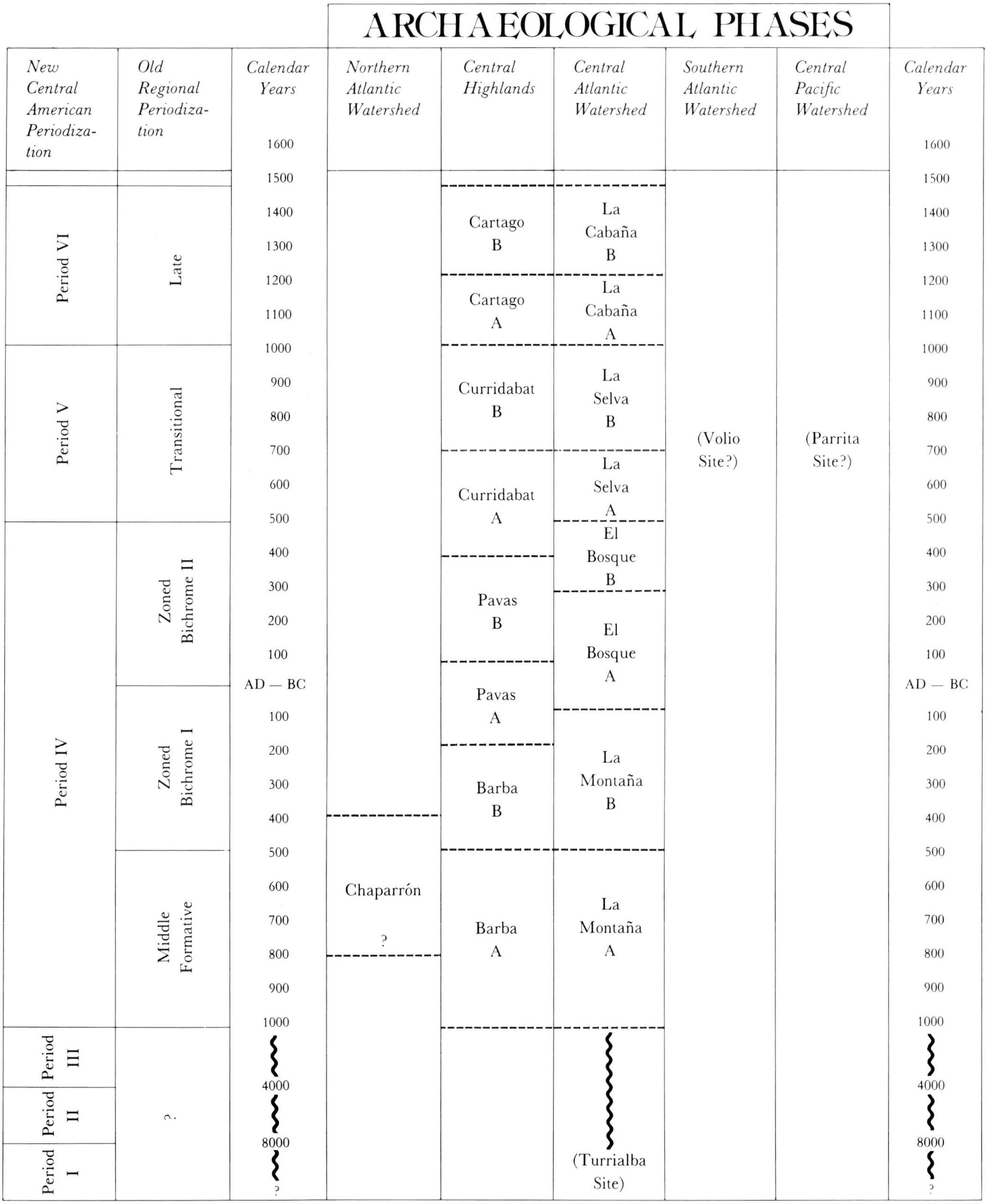

ARCHAEOLOGICAL PHASES

New Central American Periodization	Old Regional Periodization	Calendar Years	Northern Atlantic Watershed	Central Highlands	Central Atlantic Watershed	Southern Atlantic Watershed	Central Pacific Watershed	Calendar Years
		1600						1600
		1500						1500
Period VI	Late	1400		Cartago B	La Cabaña B			1400
		1300						1300
		1200		Cartago A	La Cabaña A			1200
		1100						1100
		1000						1000
Period V	Transitional	900		Curridabat B	La Selva B			900
		800				(Volio Site?)	(Parrita Site?)	800
		700			La Selva A			700
		600		Curridabat A				600
		500						500
Period IV	Zoned Bichrome II	400			El Bosque B			400
		300		Pavas B				300
		200			El Bosque A			200
		100						100
		AD — BC		Pavas A				AD — BC
	Zoned Bichrome I	100						100
		200			La Montaña B			200
		300		Barba B				300
		400	Chaparrón					400
	Middle Formative	500						500
		600			La Montaña A			600
		700	?	Barba A				700
		800						800
		900						900
		1000						1000
Period III	?	4000						4000
Period II		8000						8000
Period I		?			(Turrialba Site)			?

Figure 13. Chronological chart of archaeological periods and phases in the Central Highlands–Atlantic Watershed.

undoubtedly, a wide range of objects in perishable wood (staffs, drums, etc.), cloth, and bone. Sites of the El Bosque (middle Atlantic Watershed) and Pavas

43

(Central Highlands) phases, dating from c. 100 B.C.–500 A.D., are numerous and large.

Contact with more developed Mesoamerican cultures c. 600–200 B.C., probably through elite–oriented trade, may have resulted in the gradual propagation in northern Costa Rica of a new mythic complex, or politico–religious "world view," in which different deities, a reverence for jade amulets, and possibly intensive maize agriculture were important components. The popularity of zoned red–on–buff pottery, common in Mesoamerica, but rare in northern South America, can perhaps be traced to this interaction. The population boom may have been produced by successful, intensive maize farming, producing increasing competition for prime agricultural lands, and a need to ritualize cyclical agriculture procedures. Warrior, priest, and administrative classes probably evolved to handle related duties, creating a market for luxury articles that were badges of office.

Figure 14. Sherds of the La Montaña and Chaparrón ceramic complexes, early to middle Period IV, c. 700–300 B.C. (a) A–N: La Montaña; (b) O–Z: Chaparrón. Photo: Maritza Gutiérrez, Museo Nacional de Costa Rica.

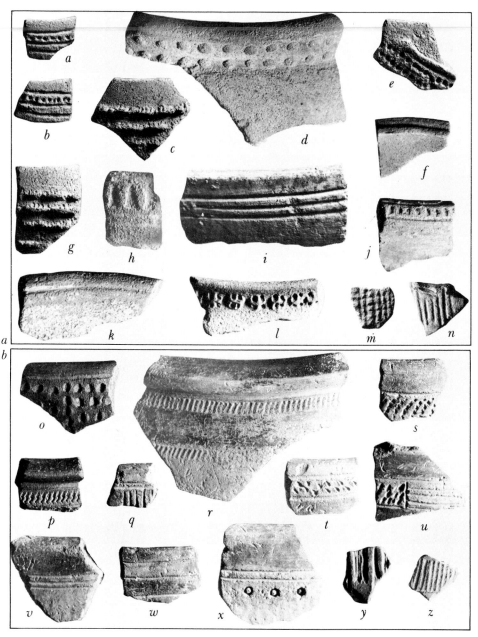

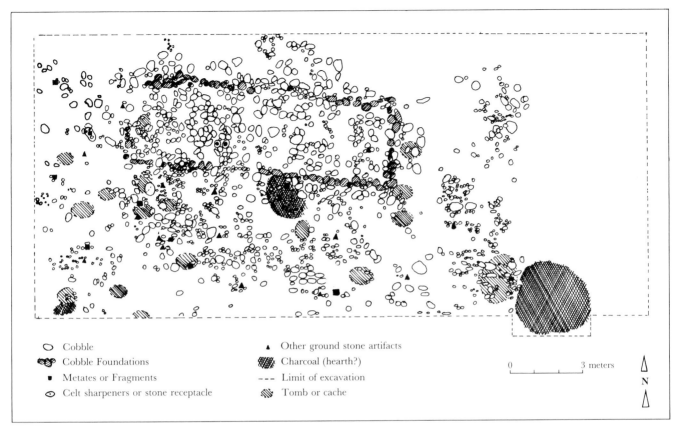

○	Cobble	▲	Other ground stone artifacts
	Cobble Foundations		Charcoal (hearth?)
▪	Metates or Fragments	---	Limit of excavation
○	Celt sharpeners or stone receptacle		Tomb or cache

0   3 meters

N

It should not be assumed that a Mesoamerican–type mythology obviated other belief systems. The predominance of toad, lizard, and especially cayman effigies is important, if one accepts Donald Lathrap's (1973) association of cayman symbols with manioc farming in South America. A patina of Mesoamerican symbolism may have combined with earlier tropical–forest animist beliefs, resulting in the menagerie of zoomorphic *adornos*, or ornaments, typical of Central Highlands–Atlantic Watershed pottery.

Recent archaeological excavations by the MNCR have provided considerable information on house forms, tomb constructions, and associated artifacts. At Severo Ledesma, near Guácimo, in the eastern lowlands, three El Bosque–phase houses were found. The two smaller ones were 3.5 x 12-meter rectangles, delimited by river cobbles stood on end; a perishable structure of wood, cane, and thatch was probably erected on this foundation, but no trace of it remains. Each house had two cobbles with cup–shaped depressions placed along one wall; these may have been mortars or receptacles. Numerous fragments of metates and other stone tools surrounded the houses, and several simple burials, excavated in the subsoil, were also associated (fig. 15). In the rainy Caribbean climate, no bones are preserved; burials are recognized by the tomb edifice and/or grave goods, mostly pottery. The third El Bosque house (fig. 16) was also rectangular, but much larger, 15 x 2.5 meters; because it was divided into rectangular segments by interior stone foundations, it may have been two adjoining structures. In any case, it housed people of a higher rank. The interior beneath the floor was honeycombed with burials and caches; one of the former contained an individual with a necklace of jade disk beads, surrounded by 27 pieces of grave furniture that included the plate of a "flying–panel" metate, fancy ceramic tripods

Figure 15. Structure 2 at the Severo Ledesma site, near Guacimo (C. Enrique Herra, Museo Nacional de Costa Rica).

OVERLEAF:
Plate 15. Female figure with child, Hacienda Tempisque, Guanacaste, ceramic (cat. no. 84).

Plate 16. Figure seated on bench, Nosara, Nicoya, ceramic (cat. no. 93).

45

decorated with animal and human modeled effigies, pottery ocarinas and rattles, and ground–stone celts.

Carbonized palm nuts of the species *Elaeis oleifera* HBK, an American oil palm related to the commercially important African oil palm, were found within this house, and a maize cob was found in another part of the site. No houses of the contemporary Pavas phase in the Central Highlands have yet been recognized, but there are considerable data on subsistence. During salvage excavation of a later architectural site at Barrial de Heredia, a deep trench bisected a large conical pit (two meters in diameter at the base and two meters deep) containing broken Pavas culinary pottery, stone tools, and a carpet of carbonized floral remains. Although botanical analysis is still in progress, it is known that the feature contained thousands of maize kernels; five maize–cob fragments, similar to Swasey 1 and 2 types from Cuello, Belize; several pieces of unidentified nuts or hard–shelled fruits; unidentified erect rhizomes; and several dessicated, pitted "cherry–like" fruits (Robert McK. Bird, personal communication). Also present were one—perhaps two—varieties of *Phaseolus vulgaris* (common bean) that are "closer to Mesoamerican than Andean types," as well as seeds of the Convolvulaceae family (Lawrence Kaplan, personal communication), which includes both sweet–potato and morning–glory species. The final identification of these seeds will be revelatory; if the former, a new cultigen will be added to the Costa Rican prehistoric subsistence complex, while the presence of the latter would be hard evidence for psychotropic drugs, a tradition well documented in other Precolumbian cultures and indirectly indicated by El Bosque–phase clay double–tubed nasal snuffers.

When he first identified conical features at the type site of Pavas, a San José suburb, Aguilar (1975) referred to them as "bottle–shaped tombs" because their contents included human skeletal remains and whole ceramic artifacts. Nevertheless, a case can be made for classifying them as "bell–shaped" storage pits, associated with the domestic–activity zone surrounding a dwelling, as in the Formative Mesoamerican pattern. Marcus Winter (1976) notes their occurrence

48

Figure 17. Complex of corridor tombs at Severo Ledesma. Note how their proportions echo those of El Bosque–phase houses (see fig. 16). Photo: C. Enrique Herra, Museo Nacional de Costa Rica.

from the Valley of Mexico to Guatemala City, and emphasizes their almost universal use as maize–storage pits, which, upon abandonment, were often "filled with household debris including burnt daub..., ashes, carbonized corn cobs and fruit seeds, animal bones, cooking pots and discarded manos and metates; some also had burials." Other Pavas–phase burials were unmarked except for associated grave goods, so mortuary patterns varied.

El Bosque–phase tombs may be one– or two–meter rectangles of cobbles; ellipses; corridors up to 12 meters long; or simply a scooped–out oval area in the subsoil, with no tomb edifice. Tombs in separate cemetery zones always have walls of cobbles and are usually long rectangles, often ordered neatly in ranks and files; these tombs repeat, on a smaller scale, the shape and proportions of El Bosque houses. Groups of 15 to 30 or more tombs, separated from other groups by empty corridors, may have corresponded to different lineages or clans (fig. 17). Although no bones or even teeth have been recovered, it seems that most burials were of the primary extended type; jade pendants, found face up in the bottoms of some tombs, were probably suspended around the neck of the deceased. Some El Bosque cemeteries cover several acres and contain hundreds of tons of volcanic–stone cobbles brought from river beds anywhere from 50 meters to several kilometers distant.

Chipped–stone artifacts are rare in El Bosque and Pavas deposits, but daggers of slate or fine basalt (cat. no. 142) were produced by this technique. Pecked– and ground–stone tools abound; mostly andesite, they are usually related to food processing or agriculture. Petaloid and trapezoidal celts, most with signs of hafting, are found frequently. Other ground–stone artifacts include bark–beaters (cat. no. 143), pestles (cat. nos. 135, 136), mortars, edge–battered cobbles, crude mace heads (probably weapons), loaf– and stirrup–shaped manos (cat. no. 137), and several kinds of metates. Loaf-shaped manos and basin– or trough–shaped metates, the typical maize–processing tools in prehistoric Mesoamerica, are found most frequently. Flat, tripod metates with raised rims and stirrup–shaped mullers are found less often and in contexts that sometimes suggest nondomestic roles—the preparation of special, ceremonial foodstuffs or drugs. Since the edges of these metates are carved in the shape of small heads, the taking and shrinking of trophy heads by warriors in battle seems to have been connected with them. Metates are also employed as a funeral bier in the most prestigious tombs; the body is laid out on two or three of them placed side by side. Many of the extraordinary "flying–panel" examples (cat. nos. 144–147) may have been manufactured especially for high–rank burial. An exceptional burial of this kind was found in a salvage excavation at Tibás (fig. 18). Besides artifacts of jade, stone, and pottery from both the Central Highlands and

Figure 18. Principal burial at Talamanca de Tibás with associated offerings. Photo:Michael J. Snarskis.

*Plate 18. Zoomorphic–effigy vessel,
Guanacaste–Nicoya zone, ceramic
(cat. no. 102).*

*Plate 19. Feline–effigy vessel,
Guanacaste–Nicoya zone, ceramic
(cat. no. 108).*

*Plate 20. Death's head effigy vessel,
Hacienda Tempisque, Guanacaste,
ceramic (cat. no. 105).*

Guanacaste– Nicoya, it contained a remarkably large Olmec jade clam shell (33 centimeters), with low relief on the interior showing a human hand holding a mythological composite animal, half feline, half moth. It is the only Olmec jade recovered in controlled excavations in Costa Rica (Snarskis 1979a).

Ceramics of the El Bosque complex in the Central Atlantic Watershed are most often red on buff (cat. nos. 116, 117) with polished dark–red lips, interiors, and bases, and a collar of naturally buff–colored clay, smoothed, but left exposed around the vessel shoulder and neck. This area may be blank or decorated by a series of tool–impressed techniques, appliqué motifs, or painted linear patterns. Shell and reed stamping, combing, scarifying, fluting, pattern burnishing, and appliqué pellets and adornos are some of the decorative techniques found in El Bosque pottery. There are also red– and orange–slipped vessels with maroon paint. El Bosque pottery may be baroque, with piled–on appliqué, or exquisitely elegant and simple. Technically, the pottery is very well made, showing a dominance of the ceramic craft that disappears in later periods.

Pavas–phase pottery of the Central Highlands is modally similar to El Bosque, but orange slip and maroon paint predominate (cat. no. 123). Vessels are generally larger. Whereas the Ticaban tripods of the El Bosque phase are rather massive solid-leg vessels with zoomorphic adornos on each support (cat. no. 125), Pavas–phase ceramics of the Molino Channeled type are usually more graceful. Small, rotund figurines in a variety of domestic and ceremonial poses are frequent El Bosque–phase finds. Men with feathered capes, large headdresses, and zoomorphic masks, sometimes holding trophy heads, give a glimpse into complex ceremonial life. Women are portrayed holding children or carrying burdens on a tumpline. Animals are shown in naturalistic postures; what look like small dogs are often bicephalic. Most of these hollow figurines (the so-called Santa Clara type) double as rattles and may be finished with black, white, or yellow fugitive paint; red-slipped varieties also occur.

Other special–purpose ceramic artifacts include maracas; small rattles made with rings, to be worn on the fingers; ocarinas (cat. nos. 126–128), flutes, and whistles, of various forms; flat and roller stamps or seals (cat. nos. 133, 134) (probably for body painting or cloth imprinting); and single– or double–tubed pipes—the last were probably used for inhaling drugs (cat. no. 132). Five C–14 dates for the El Bosque phase range from 50 B.C. to 425 A.D.

PERIOD V (500–1000 A.D.)

After maintaining close contact with Mesoamerican culture for several centuries, the Central Highlands–Atlantic Watershed, during the middle part of Period V, underwent striking changes, which can be observed in house forms, ceramics, and high–status artifacts. Most evidence suggests that an undefined "southern influence" produced these changes. It was perhaps fortuitous that the fall of Teotihuacan in the sixth century, with the consequent disruption in central lowland Maya centers and the Pacific trade route to the south, coincided approximately with the introduction to Costa Rica of metallurgical techniques from Colombia and Panama, but it may turn out that there was a causal relationship, with elite–oriented gold objects and their associated mythology being brought in to fill the vacuum produced by the sundering of ties with Mesoamerican elite groups. Guanacaste–Nicoya did not react to these influences in the same way; after c. 500 A.D., the ceramic traditions of the two zones began a marked stylistic divergence, the former emphasizing polychrome painting and the latter, plastic decorative techniques.

54

In the first part of Period V, settlements seem to have followed the El Bosque pattern of dispersed villages of several houses, usually located on alluvial terraces; one incomplete excavation of a La Selva A–phase house in the Turrialba valley suggested a rectangular form. Long "corridor" tombs are also typical of La Selva A. Examples at the La Montaña site near Turrialba were defined by rows of cobbles in two or three courses, measuring 2–2.5 x 7 meters. No domestic zones of corresponding Curridabat A–phase sites in the Central Highlands have been reported, but Aguilar excavated tombs of this date at Tatiscú, near Cartago, that were shaped like large, shallow basins and contained multiple interments. In one, he recorded a large fragment of a tumbaga figurine in the "Coclé," or Sitio Conte, style—one of the earliest metal objects found in Costa Rica.

The same kinds of ground–stone artifacts described for the El Bosque phase continue in La Selva A and Curridabat A. There is a decline in the technical skill of lapidary work, and frequently lesser stones are used as raw material. At La Montaña, we recovered a necklace composed of tiny disk beads made from *tiza*, a light–green, chalky stone; at intervals among them were strung miniature beads of jade and tree resin, with a somewhat larger jade pendant placed to hang centrally on the chest. Ceramics sometimes reflect the zoned, red–on–buff El Bosque tradition, but the simple elegance that sometimes characterized that style is lost. Shiny maroon–on–orange painted decoration appears on the interior of open bowls, and purple or maroon paint on orange–brown slip, accompanied by a variety of incised, stamped, or appliqué motifs, becomes more common. This is what Hartman called Curridabat ware (fig. 19). The massive Ticaban tripods of El Bosque are gradually replaced by the hollow–legged Africa type (cat. no. 187), whose modeled adornos, perched above the supports, display a variety of ritual and domestic poses.

In one tripod we found a carbonized maize cob. Burnt maize in a mortuary offering might be symbolic of the funeral *chicha*, a thick, fermented brew made from maize or palm-fruit. In another part of the same cemetery, a mass of 15 to

Figure 19. Curridabat Ware. Reproduced from Lothrop 1926: pl. CLXXI (p. 32).

Plate 21. *Tripod vessel, Filadelfia, Guanacaste, ceramic (cat. no. 115).*
Plate 22. *Bowl, Guanacaste–Nicoya zone, ceramic (cat. no. 114).*

Plate 23. Plate, Atlantic Watershed
zone, ceramic (cat. no. 117).

Plate 24. Bowl, Línea Vieja, Atlantic
Watershed, ceramic (cat. no. 116).

20 of the same kind of tripods was found, smashed, near the surface at one end of a corridor tomb. This discovery recalls the two– or three–day funeral *chichadas* (rowdy, drunken feasts) described for historical times by María Eugenia Bozzoli (1975) and others. Another possibility is that the tripods were incense or offertory burners, since many are smudged on the exterior.

Red-slipped Gutiérrez Incised/Engraved and the earliest brown–slipped incised types of Guanacaste–Nicoya have analogues in Zoila Red and La Selva Brown of the Atlantic Watershed. Incised triangles with simple hatching, probably symbolizing alligator scutes, are a common motif, and zoomorphic effigy vessels sometimes occur. Negative, or resist, painting—in which pottery is painted with a design in wax or impermanent clay and then smudged or repainted, after which the "resist" substance is removed to reveal a design the color of the original surface (a technique similar to the batik process on cloth)—increases greatly toward the middle of Period V. It is usually applied in curvilinear patterns (cat. no. 192) reminiscent of Colombian and Panamanian motifs.

Around 700–800 A.D., the preferred house form became circular, and tombs became what have been called stone cists: oval or rectangular boxes of cobbles or flagstones, usually with both a floor and a lid of stone. When floors and lids are missing today, they were probably made of wood, now decayed. Wooden cist tombs—used because of taboos against the funerary bundle touching earth—are recorded historically. Some of the better–made prehistoric stone cists were sealed so well with natural volcanic flagstones that today they are only half–filled with fine dirt that has sifted in over a thousand years. At about this time, a few Early Polychrome trade ceramics (usually Galo or Carrillo) from Guanacaste–Nicoya appear in Central and Atlantic sites, beginning a substantial trade in polychromes between the two zones.

The earliest known site with circular house forms is La Fábrica, near Grecia in the Central Highlands, where the MNCR did archaeological salvage. Thirteen circular foundations of field stone and river cobbles were mapped; at least as many more may be hidden in nearby sugar-cane fields (fig. 20). Most foundations varied from 10 to 20 meters in diameter, and the largest had two rectangular entry ramps opposite one another. A cobble–paved causeway, nine meters wide, enters the site from the north and runs toward the principal structure. La Fábrica shows evidence of occupation from the first few centuries after Christ until c. 1100–1200 A.D.; associated pottery of the Curridabat B phase suggests that the circular structures date to 700–900 A.D.

La Fábrica has no stone cist tombs. Instead, the mortuary patterns recall those of Guanacaste–Nicoya: tombs were marked with natural stone columns and/or accumulations of field stone. Fired adobe floors appeared 50 to 200 centimeters below the present surface in cemetery zones and beneath houses, where burials were also located. Most La Fábrica burials were of the primary extended type. One cemetery burial, laid on three decoratively sculpted metates, was accompanied by artifacts known to be indicative of high status in most of Costa Rica before c. 800 A.D.: jades, ceremonial mace heads, teardrop–shaped polished black celts, and a stirrup mano with zoomorphic motifs. A collared jade tube found in this burial is identical to examples recovered from the Sacred Cenote at Chichén Itzá, dating to the Maya Late Classic (c. 800 A.D.). While this burial is similar to the Tibás burial that contained an heirloom Olmec jade, artifacts from the La Fábrica burial place it somewhat later.

At La Fábrica, carbonized remains of maize, beans, and palm nuts were found, which, together with the large quantities of quotidian manos, metates, and

Figure 20. Archaeologists of the Museo Nacional de Costa Rica excavating and mapping the site of La Fabrica de Grecia, a Period V settlement exposed during the construction of a liquor factory. Photo: Juan Vicente Guerrero, Museo Nacional de Costa Rica.

chipped–basalt tools, indicate a nucleated agricultural village. Differences in architecture and grave goods (a copper or tumbaga bell and deer antlers were found in the principal house) reveal a rank–structured society.

Barrial de Heredia was another Central Highlands site excavated as part of an MNCR salvage program. Its architectural remains date to the transition between Periods V and VI (900–1100 A.D.). Although later than La Fábrica, Barrial did not have round houses. Of eight structures excavated and mapped, three were ellipsoidal and five were square or slightly rectangular. The two shapes apparently correspond to functional differences, for the ellipsoidal cobble foundations contained much more domestic refuse (burned food remains, broken culinary pottery, and stone tools) and large ovens and/or hearths, and lacked burials beneath the floor, while the quadrangular examples (fig. 21) showed less evidence of domestic activity but had burials with imported polychrome ceramics beneath the floor. The largest quadrangular and ellipsoidal structures directly adjoined, suggesting that occupants of the latter (wives?) were involved in the domestic maintenance of those domiciled in the former. Two kinds of tombs were noted at Barrial: a variant of the long, corridor variety, using only one line of standing cobbles and found only beneath the largest quadrangular houses, and a simple rectangular trench capped with flagstones. The latter type was found under houses and in a small cemetery zone, 100 meters away.

Basin–shaped metates and simple cobble mortars appear at Barrial; the most commonly observed stone tool was a small boxlike *mano–machacador* (combination grinder–pounder) showing use–polish on its flat facets and battering at the extremities. Carbonized maize and beans were found in and around the structures. Although Curridabat B–phase pottery was found beneath many parts of the site, ceramics associated with the architectural features were more closely

Plate 25. Pot stand, Atlantic Watershed zone, ceramic (cat. no. 120).

Plate 26. Pot stand, Atlantic Watershed zone, ceramic (cat. no. 122).

Plate 27. Ocarina, Guácimo, Atlantic Watershed, ceramic (cat. no. 126).

Plate 28. Ocarina, Guácimo, Atlantic Watershed, ceramic (cat. no. 127).

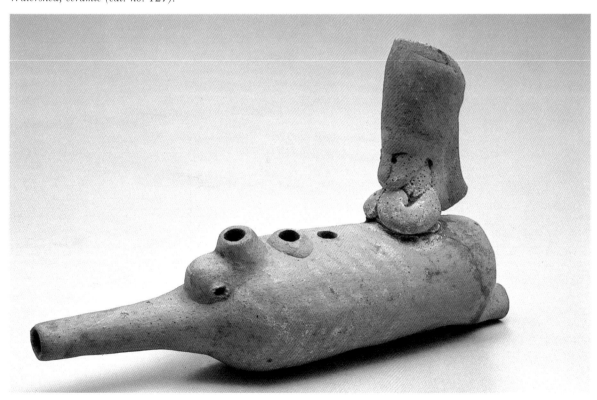

Figure 21. Excavation and mapping of a square house foundation (c. 900 A.D.) at Barrial de Heredia. Photo: Michael J. Snarskis.

related to the crudely executed appliqué styles of Period VI. Other frequent finds were small, open dishes with tripod zoomorphic–effigy head supports, a brown slip, and geometric incised panels on the exterior (Tayutic Incised), and a large number of caches of tiny *ollas*, often placed well away from burials and at no great depth.

Of the hundreds of Guanacaste–Nicoya polychrome sherds found at Barrial, a considerable percentage showed crack–lacing holes, a mending technique whereby perforations are drilled on either side of a fracture, and thongs are employed to bind the weakened part together. This bespeaks esteem for the foreign polychrome pottery—almost no locally made vessels were thus mended. The repeated presence of this polychrome in higher–status tombs at Barrial indicates a flourishing, elite–oriented trade network between these two arch-aeological zones. Since Central Highlands–Atlantic Watershed ceramics are not found in Guanacaste–Nicoya sites, we know that something else was being traded in return, possibly perishable commodities (carved wooden objects, feath-ers, poisons, drugs, cacao, or slaves). Two C–14 dates from Barrial fall between 800 and 1000 A.D.

PERIOD VI (1000–1550 A.D.)

A recent catchment analysis—in which a series of natural resource zones and environmental variables are related to the location of human settlements—of a small sample of Atlantic Watershed archaeological sites revealed an interesting trend. Through Periods IV and V—some 2,000 years—there was an increasing tendency to locate settlements on reasonably flat alluvial plains suitable for farming. In Period VI, the distribution of sites in several environmental zones becomes random, suggesting that other factors besides good farmland became important in choosing a site; these factors were probably socio–political frontiers and defense (Findlow, Snarskis, and Martin 1979).

Period VI habitation sites in the Central and Atlantic zones are usually easily recognized because of their rudimentary but distinctive architecture: round, earth–filled mounds or simple foundations with retaining walls of stone cobbles; *calzadas*, or cobble–paved causeways; small ridged enclosures or plazas; and even aqueducts and giant flagstone bridges in the larger sites. Petroglyphs (rock carvings) are frequent. Just as noticeable to the archaeologist is the degree of agglomeration—houses and other features packed together—which gives the sense of definite site boundaries. There seem to have been networks of tightly organized sites, small and large, often surprisingly close together.

The largest, most complex site known for this period is Guayabo de Turrialba (see Fonseca Zamora, this volume). Other major sites in the Atlantic lowlands are Las Mercedes, now destroyed; Anita Grande; Costa Rica Farm; and, on a smaller scale, La Cabaña. Such sites probably number well over 100 in this archaeological zone, although only Guayabo and La Cabaña have been excavated horizontally, in part. MNCR excavations in La Cabaña in 1976–77 exposed two circular mounds, 20 meters across and less than two meters high; one non–mound house circle, 12 meters in diameter; and a square, ridged enclosure surrounding an empty "plaza," with a cobble–paved causeway leading into it (fig. 22). Horizontal stripping of the two main mounds showed that Mound 1, the higher, had only a central hearth, while Mound 2—from which a curved porchlike area projects near the entrance—had along one part of the interior a series of four or five

Figure 22. Partial plan of the La Cabaña site (C. Enrique Herra, Museo Nacional de Costa Rica).

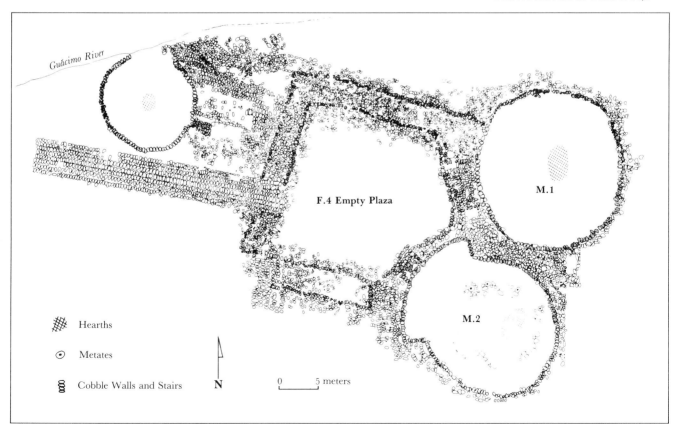

Guácimo River

F.4 Empty Plaza

M.1

M.2

⊞ Hearths

⊙ Metates

ⱷ Cobble Walls and Stairs

N

0   5 meters

boulder metates, sometimes surrounded by stone seats; one had a mano nearby. In addition to the central hearth, several smaller ones were noted. The presence of food processing on one mound and not the other would seem to indicate a different function for each. The taller Mound 1 might be construed as the residence of the ruling individual or group, with Mound 2 housing wives or others having to do with the domestic maintenance of Mound 1 inhabitants. Fray Agustín de Zevallos, writing in 1610, describes several customs of the peoples then living in eastern Costa Rica, "who live in *palenques*, which are forts built in native fashion. . . . The chiefs have the women that they desire *all in the same house*, and the common people generally have one. . . ." (Lothrop 1926: 446; author's italics).

At La Cabaña, stairways off the two major mounds, as well as one major and

a   *b*

Figure 23. (a) Stone cist cemetery at Hacienda Molino near Cartago. (b) The skeletons of both primary and secondary burials were recovered at this site, which dates to c. 1200 A.D. Photos: Ricardo Vázquez, Museo Nacional de Costa Rica.

three minor paved causeways, enter the empty plaza area. Within the walled, square enclosure surrounding the plaza were found small, stone cist tombs or caches containing prestigious ceramic artifacts. A plaza area with enclosure has been noted in all major Period VI sites, invariably near the principal mounds. At Anita Grande, two very large quadrangular plazas are connected by a causeway almost 500 meters long. It is tempting to interpret this plaza configuration as the formal place of contact between the ruling class and the lesser population of the site, perhaps for ritual redistribution of goods.

Stone cist burials predominate in Period VI, under or around houses and in special cemetery zones. Much more use was made of flagstones as floors or lids of cobble–built tombs, or as the sole element in tomb construction. Several stone cist cemeteries excavated around Cartago by the MNCR (fig. 23a) contained extended primary and secondary burials, some tombs containing both kinds. Cups made from human skulls were found above many tombs. Exhumation and reburial seem to have been practiced, for many tombs were divided, added to, or built in as many as three vertical layers. Stone cists in the Atlantic lowlands are

Plate 29. Flying–panel metate, Atlantic Watershed zone, stone (cat. no. 144).

Plate 30. Zoomorphic–effigy bowl, Atlantic Watershed
zone, volcanic stone (cat. no. 228).

Plate 31. Pedestal bowl, Atlantic
Watershed zone, stone (cat. no.
225).

Plate 32. Trophy head, Atlantic Watershed zone, ceramic (cat. no. 190).

Plate 33. Anthropomorphic–effigy vessel, Turrialba, Atlantic Watershed, ceramic (cat. no. 191).

Figure 24. Common Period VI pottery (1000–1500 A.D.) from both the Central and Atlantic zones, called by Lothrop (1926) "Stone Cist Ware." Photo: Dirk Bakker.

more often made of carefully chosen cobbles, chocked with smaller stones; no mortar was used (fig. 23b). Grave goods in stone cist tombs are usually fewer and of poorer quality than those of the preceding periods. Many tombs contain no offerings, although perishable articles may have been included. Tiny quartz crystals, used as gravers, were found in several stone cists in the Cartago valley (Hacienda Molino and El Cristo sites). One tomb yielded a copper bell with a quartz crystal inside it.

In Period VI, cobbles were used as quotidian metates. Slightly used mortars and hammerstones seem to have been frequent. Ornate ceremonial metates did not disappear, however, although styles changed. Four–legged jaguar–effigy metates appear (cat. no. 229), and round versions with pedestal (cat. nos. 199, 200) or atlantean (cat. no. 201) bases become more common. Free–standing stone sculpture increases sharply (cat. nos. 193–198, 217–224), tending to repeat "standard" or "archetypal" poses; idiosyncratic poses—women braiding their hair, a man urinating—are also seen. Some sculptures seem to be portraits of specific individuals, even depicting deformities or facial tics. While earlier stone sculpture almost always portrayed zoomorphic effigies or, at best, a human figure with a zoomorphic mask, Period VI sculpture primarily records human subjects. This must represent a fundamental philosophical shift, wherein military or political power was augmenting at the expense of the traditional "religious" power base, probably as a result of population pressure on certain resources and/or new modes of conflict resolution. The hubris of emergent

Figure 25. "Frying–pan" censer with zoomorphic handle. Photo: Dirk Bakker.

warrior–chiefs may have caused them to erect stone images of themselves as large as, or larger than, those of their zoomorphically symbolized deities.

With a few exceptions, Period VI pottery is of poor quality compared with that of earlier cultures, and there seems to have been less of it. Crude little ollas and tripod dishes of a coarse, poorly knit paste are the most frequent finds. Better–preserved examples are overloaded with decoration—incision, tool stamping, appliqué pellets, fillets impressed to look like chains, and crudely modeled heads or animal figures—Lothrop (1926) called this Stone Cist Ware (fig. 24). Brown incised/engraved types from the end of Period V continue throughout Period VI, increasingly carelessly made. Resist decoration usually appears only on high–status pieces. Dishes or slightly flaring cylindrical jars with animal–head tripod supports are found, as they are in Guanacaste–Nicoya, but the long–legged tripods of the two preceding periods virtually disappear. Seen more fre-

Figure 26. Irazu Yellow Line, a Period VI painted type from the Central Highlands–Atlantic Watershed zone. Photo: Dirk Bakker.

quently is an unusual skillet–like form, known as a frying–pan censer, apparently used for burning incense (fig. 25). Cartago Red Line begins in this period, first as simple or tripod dishes, often with a stylized feline head and tail added on; red finger–painted lines on orange slip decorate the earlier varieties. Later, the red paint becomes more vivid, a cream slip replaces the orange, and more animated design possibly attempts to copy the brilliant Papagayo Polychrome traded in from Guanacaste–Nicoya.

In other Period VI ceramic types, a Diquís or Chiriquí stylistic influence can be felt. Irazú Yellow Line shows geometric designs in thick, yellow paint on two–tone orange and brick–red slip (fig. 26), while Cot Black Line has similar motifs in weak black and red paints on orange-brown slip. Especially important are open dishes or bowls, with effigy-head tripod supports. The geometric motifs recall those of Chiriquí Polychrome, a late Diquís type that may have been inspired by Guanacaste–Nicoya polychromes. Another Atlantic type, Turrialba Bichrome, exhibits very thin vessel walls and elegant, simple olla forms in the

OVERLEAF:
Plate 34. Tripod vessel, Atlantic Watershed zone, ceramic (cat. no. 187).

Plate 35. Human–effigy vessel, Atlantic Watershed zone, ceramic (cat. no. 210).

best examples, recalling the delicacy of the exceptional Tarragó Biscuit type of Diquís. Trade sherds of Tarragó Bisquit found at Guayabo de Turrialba by Aguilar (1972b), provide more concrete evidence for ties to the south.

Metallurgy was the most important material–culture introduction from the south, reaching its apogee in the Central Highlands–Atlantic Watershed during Period VI (Bray, this volume). The disappearance of jade working by 1000 A.D. has previously been attributed to the exhaustion of local jade sources (Easby 1968), but we may now consider the possibility that Atlantic and Central cultures at this time were simply not concerned with jade as mythologically significant material, preferring gold amulets or other articles important in a southern–oriented ritual complex.

Figurines, ocarinas, rattles, and other small special–purpose ceramic articles — with the exception of a well–made brown incised type that spans the transition between Periods V and VI—are very rare in this period. Stone and wood carving may have taken precedence over the ceramic medium for figurines. Five C–14 dates from La Cabaña–phase sites range from 1000 to 1400 A.D.

Diquís

Diquís is the least known of Costa Rica's archaeological zones; an interpretative synthesis of its prehistory must of necessity be brief and tentative. The plundering of tombs has been intensive, because of the single–minded pursuit of gold, stimulating looters to smash pottery vessels and even to dynamite the famous stone spheres of this zone.

PERIODS I, II, and III (?–1000 B.C.)

Nothing is yet known about these periods in Diquís. In the Chiriquí province of Panama, however, part of the same cultural subarea, Olga Linares and Anthony Ranere (1980) have done extensive work, resulting in the most complete archaeological sequence in Central America for Periods II and III.

Figure 27. View of the Diquís archaeological zone near Palmar Sur. Photo: Michael J. Snarskis.

Figure 28. Map of the Diquís archaeological zone (C. Enrique Herra, Museo Nacional de Costa Rica).

PERIOD IV (1000 B.C.–500 A.D.)

We pick up the prehistoric thread well into the second half of Period IV with the Concepción and Aguas Buenas archaeological complexes. For specific data on chronology, settlement patterns, and subsistence, it is necessary to extrapolate from published work carried out in Panama, where highland valleys or upland ridges seem to have been preferred locations for villages, a pattern also observed in Diquís by Haberland (in press) and confirmed by a survey carried out by Robert Drolet and Robert Markens for the MNCR during 1980–1981. With the exception of a possibly oval or rectangular house (suggested by postholes) at the Panamanian highland site of Pittí–González, no house forms are known. Larger, probably ceremonial sites like Barriles, in Panama, and Bolas, in Diquís, include stone–faced earthen mounds and terraces or platforms.

Considerable uncertainty exists as to the spatial and temporal relationship of the Concepción ("Scarified Ware") and Aguas Buenas ceramic complexes, which predominated in this zone from several centuries before Christ until c. 500–700 A.D. (fig. 30). Concepción, known primarily from Chiriquí, is characterized by multiple–line incising or rough brushing on the naturally buff or brown clay exterior, giving the appearance of rough–edged, fine corrugation, hence "Scari-fied." Chimney–shaped and conical vessels, some with tripod feet, are typical. Clay roller stamps are known. Although featured prominently in the earliest archaeological monographs (Holmes 1888; MacCurdy 1911), very little of this pottery has since come to light. Aguas Buenas pottery may be red, brown, or red

Plate 36. Annular base, provenance
unknown, ceramic (cat no. 232).

Plate 37. Jar, Diquís zone, ceramic
(cat. no. 237).

Plate 38. Ocarina, seated figure,
Carbonera, Osa Peninsula, ceramic
(cat. no. 231).

New Central American Periodization	Calendar Years	Diquís Phases
	1600	
Period VI	1500	Chiriquí B
	1400	
	1300	
	1200	- - - - -
	1100	Churiquí A
	1000	
Period V	900	- - - - -
	800	Burica?
	700	
	600	- - - - -
	500	
	400	Aguas Buenas
	300	
	200	
	100	
	AD — BC	Concepción
Period IV	100	
	200	
	300	- - - - -
	400	
	500	
	600	?
	700	
	800	
	900	
	1000	

Figure 29. Chronological chart of the Diquís archaeological zone.

on buff; small recurved–rim dishes and ollas are typical, and zoomorphic modeled adornos are a frequent decoration. Certain very large urns were apparently used to house secondary burials. The unusual Carbonera figurines, reputedly from the tip of the Osa Peninsula, are suggestive of a style at once older and foreign (cat. nos. 230, 231). The Osa may have offered a convenient point of arrival for seagoing peoples, in this case from South America (Paulsen 1977).

Cobble metates, with and without tripod legs, open at one end and raised along the other three sides, are known from Aguas Buenas sites, as are many waisted, double–bitted axes of chipped stone. Some Barriles–like artifacts have been recovered; carved stone barrels of andesite and granite, with low reliefs carved at either flat end, have been found near the Costa Rican town of San Vito. It is said that 15 were found around a huge petroglyph–bearing boulder called Piedra Pintada, where they may have functioned as seats (Laurencich de Minelli and Minelli 1973: 222). Also found in that region were fragments of stone figures, some with conical headgear like that known from the famous Barriles statuary. Shaft–and–chamber tombs at Barriles contained huge ellipsoidal metates, adorned along the edge with carved human heads and supported by four legs sculpted into detailed human figures. A similar metate can be seen in this exhibition (cat. no. 233). Missing in this region is intensive lapidary work in jade; although a very small amount has come to light, it seems that other materials available locally, like agate, were used.

Some archaeologists (Stone 1977:106; Haberland, in press) believe that the giant stone spheres of Diquís began to be made at this time (fig. 31; cat. no. 235). Some spheres are over two meters in diameter, yet vary from the perfectly spherical by a mere centimeter or two; they are made of granite, andesite, and even sedimentary stone, and weigh up to 16 tons. Certain balls found on the Diquís Delta were apparently rafted and hauled to their present location from places many kilometers distant. The spheres have been found in alignments on the surface, some mounted on cobble platforms. Although no burials have been found beneath them, the spheres are often grouped in the vicinity of a cemetery zone (Lothrop 1963).

Since maize, beans, palm nuts, and avocados have been recovered from late Period IV sites in Chiriquí (Linares and Ranere 1980), we may infer a similar subsistence for Diquís populations at that time. Root crops were almost certainly important as well, but they leave few macroscopically identifiable remains.

Some Concepción–phase tombs in Chiriquí, stone–lined and incorporating metates in the walls, suggest extended primary burials. Other Aguas Buenas tombs were simple oval pits, while Barriles had well–made shaft–and–chamber tombs, a form known early from Colombia and the Andean area. Urn burials are also reported. Burials are usually found beneath or around dwellings, but appear in a separate cemetery zone at Boquete, Panama (Haberland, in press).

PERIODS V AND VI (500–1550 A.D.)

As in the Central Highlands–Atlantic Watershed zone, important cultural changes occurred in Diquís between 500 and 800 A.D., seeming to indicate an influx of South American peoples and/or cultural traditions, possibly the arrival and eventual hegemony of Chibcha–speaking peoples from Colombia.

The transition from the Aguas Buenas to the "classic" Chiriquí phase is obscure. While some pottery reminiscent of Period V complexes in Central–At-

Figure 30. Red and buff ceramics of the Aguas Buenas/Concepción complex (c. 1–500 A.D.). Photo: Dirk Bakker.

lantic Costa Rica and western Chiriquí, Panama, has come to light in Diquís, we have only the beginning of a decent ceramic stratigraphy (Lothrop 1963). For this reason, following Linares's Panamanian terminology (Linares and Ranere 1980: 111), I have tentatively indicated a transitional Burica (or late Bugaba) phase between Aguas Buenas and Chiriquí, although its validity in Diquís remains to be ascertained.

In their recent survey of the Térraba (Diquís) drainage, Drolet and Markens found that Chiriquí–phase sites were most often located on broad terraces just above major water courses, suggesting a more intensive utilization of the major rivers in later times. While increased travel and commerce along these mostly navigable rivers were probably a factor, the extraordinary amounts of river

Figure 31. Moderately sized stone sphere from Diquís. Photo: Michael J. Snarskis.

OVERLEAF:
Plate 39. Seated figure, Diquís zone, ceramic (cat. no. 243).

Plate 40. Tripod vessel, Diquís zone, ceramic (cat. no. 241).

cobbles used in the construction of Chiriquí–phase sites must also have played a part in the shifting pattern of settlements.

Several kinds of sites are known for Period VI. Special burial grounds, often incorporating cobble platforms and walls—as in the case of Sabana de Caracol (Haberland 1961a)—have been found on the summits of rather large hills. Cemeteries, rich in cast gold pendants and other metal artifacts, were discovered along high, sharp ridges, today overgrown with rain forest (e.g., the Coquito cemetery). A second class of sites seemingly combined ceremonial and perhaps funerary activities with habitations. Finca Remolino, mapped by Drolet and Markens, incorporates large, low, stone–faced platforms of many shapes, including quadrangular ones, interspersed with what seem to be house mounds. On, or alongside, the platforms were embedded large natural monoliths (of columnar basalt) up to four meters in length, some pecked to a pointed end for easier insertion. A third kind of site seems to have been primarily habitational, with circular house foundations of cobbles, terraces with retaining walls, and cobble–paved walkways. This kind of site is most frequently found along major rivers; almost all have associated cemeteries on terraces above the habitation zones.

Murciélago, a very large site (almost 4 square kilometers) of the third kind, has recently been mapped and partially excavated by Drolet and Markens, who found circular house foundations, 12 to more than 20 meters in diameter, surrounded by a gently sloping pavement of river cobbles (fig. 32). Although many manos and metates were found outside the houses, most chipped and pottery refuse was apparently deposited in unusual features composed of yellow and red oxidized subsoil rocks, which surround the houses. Whether these features were activity areas or dumps is unclear, but they were placed systematically throughout the site. A complex system of pavements and ramps connected living areas in any one part of the site. These new, important settlement data for Diquís, along with the previously known stone cist tombs, make up an "architectural" complex much like that known from the Central Highlands–Atlantic Watershed during Periods V and VI, and we may assume that both zones experienced the same pervasive "southern" influence during that time. In addition to stone cist tombs, we know that shaft–and–chamber tombs continued to be constructed into the Chiriquí phase (Haberland 1976).

There is a fairly large range of pottery types known from Diquís during the last six or seven hundred years before the Spanish arrival. Tall, hollow–legged tripods, slipped in reddish brown and usually decorated with appliqué fillets, pellets, adornos, or white–painted lines, recall somewhat similar (but earlier) vessels of the Atlantic Watershed. In Diquís, the tripod legs are often in the form of crocodiles or fish. Organic black resist decoration, often combined with positive red paint, adorns white or orange–slipped small ollas, in patterns recalling Panamanian, and especially Colombian, ceramics. It is significant that small, cylindrical, capped phials, of the kind used among Colombian cultures to carry lime for chewing with coca leaves, appear in Diquís in this ceramic type, since coca–chewing is a South American trait.

Chiriquí Polychromes (cat. nos. 242, 243) are usually executed in black and red on a cream slip, with simple, geometric motifs. While Panamanian motifs seem to dominate, there was some stylistic influence from northwestern Costa Rica, and a few Nicoya polychrome trade sherds have been found in Diquís. As in the rest of Costa Rica during Period VI, tripod supports shaped like animal (mostly feline) heads are diagnostic for this time in Diquís. Stone (1943) found this pottery (her Red and Black Line) along with Spanish iron and glass artifacts.

Perhaps the pinnacle of the ceramic craft in Period VI Diquís was the Tarragó Biscuit. This fine, buff–colored pottery may have walls less than two millimeters thick, and displays supremely simple yet elegantly proportioned shapes. Tiny modeled adornos frequently emphasize the voluptuous forms. Zoomorphic effigies include what is almost certainly an American camelid (llama, guanaco), an animal whose natural habitat extends only as far north as the Colombian Andes.

Diquís stone sculpture of Period VI is radically different from that of the other two zones of Costa Rica, and, at the same time, reminiscent of Colombian forms. A link with the Atlantic Watershed is found in the tetrapod jaguar metates and circular "Atlantean" varieties that appear in both zones; ceramic models of the latter kind probably served as seats. Large stone spheres have been found around Chiriquí–phase cemeteries.

Periods V and VI witnessed a florescence of the metallurgical craft, which produced quantities of pendants, bracelets, plaques, headbands, and other articles of gold or tumbaga (Bray, this volume). The Diquís gold–working style is basically the same as that of Chiriquí.

Conclusions

In a very general way, we can sum up prehistoric cultural development in Costa Rica as follows, starting c. 1000 B.C.: a few small and sedentary communities, with pottery and *perhaps* a northern South American subsistence pattern, i.e., mostly root cropping, were followed by a rapid increase in population and social complexity, *perhaps* stimulated by developing maize agriculture, complemented by polycropping (in regions of fertile, alluvial soils and abundant rain) and hunting. A culmination occurred around the time of Christ in sedentary, fairly

OVERLEAF:
Plate 41. Monkey pendant, Palmar Sur, Diquís, gold (cat. no. 267).

Plate 42. Avian pendant, Sierpe, Diquís, gold (cat. no. 249).

large nodes of population, which were characterized by stratified society with complex ritual connections to Mesoamerican trade networks, and probably a redistributive hierarchy. In Guanacaste–Nicoya, a gradual shift to coastal foci occurred, accentuated markedly after c. 800 A.D.; it continued, with variable links (spiritual and commercial) to Mesoamerica, revealed by the transition from "Mayoid" to "Mexicanoid" iconography and art styles. Eventually, Greater Nicoya was defined as a buffer zone between Mesoamerica and tropical–forest cultures of southern origin. In the Central Highlands–Atlantic Watershed and (probably) the Diquís zones, the first five or six centuries A.D. saw sporadic intergroup resource competition and warfare, with head hunting and sacrifice of captives possibly indicating population pressure; the apparent intromission, c. 500–700 A.D., of foreign (probably southern) peoples and tradition; changes in house and tomb forms; and the gradual degradation of ceramics, although not of other prestige items (gold replaces jade). The "balkanization" of these zones took place in the late period; they broke into relatively small, agglomerated, rudimentary–architecture settlements, for political control and defensive strategy, with occasional strong leaders who organized several centers into a site hierarchy or alliance for brief periods.

Why did the cultural evolutionary process in Costa Rica (and the Intermediate Area in general), similar in its early stages to that observed in Mesoamerica and Peru, sputter and stall? Why did no "urban" centers with large pyramid complexes appear? Robert Carneiro (1961, 1970) believes that historical evidence shows that no autonomous socio–political unit, large or small, will voluntarily relinquish sovereignty in the name of cooperation or the "greater social good." Only through forceful domination (war) are states and empires forged. Betty J. Meggers (1971: 159) postulates that endemic warfare in an "open" environment like Amazonia, overtly waged for reasons like revenge, supernatural mandates, and the taking of exogamous marriage partners, is, in reality, a regulatory device for human population in an area with a precarious ecological balance. Warfare in Costa Rica may have functioned in this fashion, and may have been even more intense, given greater population densities. Why did this conflict not result in the amalgamation of larger, more complex socio–political structures, as it apparently did in parts of Mesoamerica and Peru? The answer is that oppressed populations could successfully flee the threatened domination, emigrating to other, similar localities instead of being incorporated by force into the larger or more powerful conquering group (Carneiro 1970: 735). William Sanders and Barbara Price (1968: 130), in their essay on the development of "civilization" in Mesoamerica, note that it is not the lack of productive potential in tropical–forest areas like Amazonia that prevented the development of a complex society, but, rather, the presence of huge amounts of at least nominally agricultural land acting as an incentive to successful emigration. The juxtaposition of very different environments in Mesoamerica produced a cycle of competition and cooperation between "symbiotic regions," with growth and expansion trends in all participating "environmental niches," culminating in a socio–political whole bigger than the sum of its parts. Ironically, the abundance—not the lack–of viable ecozones may have stifled the cultural evolutionary development of much of the area between Mesoamerica and the Andes. In no way, however, did this detract from the graphic expression of a complex mythological "world view," which, in Costa Rica, combined elements of pervasive cultural traditions from both Middle and South America.

ETHNOHISTORICAL APPROACHES TO THE ARCHAEOLOGY OF GREATER NICOYA

Suzanne Abel–Vidor

At the moment of first contact with the Spaniards, the Nicoya Peninsula, adjacent Guanacaste province, and the Pacific region of Nicaragua, between the lakes and the coastal range, together formed a unit—Greater Nicoya (Norweb 1964; M. Coe 1962a)—with a geographical and cultural integrity quite distinct from the balance of Costa Rica to the east of the Gulf of Nicoya. Nicoya and Guanacaste were incorporated into the new Spanish colony called Nicaragua.

The Gulf of Nicoya was first sighted in 1519 by two lieutenants of Gaspar de Espinosa, who sailed the ships of Vasco Nuñez de Balboa northwest up the unexplored Central American coast; but they did not enter the gulf. It was not until 1522 that an expedition from Panama, commanded by Gil González Dávila, explored the coast by ship and by land from western Panama to the Nicaraguan lakes. González's route took him through northwestern Costa Rica from the eastern shore of the gulf, across Guanacaste, and to Lake Nicaragua.

Two accounts of this expedition—one written by González in 1524, from Santo Domingo and addressed to King Charles V, and the other, dated 1522, written by the official accountant of the expedition, Andrés de Cereceda—provide complementary narratives of the explorations. Cereceda's (in L. Fernández 1976, I: 33ff.) is a terse listing of settlements and *caciques* encountered, the distances traveled between them, the number of Indians baptized in each location, and the spoils gathered at each place. González's (in L. Fernández 1976, I: 36ff.) report to the king notes the striking difference in size, number, and character of the Nicaraguan Indian communities in comparison with those contacted south of the lakes region in the Nicoya Peninsula. The latter were, in turn, distinguished from those found south and east of the peninsula, which were few, scattered, poor, and small. The population and material wealth observed on the Nicaraguan leg of this expedition are much greater than those described either for the Costa Rican part of Greater Nicoya or for the region to the south along the coast into western Panama.

Several sources in print summarize the ethnographic data recorded by 16th–

OVERLEAF:
Plate 43. Pedestal jar, Guanacaste–Nicoya zone, ceramic (cat. no. 96).

Plate 44. Pedestal bowl, Guanacaste–Nicoya zone, ceramic (cat. no. 112).

and 17th–century European observers of the natural world and the Indian societies and cultures of Greater Nicoya. These are Lothrop (1926), Chapman (1960), Stone (1966c), and Ferrero (1977a). The 16th–century sources from which these modern authors have culled their information are mostly chroniclers, who wrote narratives of the exploration and characteristics of the New World and its peoples. Some were eyewitnesses to the events they described, but the scope of many chronicles is so broad as to demand heavy reliance on secondary or tertiary sources.

By far the most important chronicler for Lower Central America is Gonzalo Fernández de Oviedo y Valdés ("Oviedo"), whose *Historia General de las Indias, Islas y Tierra Firme del Mar Oceano* (1945; first 19 books originally published in 1535) supplies the bulk of the ethnographic information conventionally cited by more recent authors. Oviedo first went to the Panamanian colony in 1514 as *veedor* (inspector of mines). In 1527, he arrived in Nicaragua, where he observed in fine detail the flora, fauna, and some of the indigenous culture and society, while also participating in and recording the involvement of the Spanish in the area. In late July of 1529, he set out on foot for the Gulf of Nicoya, spending ten or twelve days in the company of the cacique of Nicoya before returning by sea to Panama.

Other important 16th-century chroniclers include Pascual de Andagoya, Girolamo Benzoni, Peter Martyr de Anglería, Fray Antonio de Ciudad Real, Fray Bartolomé de Las Casas, Fray Toribio de Motolinía de Benevente, and Juan López de Velasco. Juan de Torquemada, O.F.M., and Antonio de Herrera y Tordesillas wrote around the turn of the 17th century, and the English priest Thomas Gage traveled and worked as a missionary in Mexico and Central America from 1625 to 1637. The numerous legal documents, reports, and letters generated by the European conquerors constitute another source.

There is no doubt that Greater Nicoya was characterized by a plural society. The Nicoya–Guanacaste portion of the territory apparently supported a much smaller population than did the Nicaraguan lakes region in the 1520s, but it nonetheless formed part of the same interaction sphere (Caldwell 1964; Smith and Heath-Smith, in press). Pacific Nicaragua and adjacent Nicoya shared certain archaeologically identifiable cultural elements, but were also characterized by a diversity of languages and ethnic identities. Oviedo (1976: 36, 186) lists seven languages for the Nicaraguan colony: Chondales, Nicaragua, Chorotega, Oroçi, Orotiña, Guetares, and Maribios, although he later states that "The Indians of Nicoya and of Oroci are of the language of the Chorotegas." Ciudad Real (1873), writing about a visit to Nicaragua in 1586, lists Mangue, Marivio, and "corrupt Mexican" as the languages of the province. This use of "Mexican" is a complicating factor; while a Nahua–related language was in broad use throughout much of Central America north of Panama at the time of the Conquest, the inference that all speakers of Nahua shared a common culture or a common ethnic identity denies the recognized status of that tongue as a lingua franca.

González's narrative (in Colección Somoza 1954, I: 90) goes further into the apparent Mesoamerican character of the Nicoyan and Nicaraguan cultures. He says that he "walked CCXXIIII leagues, in which I discovered great towns and things until I encountered the language of Yucatan."[1] Later on in the letter, he repeats that "all the things of the Yucatan have we encountered, from the houses to clothing to armaments," and, again, that Nicaragua "is another Yucatan in its riches and in the language and in other matters of the Indians' dress and dealings" (*ibid.*: 101, 104; author's translation).

While it is clear that González's identification of Nicaragua with Yucatan was in a strict sense erroneous, it is equally clear that his interpretation was based, at least in part, on his observations of cultural elements and linguistic affiliation linking Nicaragua with cultures to the north, and not with those he knew from Panama. González's equation of the Nicaraguan and Yucatecan cultures has had a significant impact on the application of the concept of the Mesoamerican culture area in Nicaragua and Nicoya. A conspicuous tendency in archaeological research to seek indications of direct contact with, or "influence" from, Post-classic nuclear Mesoamerica or Central Mexico has virtually precluded appreciation of the uniquely innovative character of the archaeological and protohistoric cultures of Greater Nicoya.

Oviedo and other sources confirm that there was enmity among the Nicaraguan groups and some variation in observed religious practices, but that, despite the reported bellicosity of the Nicaraguan peoples, the wealth and settlement size and density to the north were of sufficient magnitude, and its geographical position of sufficient strategic promise, to arouse great expectations for the colonization of Nicaragua. Perceiving that area as a rich, well-populated, and eminently exploitable province, the Spanish chose to colonize it immediately, while interest in a Costa Rican colony languished.

The Pacific coast was considered by the Spaniards to be extremely dangerous to navigation because of its great winds and seas and its lack of protected roadsteads; the overland trip to Nicaragua from Gracias a Dios, Honduras, was long and perilous. The only viable supply route lay from Panama up the west coast of Costa Rica and into the well–protected Gulf of Nicoya. From there the traffic proceeded to the town of Nicoya, the sole official Indian town of Greater Nicoya, located in the western Tempisque River flood plain, which served for many years as the vital transport and supply point between the Gulf of Nicoya and the Nicaraguan settlements.

Among other reasons, a lack of concentration of labor and little readily available material wealth in the form of pearls, gold, or silver precluded the establishment of more than a very few desirable *encomienda* grants in the first years of the colonization of the Nicaraguan colony's southern portion. The encomienda, a grant of Indians for the provision of labor and tribute to the Spanish *encomendero*, depended quite directly on the perpetuation of stable, productive Indian society. The encomendero became the beneficiary of the existing economic system only if Indians were found in sufficiently organized concentration to make it worth his while (Hennessey 1978).

If the extractable wealth of both the Nicaraguan and Costa Rican Indians was very quickly exhausted, the former at least could be exploited very lucratively as slave labor (Lockhart 1968; MacLeod 1973; Radell 1976; Sherman 1971, 1979). The fact that there was a Precolumbian institution of slavery (González, in Colección Somoza 1953–57, I: 95) made imposition of the Spanish practice less problematic. Oviedo (1976: 361; author's translation) writes of his experience in Nicaragua in the late 1520s:

More ceremonies and rites and customs and noteworthy things still should be recounted that have not been said of this territory and its adjacent districts, and to recount them all would be impossible, as much because the diversity of languages precludes the sort of special treatment and understanding that one would wish, as because war and conversion of the Indians and the passage of time have consumed and put an end to the lives of the elder Indians and even to those of the young, and because of the avarice of the judges and governors and others who have had such haste to remove the Indians from that land, designating them as slaves, to sell them in Castilla del Oro [Panama] and in other places.

The issue of how large the Nicaraguan population was at the time of first contact with the Europeans, and what proportion of it was exterminated, exported, or otherwise lost, has been vociferously debated since the 16th century. The population was certainly substantial, and the density within the lakes region was very high, if not truly urban. Estimates by writers of the time seem to converge around an approximate figure of half a million, with Oviedo citing 400,000, Motolinía 500,000, and D. Herrera 600,000. The decimation was so precipitous that even contemporary testimony of its massive scale has elicited scepticism in the minds of some later scholars.

By 1548, when a very thorough tribute assessment was made for the Nicaraguan province, only 11,137 tributaries could be found (Radell 1976: 75). Applying to this total the perhaps conservative 3.3 factor for approximation of overall population figures based on tribute figures (Cook and Borah 1960), this would yield a Nicaraguan population of only 36,752, a total that is in striking agreement with the estimate of 30,000 made by a royal official in 1545 (D. Herrera 1875). Herrera further states that the original Indian population was 600,000, indicating a reduction of 95% in less than 25 years. Whether or not one chooses to accept the validity of these figures, the picture of demographic disaster is basically the same.

The historic peoples of Nicaragua were found clustering in the very fertile, well-drained plains between the coastal ranges and the two big lakes of Managua and Nicaragua, with dense populations extending up the Pacific corridor west of the volcanic cordillera to the Gulf of Fonseca. With the conspicuous exceptions of the bays and gulfs of the northern Guanacaste coast and the littoral of the Gulf of Nicoya, where a marine-based subsistence strategy remained viable in the ancient tradition of the prehistoric Nicoyan peoples, much of the rest of the peninsula and of Guanacaste province to the north would have been relatively unsuitable for the maintenance of large, stable human settlements. Oviedo's exhaustive description of agricultural practices in Nicaragua leaves no doubt as to the subsistence base of the plains communities. Two resources critical to a predominantly agricultural population would have been soil fertility and drainage, in addition to the availability of fresh water in the dry season, which lasts from approximately December through May or June. In both respects, the Nicaraguans were far better off than the inhabitants of the Nicoya Peninsula, and this difference is obvious even today (Stevens 1964; Lange 1971a, 1980; Healy 1974).

The historic documents evoke an image that unequivocally sets Costa Rican Nicoya apart from the rest of Pacific Nicaragua as a frontier zone with unmistakable connections with the lakes region, but also with a much lower settlement density and smaller settlement size. Dávila (in Colección Somoza 1954, I: 128 ff. 446), Castañeda (in Peralta 1883: 36 ff.) and Oviedo (1945, 1976) all agree that between the town of Nicoya and the lakes were many leagues of *despoblado*, unpeopled, without water, and empty.

For the lands lying between the caciques of Nicoya and Nicaragua, in what is today the province of Guanacaste, Cereceda's account lists eight caciques, several hundred baptized Indians, a minor quantity of gold, and the only quantity of pearls recorded during the expedition. González's letter does not even mention the existence of these populations, and we must consider this omission deliberate—he did not judge their presence politically significant or strategic. In many later descriptions of the Nicoya area, this impression of the emptiness of Guanacaste is corroborated; it is consistently portrayed as drought–plagued and barren.

Although the historical sources are remarkably silent on the subject, the middle and lower courses of the Tempisque River and its contiguous flood plain could have provided a complex of environmental conditions conducive to intensive agricultural exploitation. The Tempisque makes a very gradual descent from its source near the slopes of Orosí volcano, close to the present Costa Rican–Nicaraguan border, and forms many meanders and occasional oxbow lakes as it nears its mouth at the heavily sedimented head of the Gulf of Nicoya. This very gentle gradient makes the river subject to serious seasonal flooding, a condition that has important implications for human settlement. The potential destruction of human habitations along its course discourages the construction of substantial permanent housing. On the other hand, the floods deposit rich alluvial soils on the bottomlands, although these soils are subject to rapid leaching from heavy seasonal rains.

The large Nicaraguan populations were by no means totally dependent on the products of agriculture. Hunting, important in the late prehistoric period (Healy 1974; Wyckoff 1978), is documented for the early historic period (Oviedo 1976), and the rich fisheries of the two fresh–water lakes undoubtedly provided diversity in the diet. Moreover, as Wyckoff suggests, there may be a strong positive relationship between the amount of land cleared for cultivation and the abundance of certain game, particularly deer and rabbit, both of which Oviedo describes as abundant and appreciated for their meat.

The Nicoya region may have served in ancient times as a resource zone for the Nicaraguans, supplying products for which it was known in the colonial period: purple shellfish dye, honey, beeswax, cotton cloth and other natural fibers, precious feathers, indigo, cacao, and, in all likelihood, dried fish and shellfish. Salt from the extensive salt flats of the Gulf of Nicoya and the northern Guanacaste coast would have been in great demand in the Nicaraguan communities because their own coast lacked this resource almost entirely. The need for control and administration of commerce could help explain the presence of sites along the middle Tempisque that have yielded numerous elaborate Late Polychrome vessels of probable Nicaraguan manufacture. The ceramics may indicate the existence of an elite at these sites, or may at least imply that peoples along the river were receiving these vessels in payment for supplying the commodities listed above (Day and Abel–Vidor 1980.).

Micro–regional demographic and ecological distinctions between Nicoya and Nicaragua have multiple social, cultural, economic, and political implications. If Pacific Nicaragua was, indeed, better endowed for the intensive practice of agriculture in the Mesoamerican tradition and for Central American horticulture, and if it can be demonstrated archaeologically as well as historically that the Late Polychrome period was characterized by both a shift in settlement pattern favoring nucleation in the lakes region and the partial occupation by peoples speaking a language of the Aztecan subfamily, then there is every reason to believe that this period also witnessed a reorganization and reorientation of society, including a tighter integration into the broad trade–articulated Mesoamerican interaction sphere (Smith and Heath-Smith, in press).

The nature of the ties between the communities in Nicoya and those in the lakes region of Nicaragua is still poorly understood. While unscientifically excavated ceramics from the Tempisque Valley and the Bay of Culebra zone are known in some quantity and manifest some close stylistic parallels with ceramics from other Postclassic Mesoamerican complexes, these seem to be more common north of the current political boundaries. The most obvious examples are vessels with incised or painted standardized representations of Mesoamerican supernatural beings and other symbols. Local copies or imitations of these styles, which are quite abundant in collections from the middle Tempisque, strongly suggest that the originals may have been imported into the region (Day and Abel–Vidor 1980). Actual trade wares of more northerly Mesoamerican manufacture are more numerous in Middle Polychrome times than in the late period.

While we know from the Fifth Letter of Cortés (1971) and from López de Gómara (1954) that merchants in the Gulf Coast Mexican province of Xicalango painted a map for Cortés of all the roads and major geographic features between there and Nicaragua, in itself powerful evidence for the existence of pan–Mesoamerican trade routes in the 16th century, the absence of imperishable trade wares argues for one of two characterizations of that trade. Either it involved exchange of perishables, or the merchants effected exchange of goods over short distances only, attending periodically scheduled market fairs all over Central America while ranging over longer distances on some regular route. We might conceive of a quasi–autonomous *pochteca*–like class of merchants, who did not operate, in this case, as imperial agents, as they did in the Aztec system, and who would not have been responsible for the simple extraction of goods for the benefit of a single imperial nucleus; their busines would have been effected on a more localized scale for the benefit of local elites.

Evidence for Nicaragua's involvement in the Postclassic Mesoamerican interaction sphere does exist in rather compelling form in the ethnohistoric materials; the archaeological manifestations must now be actively sought.

[1]The transcriptions of this letter that I have had access to do not agree on the number of leagues covered by land. While the transcription in Colección Somoza gives 224, that in L. Fernández (1976, I: 36) gives 125 leagues. Hubert Howe Bancroft (1886: 494), on the other hand, citing a manuscript copy of the document, states that 324 leagues were covered by land.

ETHNOHISTORY AND ETHNOGRAPHY IN THE CENTRAL HIGHLANDS— ATLANTIC WATERSHED AND DIQUÍS

Luis Ferrero A./Translated by M.J. Snarskis

When Costa Rica was discovered by Christopher Columbus in 1502, he found a "high land, with many rivers and full of tall trees" (Colon 1947: 280). The Indians gave the Spanish fruit, meat, and gold ornaments, all the while exhibiting friendliness, cleverness, and intelligence. The Spanish admired the native wearing of gold jewelry, the many strange animals, and the custom of embalming the dead and then covering the tomb with wooden slabs carved with figures of men and animals. So reported Columbus in his *Lettera rarissima*, the first ethnographic document for Costa Rica.

Most Costa Rican colonial records were kept by soldiers or those who lacked the objectivity to describe accurately what they saw. Many years later, a few missionaries wrote reports that included ethnographic data, but without much detail. Since the first part of this century, historians, archaeologists, and anthropologists have used the Spanish chronicles to a greater or lesser degree in their works on central and eastern Costa Rica. They include Fernández Guardia (1913, 1918), Gagini (1917), Lehmann (1920), Lothrop (1926, 1942), Lines (1938, 1941, 1942), Johnson (1948), Skinner (1920), Aguilar (1952, 1965), Castro–Tossi (1968), Stone (1961, 1964, 1966a), Ferrero (1975, 1977a, 1977b), Bozzoli (1975, 1979), Snarskis (1978), Golliher (1977), and Rivas (1979).

Most of Costa Rica was populated by groups with northern South American cultural traditions, speaking languages of the Macro–Chibcha group (fig. 33). In 1564, the Spaniard Juan Vázquez de Coronado traveled with two interpreters from Coto to the Diquís zone, across the Talamancas to the Alto Lari, down to the Caribbean coast, and back through Limón and the Turrialba valley to the central highlands, with no problems in communication. This is testimony, without a doubt, to the existence of an interrelated group of languages or dialects.

The adaptive systems of the indigenous population of Costa Rica were not as striking as those of Mexico and Peru. Perhaps the first impression the conquerors had was of a low level of culture, with root–crop swidden agriculture and

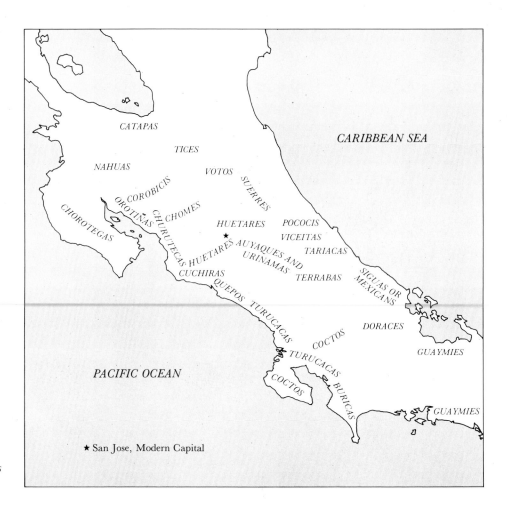

Figure 33. Map indicating the approximate distribution of indigenous groups in the mid–15th century.

small dispersed villages of pole–and–thatch houses. The Spaniards did not immediately comprehend the wealth and variety of sophisticated craftsmanship in wood, stone, and metals, nor the socio–political and religious complexity that had shaped an apparently simple way of life. The first Spaniards had only one goal: to obtain gold. The indigenous population was dealt with only insofar as it served that end.

The first Spanish capital, Cartago, was founded in the fertile central valley, where many important *caciques*, or native chiefs,[1] had their settlements (fig. 34). From there, Spanish expeditions explored the Atlantic Watershed and the Talamancas. A few small towns were founded in the eastern lowlands, but after a few years the settlers succumbed to disease and Indian raids. Around Cartago, however, the Spanish succeeded in fragmenting and dominating indigenous cultural groups. The native population was divided into work details apportioned to various local *conquistadores*; this was actually thinly disguised slavery. In more isolated regions, indigenous ways persisted. The Talamancan tribes survived in great part because of their bellicosity: although Franciscan missions, guarded by soldiers, were established in their midst, these never took root, and eventually the region was set apart as an Indian reservation.

Today, we understand the indigenous cultures of these parts of Costa Rica better because of the accounts of travelers and explorers like Angulo (1966), Gabb (1875, 1978), Thiel (1884), Bovallius (1887), Pittier (1883, 1898, 1903a, 1903b), Sapper (1900), and Blessing (1900, 1921). Although they all made their

94

forays more than three centuries after the Spanish arrival, the fact that they traveled in the eastern and southern parts of the country, where the traditional customs of the indigenous cultures were still preserved, makes their data valuable.

Figure 34. The last cacique of Talamanca, Antonio Saladana (far left), photographed with his family. Photo: Luis Ferrero A.

Tribal Groups

In the northernmost Atlantic plains, from just below Lake Nicaragua to about the middle of Costa Rica, lived the Catapas, the Tices, the Votos, and the Suerres. On the rest of the Atlantic Watershed were found the Pococis between the Reventazón and Matina Rivers up to the Turrialba valley, while the Viceitas occupied the banks of the Lari River, tributary to the Sixaola, which forms the border between Costa Rica and Panama. The Cabecars lived between the Coen and Tarire Rivers, and the Auyaques and Urinamas between the Tarire and the Uren. The Térraba lived near the Tilorio River, close to Panama. The Siguas ("foreigners") were Mexican interlopers, probably Aztec *pochtecas* on a trading mission to Central America; they also lived near the present Costa Rican–Panama border when the Spanish encountered them, in the Valley of Duy or Coaza, between the Sixaola and Changuinola Rivers. The Changuinas lived along the Puan River, tributary to the Changuinola, and the Doraces were found on what is now called Almirante Bay, in Panama. The entire Ara valley, from the Cricamola River near the Chiriquí lagoon all the way over the mountains to the Pacific

Watershed, was occupied by the Guaymís. From these groups recorded in the 16th century came the cultural traditions still preserved by the modern tribes called the Térrabas, Cabécars, and Bríbris. The cultures inhabiting the Central Valley and the Atlantic Watershed have been known traditionally as "Huetar," because the *cacique* Huetara (cacique is a Taino word meaning "head of house-hold") had his domain near the Turrubares Hill, toward the south of the Río Grande de Tárcoles on the Central Pacific drainage.

The Corobicís inhabited the Guanacaste mountains near Tilarán, controlling a zone that extended down to the Tempisque River. Bordering this zone were the lands of the Chorotegas—Mangue (also known as the Orotina or Gurutina), a Mexican people, who lived between Chomes and the Río Grande de Tárcoles; there was probably a reciprocal influence between them and their neighbors of South American tradition, the Corobicís, Huetars, Cochiras, and Quepos. In the Central Pacific zone, toward the Paquita or Savegre Valley, were the Cochiras, and farther to the south, the Quepos, whose territory was defined by the Coto highlands to the north, the Pacific coast to the south, the Savegre River to the east, and the Naranjo River plains to the west (Barrantes Ferrero 1971: 27). The Turucacas occupied the coastal mountains of Diquís and the plains of San Andrés. Finally, the Coctus or Cotos were in the Coto—Brus Valley, and toward the Osa Peninsula, while the Buricas lived on Burica Point, the modern border between Costa Rica and Panama.

Subsistence

The prehistoric inhabitants of Costa Rica depended on a combination of culti-gens and natural flora for food, medicines, material for house construction, clothing, weapons, ceremonial articles, dyes, resins, etc. They seldom modified the natural vegetation drastically, although the Buenos Aires plains of the Diquís zone are thought to have been created artificially before the Spanish arrival by intensive slash—and—burn agriculture (Haberland 1961a: 38) and the setting of fires during warfare (Vázquez de Coronado 1964: 47). In general, each family group was allotted a parcel of land for agriculture, which was shifted when fertility dropped off. Men cleared and burned the vegetation, while women planted and harvested the crops (Fernández Guardia 1918: 21). There were communal labor projects, a tradition that still exists among the Talamancan tribes, where the men assemble at the residence of the landowner to sing and lift their spirits for the work ahead. At day's end, copious amounts of *chicha* are served. Men also hunted, made war, and sewed, while women had other domestic duties.

Diet was based primarily on root and tree crops. The former included *yuca* (manioc or cassava), *ñampí*, and *tiquisque* (taro–like roots); among the latter were *guayaba* (guava), *mamey*, cocoa, and many others, especially palm fruits like the *pejibaye*—almost as rich as the peanut in proteins, minerals, and oils—which could be dried and stored. The Spanish described a single valley with as many as 50,000 pejibaye trees. Pineapples were also grown. Animal–protein sources included two kinds of peccary, wild goat, tapir, armadillo, and large rodents. Wild turkey, quail, and partridge were hunted. Marine and riverine protein sources included manatee, turtles, crustaceans, and many kinds of fish. Nets, spears, traps, weirs, and poisons obtained from certain trees and vines were

Plate 45. Tripod urn containing other vessels, La Zoila, Turrialba, Atlantic Watershed, ceramic (cat. no. 209).

96

used in fishing. Hunters employed blowguns, spears, bows and arrows, pit traps, and snares. A subsistence pattern based on manioc, pejibaya, and forest/fluvial animal protein is diagnostic of Amazonian tropical–forest cultures. Relatively rich soils in Costa Rica allowed a short–fallow system, which in turn permitted sedentary settlements. A combination of root, tree, and grain crops, with emphasis on the first two during historic times, simulated natural tropical–forest structure in individual garden plots, and was thus ecologically sound.

Settlement Patterns and Demography

Although the so-called zone of South American influence in Costa Rica displays a reasonable homogeneity in settlement and demographic patterning, myriad slight differences in rainfall, temperature, topography, drainage, soils, flora, and fauna produced local variations. Usually, a small settlement consisted of two or three pole–and–thatch structures near a water source and arable land. Such small settlements were several kilometers apart. In each house lived a matrilineal family clan, practicing exogamy. One chronicler noted that "a lineage of fathers, sons, and grandchildren is called a people, or a province depending on the number of relations" (L. Fernández 1881–1907, III: 37). "Partiality" was another term used in place of "people."

Findlow, Snarskis, and Martin (1979) have noted a pattern of settlement location in Period VI (1000–1550 A.D.) that suggests that political boundaries and defense were of prime importance. Site agglomeration or nuclearization increased during that period, perhaps because of population pressure, but a dispersed pattern was still predominant. It is notable that the present indigenous population of Talamanca, living in dispersed hamlets, has no word for "city." The same dispersed settlement pattern explains why the Indians of this part of Costa Rica resisted Spanish conquest for so long; where population was more concentrated (as in Guanacaste and the Central Highlands), indigenous groups were more rapidly dominated.

Agglomerated (and architecturally more elaborate) settlements contained the residence of the major and principal chiefs. These sites (like Guayabo de Turrialba) were a kind of capital of the province.

Village and House Structure

The Spanish used the term palenque to describe a stockade–village, surrounded by walls of cactus or other spiny plants, in the Diquís or Central Highlands–Atlantic Watershed zone (fig. 35). Palenques often occurred in strategic sites; it is uncertain when the term came to mean any indigenous settlement. Juan Vázquez de Coronado (1964: 33–45) described a palenque in the Turucaca–Coto region of Diquís as follows:

The fort of the Coto, built on a ridge, was the largest and strongest. It was shaped like an egg and had a small door at east and west that could be pulled up and down like a drawbridge. On the north and south were two deep creeks on whose slopes grew flower gardens. Two stockades surrounded the fort, the ground between them punctuated with holes. Inside the fort stood 84 circular houses raised about half a meter off the ground

Figure 35. Luis Sanclemente, Painting of a palenque, *or conical house, in Talamanca, c. 1892. Museo Nacional de Costa Rica.*

and roofed with spire–like peaks. At each end of the fortified "egg" the houses were set in a triangle; then as the egg–shape widened, three houses and finally four were accommodated in a block with 1.2 meters between the houses. Each block of houses had a small square between it and the connecting streets. An enemy could easily find himself a target for shots launched from the embrasures and windows of four houses, whose positions did not let him see who was shooting at him. He had to take one block of houses before going on to another. Each building could house 400 men but normally it was occupied by 25 men with their women and children.

Many Turucaca–Coto houses were built on stilts because of heavy rainfall and the flooding it caused. On the Atlantic Watershed, circular houses were built with conical roofs reaching to the ground. This type of house was carefully described by Gabb (1978: 147); some still exist in isolated Talamancan valleys. Matrilineal family groups occupied separate sectors inside the house, each with its own hearth. Gabb described it thus:

...they are generally circular, about 30–50 feet in diameter and of almost the same height. The framework is of long poles, which reach from the ground to the apex of the conical roof in some parts. The roof is supported by concentric rings of bound saplings or strong vines, which are in turn supported by more poles resting on the floor of the house, a third of the way in from its perimeter, as well as more poles placed obliquely along the line of the roof itself. The whole roof is thatched thickly with palm leaves, and the hole at the top of the cone is often covered with an old pottery vessel in order to keep out the rain. There is only one door to such houses, a large, square opening on one side. Sometimes a small roof is constructed over the entryway to shelter it from rain. Hearths and sleeping quarters are inside.

Another kind of structure reported from the Atlantic Watershed in the 16th century was oval:

> ...shaped like an egg, in length about forty-five paces, and nine in breadth. It was encircled with reeds, covered with palm branches remarkably well interlaced; there were also a few other houses but of a common sort (Lothrop 1926: 33, quoting Benzoni 1545).

Houses in the northern Atlantic plains, on the other hand, were rectangular, about 15 x 40 meters. They had no walls, and the roof did not reach to the ground. Each of the nuclear families that occupied them had its own hearth and space to hang sleeping hammocks.

Social Organization

The predominant social organization was the matrilineal exogamous clan, divided into moities. This structure persists among modern Talamancan groups, in which power or status is inherited through the matrilineal line, and land is owned by the clan, which in turn organizes familial socio–economic matters. Each communal house made up a work crew, many of which joined together on certain projects. In this manner, familial and social structure inculcated in the individual values that reflected an efficient human ecology in the tropical forest (Ferrero 1978: XLIX–L, LV–LVII). Certain clans were proscribed from hunting certain animals or utilizing other kinds of resources, having to deal instead with the clan that was allowed to do so. Man–nature relationships were systematized, and a knowledge of clan duties and proscriptions gave the individual an insight into the structure of his society, and, by extension, into the universe as his religion perceived it.

Political and Religious Organization

The Spaniards apparently encountered two basic social levels, elite and commoners. A careful analysis of the chronicles shows, however, that there were many subdivisions of this general structure. At first glance, words like "nation," "region," "province," "people," and "partiality" seem to be synonyms, but examination of the 16th–century meaning of each reveals a subtle socio–political hierarchy. However, we have few details about these political strata. Each village had a chief whose status was sacred, lifelong, and inherited. His activities focused on foodstuff redistribution, political contacts, and the resolution of conflicts. A close reading of Spanish documents shows two kinds of chiefs: the "grand chief" (*cacique mayor*) and the "principal chief" (*cacique principal*). They controlled other "bosses" (*mandones*), as well as warriors. Usually, a "grand chief" dominated quite a large area, always of the same language, while the "principal chief" carried out missions of trust—for example, as emissary between two peoples, or as organizer of war parties. The chronicles are less clear about warriors; it seems that there were three classes. Bozzoli (1979: 55) notes that the modern Bribri still recall that, in the past, three warrior classes were recognized: the jaguars, the red monkeys, and the "two-headed" ones. It is also remembered that the settlements of the jaguar and monkey clans (from which chiefs were elected) were located systematically between the settlement zones of other clans (*ibid.*: 43). This spatial arrangement suggests a military strategy on the part of the "grand chiefs" to control large areas, especially those with lineal settlement systems, as along a river course. It also tended to equalize the exploitation of resources.

Both "grand" and "principal" chiefs adorned themselves with gold ornaments, indicative of elite status and political power. For this reason, gold articles were esteemed gifts during hospitality ceremonies. High–ranking personages, when going to war, covered themselves with bracelets, pectorals, headbands, and many other ornaments of gold, the better to inspire terror in their enemies. Other symbols of power were the ceremonial wooden staff and a kind of cape of cotton worn over the shoulders, often decorated with feather plumes and other attachments.

In cases of intertribal warfare or other large–scale emergencies, several chiefs would form an alliance, maintaining within it their respective powers. Even defeated chiefs did not lose social or religious powers; they simply dominated a smaller area. Intertribal wars were usually the result of boundary disputes, raids to secure prisoners for sacrifice, or attempts to steal treasured and sacred artifacts from another group. Endemic warfare probably stimulated the building of easily defended fortresslike sites. Often several chiefs and their followers inhabited a single fortress–site; the Spanish were surprised to find ten chiefs in a site containing thirteen houses. This was variable, however: one site with eight houses had no chief; another of eight houses had three, and a site with two houses had one chief.

Chiefs apparently did not have to depend on vassalage or corvée labor. All clan members recognized their obligation to contribute a reasonable amount of their time to projects or duties of their lineage, but just enough to provide the chief with his needs; the chief's share did not increase automatically if the wealth or produce of the community was augmented. Each chief had a symbol or "logo" of his reign, usually a wooden staff of power carved with totemic zoomorphic figures; frequently he caused this symbol to be tattooed on all his subjects. Some of the "grand chiefs" controlled huge areas. One of them had four properties, ranging from the Central Highlands to the Atlantic coast, on each of which he had constructed "recreational" houses to which he repaired during certain times of year (L. Fernández 1881–1907, VIII: 405). Each of the houses was located in a region with different, easily obtained sources of animal protein. Cobble–paved *calzadas*, or causeways, crisscrossed these regions, and several segments of these "Indian roads" have been discovered by landowners and archaeologists during the 19th and 20th centuries. The Spanish noted that some causeways connected zones with gold–bearing rivers and that others were provided with vine suspension bridges over torrential rivers or deep canyons.

The Costa Rican Indians communicated with each other quickly over long distances, usually in relation to the movements of Spanish exploring parties. Were drums used, or relays of runners? If the latter, they must have used paved causeways like those described by Hoffman (1976: 110); he saw lines of Indians traversing these roadways with large baskets of cargo on their backs. There were also causeways in the northern plains, but the Spanish mentioned more often the skillful river boaters they observed in that region. Sometimes there were as many as 12 rowers seated in pairs, in a 15–meter boat filled with goods for trading (Peralta 1883: 733–735). Aztec traders from Mexico came to the San Juan River (now the border between Costa Rica and Nicaragua) to collect tribute in gold for the ruler, Moctezuma (*ibid*.: 117)

In the territory of the Votos (the northern piedmont of the Cordillera Central), many chiefs were women. Houses there were rectangular, not unlike those built by the Guatuso people until recently. Among the Votos, chiefs distinguished themselves from commoners by wearing sleeveless jackets of cotton, while most of the people wore only breechcloths of bark cloth (*ibid.*: 401, 733–735, 766). Women of high rank were allowed to wear cotton robes, richly adorned, that reached to the ankles. Victorious warriors were permitted to wear small bones in their perforated noses, lower lips, or ears, as well as red feathers, the whole designed to inspire fear and awe. Commoners who did not have tattoos could paint their bodies with vegetable dyes or wear necklaces of the teeth of animals they had hunted (with the exception of the jaguar, reserved for shamanistic use). Painted or tattooed patterns sometimes distinguished social classes, especially warriors.

Among all groups, the integrative power of the prevailing mythic or religious system was of great importance. "Priests" or shamans had among their duties the preservation and transmission of songs and legendary stories of heroes and origins (Stone 1961: 108). There could be several priestly ranks; it was not uncommon that the "grand chief" was also the highest–ranking shaman (L. Fernández 1881–1907, II: 153; V: 23; VII: 218, 351, 379–380, 395, 405). Functions of the shaman included serving as intermediary between the individual, the community, and the supernatural world; he controlled spirits and climatological phenomena; he maintained taboos and castigated transgressors. He cured the sick, divined the future, dealt with "impure" objects, and guided the souls of the dead (Aguilar 1965: 28). A Franciscan missionary described shamanistic activity as follows:

> . . . there are three kinds of shamans among them; one class is called *capar*, and they are the ones who speak with the devil and predict things to come; of these there are few, greatly respected. Others they call *jaguacs*; these manipulate small pebbles to tell fortunes, and apply medicines along with blowing [see the seated *sukia* figures carved of stone, from Period VI in the Central Highlands–Atlantic Watershed (cat. no. 217)], and incantations. A third class they call *isogros*; these are summoned for funerals, where they call the souls of the dead by singing, for *isogro* means singer (Fernández Guardia 1918: 24).

Stone (1961), Aguilar (1965), and Bozzoli (1979) have published detailed commentaries on similar shamanistic orders in the historic Talamancan tribes.

Most historical sources agree that the capar of the Cabecar, a Talamancan group later conquered by the Bribri, was the most revered, and that San José Cabecar, a town that still exists today, was the major "indoctrination center" for shamans. Many "adoratories," or shrines, were located in that region, with idols of gold, shells, stone, and wood. The looting of one of these shrines caused the great Indian uprising of 1610 (L. Fernández 1881–1907, II: 152). Although we cannot speak of a distinct priestly *class*, the indigenous peoples of Costa Rica had well–developed ritual traditions, perhaps best exemplified in funerals. Until very recently, Talamancan tribes practiced a secondary interment with complex rites and symbolism, emphasizing the continuity and immortality of the clan and the return of the spirit to another corporal existence (Gabb 1978: 117–120; Pittier 1938: 24–26; Stone 1961: 63–74).

Animistic beliefs in the spirits of mountains, bodies of water, rocks, and forest–dwelling creatures were common. Taboos and proscriptions for certain clans tended to create social harmony, as far as resource exploitation and succession to power were concerned. In historic times, at least, the Talamancan tribes conceived of a single, principal deity, which they called Sibö. Sibö—associated with a long–beaked bird, apparently a kite or buzzardlike carrion–eater—brought the "seeds" from which all people sprouted, and later selected the clans upon which the rights to produce shamans, etc. were bestowed. Sibö charged his son with the duties of distributing different kinds of jobs or work to all clans and of teaching agriculture, song, and dance.

Talamancan peoples also believed in lesser deities typical of South American tropical–forest religions, such as water and celestial spirits and the "master of all animals." The last, who could take a human form, permitted unlimited hunting of animals for food, but punished severely those who killed more than was their need.

Crafts and Commerce

Each clan had a particular craft in which it specialized. Perishable products included woven mats, carved gourds, arrows, hammocks, capes, drums, maracas, animal skins, baskets, nasal pipes, necklaces of animal teeth, featherwork, carved wooden staffs, and bark and cotton cloth. Many articles had a ritual use, and their makers may have been considered as links between the clan and the supernatural world. The designs and motifs on such objects (and other artifacts, like pottery) are graphic or symbolic expressions of the concepts and structure underlying the politico–religious system. These objects communicated precise messages to those who owned, used, or saw them, and were constant reminders of the omnipresence of the supernatural in daily life.

Crafts were intimately connected with political powers, too. Carved wooden staffs and gold ornaments are the most obvious examples. The clans responsible for manufacturing the cotton capes worn by high–status personages dyed their designs only on the warp of the cloth, rendering them unintelligible on the reverse side, a technique known also from Ecuador and Peru (Stone 1949: 17).

The Spanish, upon their arrival in Costa Rica in 1502, saw large "boards" or monoliths, carved on all sides with animal effigies, which served as funeral biers for embalmed bodies. These animal figures were clan symbols. The circular metates of Period VI are adorned with zoomorphic carvings, and some ethnographic references state that similar "tables" were used to grind tobacco and other drugs for aspiration with double–reed nasal snuffers. Hallucinations produced by this activity may have given rise to the multitudinous and fantastic composite animals or man–animals that populate the iconography of eastern and southern Costa Rican indigenous cultures. The power of a shaman to transform himself into several kinds of animals is documented from many primitive cultures; often, such transformations were related to ritual drug consumption.

Many 16th–century artifacts were destroyed by missionaries when they realized that the objects were being used in rituals involving human sacrifice (every full moon, prisoners captured during battles and raids were decapitated). Moreover, the Spanish recorded very little of the indigenous cosmology, so we lack understanding of the complex iconography visible in archaeological material culture. Yet archaeology has confirmed belief in the importance of the trophy head (probably shrunken, another northern South American custom), the association of the long–beaked bird with Sibö, and the faith in the natural environment as a source of fertility and plenty.

GUAYABO DE TURRIALBA AND ITS SIGNIFICANCE

Oscar Fonseca Zamora/Translated by Michael J. Snarskis

The area around the Costa Rican site of Guayabo de Turrialba shows ceramic evidence of human occupation from at least c. 500 B.C., but, as seen today, its architectural features—stone house foundations, cobble–paved causeways and streets, stairways, retaining walls, mounds, plazas, and aqueducts—appear to date to the last five or six hundred years before the Spanish arrival. Although Guayabo is not the only site in Costa Rica that displays these features, it is the largest site of its kind known in the country thus far and has received the greatest attention from students of Costa Rican archaeology.

Guayabo de Turrialba is located 19 kilometers to the north of the modern town of Turrialba, on the slopes of a volcano of the same name at about 1100 meters above sea level (fig. 36). The position of the site between Premontane and Montane Rain Forest zones, and its relatively easy access to Perhumid Rain Forest (L. Holdridge 1978), would seem to be strategic in terms of resource procurement, suggesting economic stability and a capacity for sustaining populations both directly and indirectly associated with the site. The climate is temperate, humid to rainy; there is no well–defined dry season; annual precipitation averages 3 meters; temperature ranges from 18° to 22° C. Broadleafed evergreen forests, supporting a varied fauna, are typical of this region, although today many types of crops are grown. Farmers call the local soils very fertile. The streams and rivers of the region, always full from frequent rains, rush with white water down the steep sides of the Turrialba volcano for much of their courses. Between them, more gently sloping headlands and terraces are occasionally found; the site of Guayabo de Turrialba was constructed on one of these.

Guayabo has been known as an archaeological site since the last part of the 19th century, when several nonscientific expeditions were mounted to obtain pieces for museum and private collections like that of Don Ramón Rojas Troyo, then owner of the land on which the site was found. Only one scientist of that time, Anastasio Alfaro (a botanist), took an interest in recording the site and the details of the tombs he himself opened (Alfaro 1892, 1893). From that time until 1968, when Carlos Aguilar of the Universidad de Costa Rica began controlled excavations, Guayabo has suffered severe looting. This is the saddest part of the site's history, reflecting the uninformed and misdirected interest of collector and scientist alike for the prehistoric object itself, out of context, as a "curiosity." Through Aguilar's personal lobbying, Guayabo was declared a national park in 1973, an act which has resulted in the protection and maintenance of its exposed architectural features. Aguilar's published work illustrates the layout of the major architectural features at the site, and the stratigraphic pits he dug allowed him to suggest a tentative cultural sequence (Aguilar 1972b).

In 1978, the Universidad de Costa Rica reinitiated excavations at Guayabo, which continue today. The entire site has been carefully gridded, and investigation of the surrounding area has begun (Fonseca 1979). Participating students come from diverse fields (biology, geology, and engineering, among others), and the project's objectives have been broadened. We hope to learn more about the function of the site, how it was maintained, the factors that caused it to be founded, and its role in the hierachy of contemporary sites in the region.

Architectural Features

Although work since 1978 has been limited mostly to clearing, it is possible to see a few significant patterns. The architectural features vary in form and size. Mounds (hereafter M) are usually circular, but may be ellipsoidal or rectangular; others—for example, M 5, 10, 15, and 18 (fig. 36)—show irregular shapes as a result of forming part of the juncture between two or more features. To date, fifty features have been excavated: forty–three mounds, three aqueducts, two plazas, one causeway, one enclosure (hereafter E), and several paved walkways between features.

The architectural features vary in size from 4.2 square meters to 888 square

Figure 36. General site plan of Guayabo (Martín Chaverri).

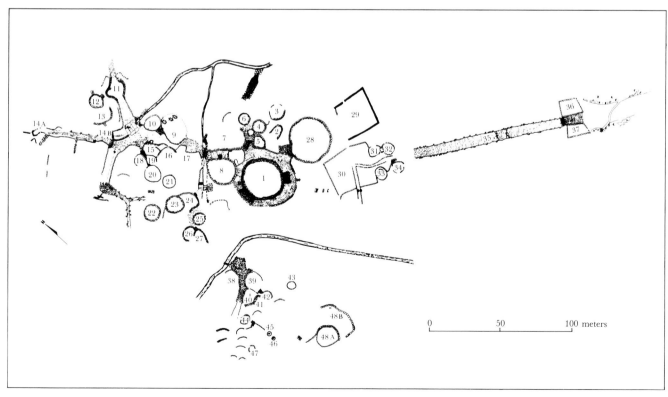

meters. Although excavations are far from finished, and survey has revealed a great deal more to be done, we have found in the placement of the architectural features a pattern that allows us to take the first steps in a functional analysis of the site. Its organization has been analyzed by observing the way in which features divide, group, or connect, in the hopes of establishing generic spatial units that might have social significance. From smallest to largest, these units are: (1) the group, a formation of structures directly interrelated by sharing structural elements like walls and/or stairs; (2) the sector, an assemblage of interrelated groups, separated from other sectors by natural limits (streams, ridges) or cultural ones (other architectural features); and (3) the site or community, an assemblage of sectors, which, although separated by well-defined boundaries, have clear zones of linkage. A stylistic and environmental unity is apparent among the architectural features, which allows them to be subsumed in this largest unit.

The site of Guayabo is generally oriented along a northwest–southeast axis, an orientation emphasized by an eight–meter–wide causeway, which apparently served as the entrance to the site from the southeast. At a point some 150 meters below the center of the site, the causeway is flanked by two rectangular mounds (M36, M37). A small stairway rises between them, and, on the side away from the site, the causeway diminishes to two-three meters in width. This "gateway" to the site (Group A) was easily guarded. Once past the stairway, the causeway, now 8 meters wide, runs directly into Plaza (hereafter P) 30 near the center of the site.

During our recent investigations, the causeway was followed one kilometer farther southeast, where it meets two mounds of seven meters in diameter. To the northwest, the same axis is defined by a causeway (which picks up on the other side of M1) formed by paved zones lying between M 1, 5, 7–10, 15–17, and the retaining walls that surround them. Near the center of the site, two other roadways break off in a Y–form, one leading to a long stairway that debouches in the Lajitas creek, while the other crosses the Chanchera creek in the direction of the Guayabo River.

The builders of Guayabo showed a notable ability to harmonize architectural features with the natural topography, using the undulating, sloping ground surface to produce a multileveled, sequential site layout, which resulted in a richness of perspectives. There is little doubt that the radial system of streams flowing down the cone of the Turrialba Volcano played an important role in the orientation of the site and its aqueduct and drainage networks. Although we do not yet know the full extent of the Guayabo site, four main sectors, including all features so far known, have been established. These sectors appear to have been defined by natural or artificially controlled water courses, which influenced the architectural forms contained in each. The Central Sector (I) is so designated because its architectural features are the largest; they are associated with what may have been ceremonial objects (petroglyphs, offertory receptacles), and form part of what was probably the main entrance of the site. The Central Sector's limits are Lajitas creek, Chanchera creek, Aqueduct (hereafter A) 49, and Group A, the "gateway." All its architectural features (M1–8, M28, M32–34, E29, P30) are connected by a series of paved roadways and a system of stairs between M5 and M7 (fig. 36).

The special character of Sector I is immediately apparent. It is considered to be the main entrance to Guayabo because the principal causeway leads directly to it, through P30, the largest feature at the site (888 square meters). Where the

Figure 37. Partial view of circular house foundations in Sector II, Guayabo, also showing part of Sector I with Mound I. Note the stairway of Mound I. Photo: Ricardo Luna.

causeway enters P30, it is flanked by two pairs of mounds (Group B), each of 50 square meters, and joined by a possible stairway. The walls of M31 and M33 form part of the perimeter of the plaza. Within the plaza, there is direct access to the largest mounds. M1 stands out, with its large eastern stairway that lines up precisely with the entry into the plaza of the main causeway on the other side (fig. 37). M1 is surrounded by a paved walkway nearly ten meters in width in some parts, and has two trapezoidal stairways, one to the east and one to the southwest (fig. 38). Petroglyphs on cobbles incorporated in the walkway are numerous; some are of considerable size. At the base of the eastern stairway, there is a cup–shaped depression carved out of the first step, in the manner of an offertory receptacle. Other sizable mounds are M7, M8, and M28. The smaller mounds within this sector (M2–5) are on lower terrain, perhaps indicating that they sustained people involved in the domestic maintenance of the higher–ranking inhabitants of the larger mounds, where, it is suggested, ceremonial activities took place.

The boundaries of Sector II are Lajitas and Chancera creeks, A14, and A49. It includes M9, 10, and 15–27. Mounds in this sector are smaller than those in Sector I; they can be divided into the following groups, from north to south: Group C (M9–10), Group D (M15–16, 18–20; M21, probably part of another group in the unexcavated area to the east), Group E (M22–24), and Group F (M25-27). These groups are defined by the sharing of a single access system, generally a ramp or stairway, or by simple proximity and morphological similarity (fig. 39). Group D is somewhat different than the others, perhaps because some of its features form part of the causeway that enters from the east; it may also have had a functional difference.

Sector III, located at the highest part of the site, is bounded by Chanchera creek and the canyon of the Guayabo River; it cannot be delimited to the east and west until our excavations have progressed further. It contains M38–48. Within

it, we can define Group G, formed of M39–42, elements that share walls or entryways. In general, architectural features are far apart, but much more horizontal cleaning must be done to clarify relationships. The smallest mounds or house circles are found here; they range from 4.5 to 28.3 square meters. M48, one of the largest in Sector III (176.7 square meters), is notable for several reasons. Its entrance, in the form of a ramp, terminates in a retaining wall of very large stones on the downhill side. Surrounding it were found nine free-

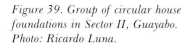

108

standing stone sculptures, mostly anthro– and zoomorphic effigies, 30–40 centimeters in height. Nearby is a petroglyph done in low relief on a sizable boulder; its zoomorphic motifs, reminiscent of some Panamanian gold work, are the most realistic, well–executed examples of stone carving found at Guayabo during recent excavations (Aguilar 1974). These associated features suggest a special, perhaps religious, character for M48.

The southern and northern limits of Sector IV are the Lajas River and A14; to the east and west, the limits are as yet undefined. A branch of the causeway, which enters the site from the east, as well as a bridge made from giant flagstones, or *lajas*, connect Sector IV with Sector II. Like Sector III, Sector IV is still imperfectly known; so far, only M3, M12, and P11 have been recognized. P11 is sunken, and one enters by stairs. It appears to be an expanded node along the passage of a causeway, which enters on one side and leaves on the opposite one. Its size is considerable (572 square meters), seeming to indicate that it was built as a plaza, not just as a wider part of the causeway.

Comparisons and Conclusions

Guayabo de Turrialba is not the only site in Costa Rica with the kinds of architectural features described above, although it is the largest presently known. Sites similar to Guayabo include Las Mercedes (Hartmen 1901), Costa Rica Farm and Anita Grande (Skinner 1926), Nájera (Kennedy 1968), and La Cabaña (Snarskis 1978; in press), all located in the Atlantic Watershed. Outside Costa Rica, we see amazing similarities between Guayabo and the site of Pueblito in northern Colombia (Reichel–Dolmatoff 1954a, 1954b).

Las Mercedes, Costa Rica Farm, and Anita Grande all included circular mounds, house foundations, and causeways, which varied in size, height, and system of access, as they do in Guayabo. The major mound at Las Mercedes is similar to M1 at Guayabo in height and diameter. Hartman noted the presence of free–standing stone sculpture at the perimeter of the feature; this is very like the situation at M48 in Guayabo. We also appear to have located a completely buried stone sculpture in the vicinity of M1. The other mounds at Las Mercedes, as well as those reported by Skinner in Costa Rica Farm and Anita Grande, are like those found in Guayabo, with systems of stairs providing access. It is notable that the stairways of two mounds at Costa Rica Farm appear to connect; at Anita Grande, two large rectangular plazas are joined by a paved causeway, over 200 meters in length, implying a considerable size for the site (Michael J. Snarskis, personal communication).

Although other architectural features are almost certainly present at the Nájera site, three were described: a retaining wall of cobbles built around a small, natural elevation; a circular house foundation; and an "enclosure," circular in form, with several open entryways. The circular house foundation is typical of most Atlantic Watershed sites after 1000 A.D., but the round enclosure is unique so far. Perhaps the feature most similar to it is P11 in Guayabo, the only nonrectangular plaza known. In general, plaza–enclosure features form a unit, the lower, open plaza space being surrounded by raised ridges of cobbles and earthfill. The plazas are always of considerable size (compared with the mounds), and have at least two entrances, suggesting a community or "public" function of some kind. The retaining wall is also seen at Guayabo, and there is some indication that there, as well as at other late sites in the Cartago valley excavated by

Hartman and the MNCR, such features were employed to delimit cemetery zones.

The part of the La Cabaña site that was carefully excavated horizontally has a quadrangular plaza with accompanying enclosure, two raised mounds abutting it, and a smaller circular house foundation outside it; all these features are connected by paved causeways, ramps, or stairways. The obvious functional unity of this group of features is reminiscent of Sector I at Guayabo and its hypothesized "public" or ceremonial nature. Small features discovered on the La Cabaña mounds (metates, hearths, stone tools) allow us to infer the existence of different kinds of activity areas within the former structures. It is assumed, on grounds of ethnohistorical analogy and remnants of burnt cane and thatch recovered at La Cabaña, that all mounds and house circles had a perishable, roofed structure built on top (Snarskis 1978: 253–254; in press). The La Cabaña plaza had clear similarities with those at Costa Rica Farm, Anita Grande, and P30 at Guayabo, both in shape and in size. Furthermore, all are entered at one side by a major paved causeway; that of Guayabo measures 8 meters in width and 1250 meters in length in its excavated portion.

Built by people of the Tairona culture, the Pueblito site in Colombia presents striking similarities to Guayabo—it includes circular mounds, retaining walls of cobbles, systems of stairways, cobble–paved causeways, aqueducts, and bridges. Gerardo Reichel–Dolmatoff (1954a), the excavator of Pueblito, subdivided the site using units much like the sector and group concepts applied at Guayabo. This organizational relationship is emphasized further by the use of water courses, natural and man–made, as borders between population clusters at Pueblito (*ibid.:* 162). A plaza, although larger than those at Costa Rican sites, shows the same rectangular form, and aqueducts appear to have been constructed in the same way as at Guayabo (*ibid.:* fig. VI) (fig. 40).

This series of shared architectural features constitutes evidence for placing parts of northern South America and Lower Central America in the same interaction sphere in the last several centuries before the Spanish arrival; similarities in ceramic styles and metallurgical techniques, and especially language,

Figure 40. Partial view of a pool incorporated into one of the aqueducts at Guayabo. Photo: Oscar Fonseca Zamora.

have long been noted. The presence of many paved causeways, some perhaps linking prehistoric sites in Costa Rica (Stone 1977: 169), the accounts of the Spanish chroniclers describing such roads (Vásquez de Coronado 1964), the reports of 19th–century travelers and explorers of road systems linking coastal and inland indigenous villages (Hoffman 1976: 110), as well as the results of our own and other anthropologists' surveys in the field (Bozzoli 1977, 1979), make us suspect that a situation like that described for northern Colombia prevailed in eastern Costa Rica during Period IV (1000–1550 A.D.). As Reichel–Dolmatoff (1954a: 148) puts it:

.... the Indians of the Sierra Nevada had constructed a network of wide, paved roads which connected the mountains with the coast, and the villages from valley to valley. These roads made for rapid communication between population centers....

Obviously, these road systems were a product of socio–economic processes that put a premium on fast, efficient communication between settlements, and between their zones of resource exploitation.

At Guayabo, we are attempting to expand our base of enquiry to include all parts of the surrounding locality and to define how the site interacted with other regions. This kind of study leads us to consider an important socio–political process, the formation of the chiefdom, and its function in prehistoric Costa Rica. I believe that sufficient evidence exists today to postulate the formation of chiefdoms from at least about 1000 A.D., if not hundreds of years before. In addition to the architectural features described above (which are found in many other sites), a mastery of difficult crafts (wood, stone, and jade carving, metallurgy, specialized pottery) indicates the existence of specialized artisans whose products were primarily of social and/or ideological importance.

Even though no one archaeological project with a truly regional, long–term focus has been completed in Costa Rica, three are now underway, including that of Guayabo. Work done to date has suggested some factors that may have been important in the development of the chiefdom social structure: (1) a diverse natural environment, with different zones at no great distance from one another, thus enhancing possibilities of resource exploitation and long–term productive stability; (2) trade or commerce with adjacent regions in high–status or luxury goods; and (3) long–distance trade with Mesoamerica or South America. One must remember the importance of trade as a means of transmission of ideas as well as of objects (Rathje 1974; Conrad 1974). Trade and increasing competition for productive agricultural or other territories must have resulted in a greater need for military–like controls and a higher incidence of small–scale warfare. These processes may well have stimulated the federation of major sites and their satellites, creating hierarchies of sites based on economic interaction.

Flannery's model (1972) for the passing of a social structure from one level of complexity to another appears to be sufficiently general to apply to the Guayabo site system. He uses the socio–environmental variables discussed above—trade, a varied natural habitat, increased competition for desired resources—to show how processes of *promotion* (ascendancy within a site hierarchy) and *linealization* (replacement of local, lower–order social controls with controls imposed by a higher, thus more powerful, authority) can occur in any social system, given the proper conditions. I think that this is the process that created Guayabo and sites like it; it only remains for scientific archaeological investigation to confirm the model, or to propose alternative ones.

TRADITIONS OF COSTA RICAN STONE SCULPTURE

Mark M. Graham

The first true traditions of stone sculpture in Costa Rica emerged late in Period IV (1–500 A.D.) in Nicoya and the Atlantic Watershed. The three most important types of functional stone sculpture were tripod metates, jade or pseudo–jade axe pendants and other ornaments, and hard–stone mace or club heads. The most important regional differences reside in the form of the special–purpose metates. Those in Nicoya have a longitudinally curved and rimless plate, while in the Atlantic Watershed the plate is horizontally flat and rimmed. In both regions, the archaeological contexts are mortuary and suggest the beginnings of differentiated social status and wealth, and their related symbols. Early attempts at figural stone sculpture were worked out on metates, first in relief and then in a projecting, nearly full–round technique. The tripod–metate traditions, along with their associated jades and mace heads, climaxed and declined in Period V (500–1000 A.D.)

In Nicoya, stone sculpture never regained its former importance. In the Atlantic Watershed and Diquís regions, Period V saw the emergence of independent figural sculpture, and, by the beginning of Period VI (1000–1500 A.D.), new metate–like forms or ceremonial lithic platforms. These regional trends in Diquís and the Atlantic Watershed were inspired, in part, by the short–lived tradition of monumental functional and figural sculpture developed by the stone carvers of Barriles, in western Panama, early in Period V. In the Atlantic Watershed, Period VI was marked by the near–mass production of figural sculpture, and by a variety of figure–decorated "metates" and bowls, some types of which were made or distributed through western Panama.

The Early Tradition

GUANACASTE–NICOYA

The early tradition of stone sculpture in Nicoya is first seen in cemeteries such as Las Pilas (Lange and Scheidenhelm 1972) and El Hacha (Stone 1977: 32-34) in the far northern part of the region. Both sites were excavated after they had

Plate 46. Warrior with trophy head, Atlantic Watershed zone, stone (cat. no. 205).

been looted, and have been dated by ceramic associations to the local Chombo phase (300 B.C.–300 A.D.). Sherds of Maya Chicanel–phase (300 B.C.–150 A.D.) ceramics support this dating, and may suggest northern contact in the early part of Period IV, perhaps around 100–200 A.D. Some of the burials at El Hacha were furnished with three important lithic types: plain rimless tripod metates (no manos were reported), jade or jadelike axe pendants, and hard–stone mace or club heads. Burials at Las Pilas were similar, but for the apparent absence of mace heads.

The development of this tradition and of the social differentiation that accompanied it is evident from a comparison of two slightly later sites in southern Nicoya, Bolsón and Las Huacas. Bolsón is a small cemetery at the middle Tempisque River, excavated by Baudez (1967: 37–44). Ceramics provide firm dating extending through the local Ciruelas phase (300–500 A.D.). The 12 burials were mostly secondary, with ceramic offerings predominating. Diagnostic lithics were limited to three jadeite beads and two small, plain, tripod metates. Of the latter, one was a fragmentary surface find; the second had been placed in Burial 3, one of the richer ones, and was accompanied by a tapered cylindrical mano. Manos of this type are rarely encountered with metates in Nicoya. Aside from the jade beads and the metate and mano, obviously special–purpose and wealth–associated artifacts were limited to a few ocarinas and zoomorphic vessels. The Bolsón cemetery appears to have been a provincial site.

The famous site of Las Huacas, however, which lies near the town of Nicoya, was surely one of the local centers at this time. Its rich cemetery had already been extensively looted when Hartman worked there in 1903, but Hartman's (1907a) carefully recorded excavations enabled his successors, Baudez (1967: 196–199) and, more recently, Oscar Fonseca Zamora (Fonseca and Richardson 1978: 299–317), to establish the temporal dimensions denied him. Baudez, from his work at Bolsón and stratified sites in the Tempisque valley, determined that Las Huacas was a multicomponent site, with ceramics extending from the local Catalina phase (300 B.C.–300 A.D.) to the San Bosco phase (500–800 A.D.), and that the principal use of the cemetery occurred within the Ciruelas phase (300–500 A.D.). The variety of functional stone sculpture at Las Huacas and Baudez's observations about ceramic associations provide a wide view of the development of stone sculpture in Nicoya.

The Catalina phase at Las Huacas includes plain tripod metates and serpentine axe pendants of humans with a bifid tongue (Burials IX, XIII; Hartman 1907a). This datable context at Las Huacas supports the coeval dating of Las Pilas and El Hacha. The Ciruelas phase at Las Huacas saw the emergence of low–relief geometric and figural decoration on tripod metates with conical legs. At its simplest, this is limited to geometric interlace motifs on the upper and lower borders of the thin, curving plate. One metate from Burial VIII adds to this format a germinal effigy concept, with the front leg incised as the head of a raptor (or parrot), the rear legs representing the feet, and the body and wings thickly incised underneath the plate (*ibid.*: pl. VIII). Two Nicoyan metates in the exhibition display important variations on this concept: one has an inverted human head carved at the top of the front leg (cat. no. 15), and the other has a crocodile or cayman spread out in low relief underneath the plate, with the front leg of the metate transformed into the creature's raised head (cat. no. 16). Plain tripod metates continued in use in the Ciruelas phase.

A disturbed part of the cemetery, without definable graves but with Ciruelas–phase ceramics, yielded a "toy" tripod metate (minus a mano) associated with a red mineral thought by Hartman (1907a: 26) to have been used in painting ceramics. One function of the small undecorated metates may have been the grinding of earth pigments. An avian axe–god and avian–headed mace heads were also found in this part of the cemetery (*ibid.*: 27–32).

A San Bosco–phase ceramic context (Burial I) yielded two small, plain, worn metates and a large tripod metate with conical legs, guilloche and "net" or "mat" designs on the upper border of the plate, and meander and mat designs on the border underneath. A small bird was carved in low relief in the center of each end of the plate, and the tips of the legs were carved in a motif suggesting a bundle of reeds or sticks (*ibid.*: 16–17).

While the conical–leg tripod metates were being made more elaborate in the San Bosco phase, a new type, showing a more difficult carving technique, was introduced. The metate from Burial XI is the only example excavated by Hartman which had carved slab legs with openwork decoration. The legs are carved as inverted stylized monkeys with erect tails; two similar heads decorate the lugs that project from the single–legged end of the plate (*ibid.*: 22–23). There is a nearly identical metate, with a mano in the form of a reed bundle, in the exhibition (cat. no. 72).[1] This metate form, and the carving technique employed, were the basis for the most complex of Nicoyan metates, effigy types with a single projecting head and slab legs, carved in a lacy open-work technique (see cat. nos. 77, 78). The development of this type began in the San Bosco phase, and the most elaborate versions probably were made later in that phase.

In sum, the dated graves at Las Huacas appear to represent the major stages in the development of the early tradition of stone sculpture in Nicoya during the period 300–800 A.D. In terms of labor expended in production, decorated tripod metates were the most important component in a complex of functional stone sculpture which also included mace heads and axes.

The Nicoyan objects have their closest formal link with a particular type of metate used for grinding maize in Mesoamerican highland regions.[2] Tripod metates with a horizontal plate occur in Central Mexico at least by the beginning of Late Formative times, apparently as a counterpart of the utilitarian basin or slab metate (Tolstoy 1965: 288). Both types were used for grinding maize, with the finer tripods probably reserved for special occasions and limited to wealthy or high-status households. From the Late Formative period on, tripod metates are found sporadically outside of Central Mexico, invariably in ritual or elite mortuary contexts (Chadwick 1965: 665, 671; Long 1966).

The plain tripod metate first appears in Nicoya at this time, 300 B.C.–300 A.D., apparently a selective local adaptation of a highland Mesoamerican ritual––mortuary trait. In Nicoya, the function and meaning of tripod metates seem quite different from what we know of the Mesoamerican tradition. Since the fine tripod metate was already established as a special–purpose artifact in Mesoamerica before it appeared in Nicoya, there is no necessary relationship between these mortuary symbols and intensive maize agriculture in Nicoya. The Nicoyan metates are fundamentally symbols separated from any domestic function; those that do show signs of wear were probably used to grind maize for ritual consumption, not as a staple.

At Las Huacas, in the 16 graves that Hartman (1907a) excavated and recorded, there were 15 metates and not one mano. It is unlikely that incomplete tools would have been placed in the graves, if the intent were to allow their use in the world of the dead. Since the metate as a tool was originally used to transform

Plate 47. Relief–decorated metate,
Guanacaste–Nicoya zone, stone (cat.
no. 16).

Plate 48. Relief–decorated metate,
Santa Cruz, Guanacaste, stone (cat.
no. 14).

Plate 49. Avian–effigy metate,
Guanacaste–Nicoya zone, stone (cat.
no. 75).

Plate 50. Decorated metate with mano, Guanacaste–Nicoya zone, stone (cat. no. 72).

Plate 51. Flying-panel metate, La Unión de Guápiles, Línea Vieja, Atlantic Watershed, stone (cat. no. 146).

maize into flour for human consumption, the metate as primary mortuary symbol may have extended this concept, so that the object came to represent both elite control over food production and a place of transformation, above all in the realm of human life and death. In Nicoya, paradoxically, where maize was apparently not a staple at this time, the metate became a vital symbol, associated with death and perhaps with the promise of rebirth and new life.

The other two components of this early complex in Nicoya also have instrumental prototypes. Figure–decorated hard–stone axes appear to derive from the Middle Formative Olmec tradition, and to represent a deliberate revival of a ritual symbol associated with Olmec and "Olmecoid" influence in southern Mesoamerica. In Middle America, plain stone axes are commonly identified with clearing land for agriculture and with woodworking, both vital tasks in the tropics. Such axes were almost certainly produced by specialists under strict control of the ruling group, so that the display and ritual use of ceremonial axes, decorated or not, suggests that their primary symbolic value was the expression of elite authority over labor and land.

The Nicoyan hard–stone mace heads may well be similarly ceremonial versions of plain stone weapons. The display and ritual use of these versions of close–combat weapons could have been emblematic of prowess in warfare and the status it conferred. Decorated mace heads must also have been made by specialists, and their distribution controlled by the ruling group.

Thus, given the probability that the production and distribution of ceremonial versions of metates, axes, and mace heads was in the hands of ruling groups in Nicoya, their primary symbolic value should logically be the visual expression of elite control over food production and processing, land and labor, and warfare or the defense and acquisition of land and people. The prevalent mortuary associations of all three objects connect these symbols of social control with elite ritual activity and presumably with elite concepts about death and the underworld.

In the early tradition of Nicoyan sculpture, the great majority of metate images represents but four animal families: saurians (crocodiles or iguanas) (cat. no. 73), avians (raptors and parrots) (cat. nos. 75, 76), felines (jaguars) (cat. no. 78), and canines (dogs or coyotes) (cat. no. 77). In addition to the above imagery, mace heads also show bats, owls, and human heads (cat. no. 45) and skulls (cat. no. 46). Nicoyan metate and mace–head imagery can be shown to have significant parallels with Classic–period Mesoamerican iconography as it relates to the sun and the underworld. As synthesized by Esther Pasztory (1978: 130), Middle Classic–period Mesoamerican imagery reveals six important clusters or "cults": agricultural fertility, warfare, ball game, dynastic rulership, elite burial, and patron deities, all concerned with the cyclical nature of cosmic phenomena, and their relationship with the cyclical patterns of agricultural and natural fertility. A major theme in these cults was "transformation through death and rebirth"; the "primary metaphor for all transformation was the diurnal cycle of the sun" (ibid.:131).

Three of the six Mesoamerican "cults" correspond to the probable symbolism of components of the early Nicoyan tradition. The concepts and imagery associated with the Middle Classic cults of agricultural fertility, warfare, and elite burial may provide an explanation for the particular combination of artifacts and imagery that make up the early tradition of Nicoyan sculpture. According to this hypothesis, the predominant metate imagery represents a cosmology in which raptors and parrots are the daytime sun, felines are the night sun in the underworld, canines are the night sun's escort, and saurians are the earth's surface. The imagery of mace heads, particularly the frequent human heads and skulls, owls, and bats, corresponds closely to the themes of aggression and death in the warrior and ballgame cults. Axes, plain and decorated, may relate equally to themes of agricultural fertility and warfare. Distinct "cults" of Mesoamerica appear to have been synthesized and symbolized by decorated versions of three ritual tools.

CENTRAL HIGHLANDS–ATLANTIC WATERSHED

The early tradition of stone sculpture in the Atlantic Watershed emerged during early Period IV (1–500 A.D.) and climaxed and declined in the first half of Period V (500–1000 A.D.). This tradition is essentially coeval with the early tradition in Nicoya, and, in some respects, the two regional traditions appear as divergent developments from a similar basis, notably special-purpose tripod metates of Mesoamerican origin.

The El Bosque phase (1–500 A.D.) is characterized by widespread production of utilitarian lithics used in land–clearing and plant exploitation, and the related emergence of finely made special–purpose ground–stone artifacts, the ultimate content and function of which were mortuary (Snarskis 1978: 152ff.). The typical domestic metate was a trough-shaped tripod, used with a simple, loaf–shaped mano. This type is remarkably close to being a synthesis of two metate types from Mesoamerica: the Lowland Maya domestic "turtle–back" type, with a use–made grinding trough; and the highland Mesoamerican flat–topped tripod type, the common special–purpose metate (*ibid.*: fig. 33b; W. Coe 1965: 599, fig. 1).

The simplest, and apparently the earliest, special–purpose metate of this tradition is an oblong or round tripod, with a horizontal rimmed plate. Snarskis (1978: 159) observes that the frequent wear–patterns on these metates were probably made by pestles, perhaps in the preparation of special foodstuffs or drugs. The rim is often notched, or carved with very stylized human heads.

As in the Nicoya region at this time, the basic special–purpose metate was elaborated by carved motifs underneath the plate, in the form of a longitudinal row of seemingly geometric projections (on oblong metates), and radial rows (in round metates) (Stone and Balser 1957: fig. 14). Snarskis identifies this motif as the dorsal scutes of the cayman, noting the ubiquity of more realistic images of this lowland saurian (Snarskis 1978: 157). Thus, in both Nicoya and the Atlantic Watershed, the first phase of metate figural decoration involved saurian imagery underneath the plate, probably reflecting an incipient cosmology in which saurians represented the fertile surface of the earth and the source of agricultural fertility.

These simple underside motifs initiated the development of that unique and most spectacular type of Costa Rican stone sculpture, the so–called "flying–panel" metates of the Atlantic Watershed (cat. nos. 144–147), which were apparently made from late Period IV into Period V (Snarskis 1978: 157).

Mace heads were also made during the El Bosque phase, some apparently indistinguishable in style and technique from those of Nicoya. Lapidary production of beads, axe pendants, and other ornaments was also similar to that known

Plate 52. Jaguar metate, Finca La Colombiana, Línea Vieja, Atlantic Watershed, volcanic stone (cat. no. 229).

Plate 53. Ceremonial metate, Guayabo de Turrialba, Atlantic Watershed, volcanic stone (cat. no. 199).

Plate 54. Seated figure, Atlantic Watershed zone, volcanic stone (cat. no. 219).

from Nicoya. Archaeological contexts show a correlation of special–purpose metates, mace heads, and jades in high–status burials, a pattern that is familiar from Nicoya.

The basic stone–sculpture types of the El Bosque phase continued through the La Selva phase, reaching a climax in the first half of Period V and declining c. 700–900 A.D. (Snarskis 1978: 234). Carving techniques developed to the point of virtuosity. The rimmed tripod metate grew larger and much more complex, with the vertical flying panel underneath the focal point of a bizarre tableau overflowing with predators and trophy heads. These monumental metates were apparently the most important ritual objects at this time, but their imagery remains poorly understood. The most complex ones are reported to have come from graves in the Turrialba Valley and the Línea Vieja subregions (*ibid.*: 157).

The technical progress evident in metates is also reflected in other stone sculpture in this period. While production of polished hard–stone mace heads may have continued from the El Bosque phase, a new type emerged, made of the same porous basalt as metates, and representing a long–beaked bird with trophy head (cat. no. 139). This repeats, in portable form, a recurrent motif of the flying–panel metates.

The technical achievements of metate carving may have contributed to the emergence of the first free–standing figural sculpture in northern Costa Rica. Evidence for this exists in the form of a small anthropomorphic figure from the Atlantic Watershed, which wears a saurian buccal mask, a tubular bead pendant, and a multitiered feathered(?) headdress (cat. nos. 196–198). Rather similar masked figures, perhaps deity impersonators, are commonly shown on La Selva–phase tripod vessels and in the central position underneath flying–panel metates, suggesting that this is another example of a portable, and less socially restricted, image taken from the monumental metate.

Most other developments in stone sculpture were minor. The stirrup–shaped muller and the flared–head pestle were refined and elaborated (see cat. no. 137, probably El Bosque phase, and cat. no. 135, probably La Selva).

There are two quite unusual objects in the exhibition, which almost certainly were made during this period, probably in the Línea Vieja (cat. nos. 148, 149). One may represent the trunk of a tree, which has been fashioned into a mortar; a small primate, either monkey or human, is seated in the hollowed-out top, while another figure, perhaps a jaguar, is carved head-downward on the backside. A nearly identical representation is found on a large jade "bead," reportedly from Guácimo in the Línea Vieja (Easby 1968: fig. 50). Since jade use virtually ceased in Costa Rica by the second half of the La Selva phase, this provides a terminus ad quem for the bead, and probably also for the mortar (Snarskis 1978: 160).

The early traditions of stone sculpture in both Nicoya and the Atlantic Watershed are marked by the increasing elaboration of tripod metates. The presence of a rim on the Atlantic Watershed metate may be a refinement of the domestic trough or basin metate of the Maya Lowlands (Willey 1972: 106–110).[3] If so, exclusive characteristics of northern Costa Rican metates—the curved plate of Nicoyan types and the rimmed plate of Atlantic Watershed types—would be design features based on heavily worn Mesoamerican prototypes, with the Nicoyan design based on a wear pattern made by overhanging manos, and the Atlantic Watershed design on the use of a loaf–shaped mano.

The symbolic connotations may also have been very similar. In the earliest forms, as in Nicoya, the saurian imagery probably signifies the surface of the earth. The metate as an implement of food transformation was the basis for its function as a symbol of transformation in the human life cycle. Apparently, a primary use of these metates was as a burial platform. The juxtaposition of decapitated human heads with the grinding plate equates the heads with the completion of the agricultural cycle, since human heads were represented as the seeds or fruits of the human life process.

The radical expansion of imagery on the flying–panel metates further elaborates on this theme. Complex metates have three fields of imagery: the plate border, the flying panel, and the three supports. Flying–panel images show considerable variety. The standing central figure is almost always anthropomorphic with a saurian (cat. nos. 146, 147) or avian (beak–bird) (cat. no. 145) mask. This figure usually stands on another with telluric associations, a jaguar, a bicephalic saurian, or a crab. While the supporting figure may symbolize the earth, the central figure is probably a deity impersonator, with both hands raised in a presumably ritual attitude. The most common images on the three supports are beak–birds, clutching a decapitated human head, or a complete figure that appears to represent a captive; monkeys, felines, and saurians are also shown. The human heads bordering the plate are a standard feature.

The basic theme of the flying–panel metates appears to be the religious ideology of human sacrifice as the generator of agricultural fertility. The deity impersonator (?) orchestrates a variety of natural predators who feed on human heads, the "fruit" of human life. If, as Snarskis (in press) suggests, the expanding polities of this time were competing with their neighbors for the choicest land (and access to exchange networks), then, in a very real sense, social predation, warfare, and the taking of trophy heads would have been the basis for both agricultural fertility and the continuation of human life.

DIQUÍS

A clear picture of the Diquís region depends heavily on the dating of monumental sculpture at the site of Barriles, in the highlands of western Panama. The stone sculpture of Barriles includes giant tetrapod metates, nearly life–size human figures on shaft bases, and the decorated cylinders or "barrels" that give the site its name.[1] The dating of Barriles sculpture has been tied to the dating of Aguas Buenas ceramics, for their association is fairly well established. Haberland (1955), who first reported on Aguas Buenas ceramics, was unsure of their date, suggesting either 1–300 A.D. or 300–500 A.D. Recent work by Linares and others (Linares, Sheets, and Rosenthal 1975) indicates that the ceremonial part of the site, where the sculptures were found, dates rather late in the first occupational sequence, perhaps c. 400–600 A.D. or even to 800 A.D., supporting the later dating of Aguas Buenas ceramics.

The Barriles sculpture development thus appears to have been more or less coeval with the early traditions of Nicoya and the Atlantic Watershed. Barriles sculpture, however, emphasizes tetrapod "metate" platforms and explicit imagery of human sacrifice with a monumentality that is rare in Costa Rica. The tetrapods commonly have a border of stylized human heads, while the supports may be plain (cat. no. 234) or take the form of human Atlantids or caryatids, or large human heads (cat. no. 233). The last is a virtual copy of the largest whole "metate" from Barriles; at each end of its oval plate there was, originally, a chiseled low relief of decapitated human figures (Torres de Araúz 1972: pl.85). This decapitation imagery suggests a new function for the Barriles "metates,"

Plate 55. Female figure, Atlantic Watershed zone, volcanic stone (cat. no. 221).

Plate 56. Female figure, Atlantic Watershed zone, volcanic stone (cat. no. 220).

Plate 57. Head, Atlantic Watershed zone, volcanic stone (cat. no. 216).

Plate 58. Head, Atlantic Watershed zone, volcanic stone (cat. no. 215).

and, by extension, for the smaller versions made in Costa Rica. The Barriles "metates" may have been sacrificial platforms used to prepare the bodies of war captives for ritual consumption. The cylinders are, apparently, monumental manos. The Costa Rican versions can hardly have been made before late Period V, thus providing further evidence that the Barriles prototypes are somewhat later than commonly thought. The Barriles site was abandoned sometime after 800 A.D., and this may account for the selective diffusion of Barriles sculptural traits in the later Transitional period in late Period IV Diquís and the Atlantic Watershed.

The early tradition of stone sculpture in Diquís, emerging in early Period V, is limited to peg–base figures, zoomorphic effigies, and stone spheres, the latter often of monumental size. The independent anthropomorphic figures may have either a functional peg or shaft base (cat. no. 245), apparently used to mount them in cobble foundations, or only a small rounded base (cat. no. 244) or plinth of doubtful utility. The Barriles ancestry of these figures can be seen in the semi–round treatment of the limbs, which are never freed from the body. The human axe–bearer or sacrificer of Barriles, however, has become, in Diquís, a less realistic anthropomorph, often with a single or bifid serpent tongue, or hair ending in serpent heads, and with an important feline trait, the N–shaped incisors that are common in composite figures of the San Agustín tradition of southern Colombia. Somewhat similar composite imagery is found in the central masked figures of the Atlantic Watershed flying–panel metates (see cat. no. 147), suggesting contemporaneity. Iconographically, however, the composite human–feline–serpent imagery of Diquís figural sculpture has no local ante- cedents, and is thematically similar to the monumental sculpture tradition of San Agustín. Portable metalwork was probably the primary vehicle in the northward diffusion of San Agustín–related traits, since the Diquís figure style is notably more "sculptural," more fully round, than that of San Agustín. These Diquís figures may have been deity impersonators or priests projecting a model for predatory human activity.

The carved stone spheres that are a hallmark of the Diquís Delta subregion are yet another surprising and enigmatic type of sculpture from Costa Rica (cat. no. 235). These spheres are very numerous and often very large (Lothrop 1963: 15ff.), numbering perhaps in the thousands and ranging up to more than two meters in diameter. When found in situ in groups, the spheres were arranged in what were probably astronomical alignments, the significance of which has not yet been determined. Smaller spheres have also been reported from graves. Stone spheres have been found in the Chiriquí highlands of western Panama in association with Barriles–style figures, and with Barriles–style cylinders and Aguas Buenas ceramics in the Diquís highlands of Costa Rica (Torres de Arauz 1972: 69; Haberland 1973: 139). The spheres of the Diquís Delta thus appear to have a direct Barriles ancestry, with a probable Period V date for the com- mencement of their production in the Delta.[5]

The closest analogues of the spheres appear to be the pedestal–mounted spheres at the Late Preclassic site of Izapa, Chiapas, Mexico (Norman 1976: 251, 257, 275). Relatively small stone balls are found sporadically in Nuclear America, and their Mesoamerican distribution, chiefly from Veracruz to Guatemala, may be related to the ball game and associated cosmological symbolism (Parsons 1978; Stone 1943). The stone spheres of Diquís exceed all others in size and technical perfection, probably indicating their greater importance to the people who made them. Both Stone (*ibid.*) and Lothrop (1963) have shown that the

126

monumental spheres were placed in groups on or near mounds that presumably were the foundations of elite residential and ritual centers; the stone balls were probably originally associated with peg–base figural sculptures, to which they may have been symbolically related. Sacrifice by decapitation after the ball game in Classic–period Mesoamerica may perhaps be related to the Diquís trophy–head imagery and stone balls. The process of quarrying, carving, and installing the large stone spheres calls to mind the production of Olmec colossal heads. In both cases, the ability to carry out such projects must have been a demonstration of economic and political authority.

The early tradition in Diquís appears to provide the earliest evidence in Costa Rica of stone sculpture intended for public ritual, installed in at least a semi-architectural context. Whereas the components of the early traditions in Nicoya and the Atlantic Watershed were all destined for individual use, only the zoomorphic stools of Diquís can be so considered. The spheres certainly, and the peg–base figures probably, must have been essentially fixed monuments. Public monuments are primarily a "high-culture" trait; their presence in the Diquís region may reflect a local synthesis, with Barriles, of both southern Mesoamerican and northern Andean concepts.

The Late Tradition

Period VI (1000–1550 A.D.) was a time of uneven development of stone sculpture in Costa Rica. In Nicoya, the old tradition of functional stone sculpture appears to have ended by late Period V, but the new type of monumental figure sculpture from Nicaragua never became widespread. In the Atlantic Watershed, this period saw some remarkable changes; there was some continuity, but there were also new forms, a more refined style, and reinterpretation of earlier themes.[6] Functional stone sculpture remained important, but independent figural sculpture gained prominence for the first time, probably as the result of a change in ritual activity. Sculpture style in the Diquís region appears to be a simplified regional variant of the Atlantic Watershed tradition.

CENTRAL HIGHLANDS–ATLANTIC WATERSHED

Iconographic features of the late tradition reflect a variety of sources, local and foreign. Foreign features appear to have been selectively adopted, no doubt for their relevance to local ritual concerns.

Metate–like lithic platforms were made in two basic types, oblong or oval and circular. The oblong or oval platforms, made in a variety of noneffigy and effigy forms, are all based on tetrapod supports. The single exhibited example of the tetrapod effigy platform (cat. no. 229) is basically a feline effigy, but the side supports are connected by a large septum which serves as the perch for a monkey, a technical device obviously derived from the flying–panel metates of the Transitional period. Further variations, mostly from the Línea Vieja subregion, are shown by Mason (1945).

The feline–effigy "metates" appear to have been inspired by Late Classic or Early Postclassic Mesoamerican jaguar thrones. The crude, blocky carving of Maya thrones—e.g., at Uxmal and Chichén Itzá (Robicsek 1975: figs. 83–89)—is in contrast to the assurance with which the Costa Rican stone carvers handled

Plate 59. Jaguar head, Atlantic Watershed zone, volcanic stone (cat. no. 211).

Plate 60. Pestle, Atlantic Watershed zone, stone (cat. no. 136).

Plate 61. Pestle, Atlantic Watershed zone, stone (cat. no. 135).

their material. The geometric interlace designs on the feline effigies of the Atlantic Watershed may represent the woven mat, a common sign of authority in Mesoamerica, especially among the Maya (*ibid.*).

Among the largest lithic platforms of this tradition are circular pedestal tables, with vertical slots carved out of the base, and small feline figures or heads pendant from the table surface (cat. nos. 199, 200). Wooden versions of these tables are known from the unique cache at Retes (Aguilar 1953). A second type has an openwork ring base, with atlantid felines or monkeys supporting the table surface (cat. no. 201).

The Línea Vieja subregion, in this period, is especially notable for the great variety of figure–decorated stone bowls. In the exhibition are two round, atlantean bowls, one supported by humans (cat. no. 225), the other by monkeys (cat. no. 226). Another round bowl is supported by a ring base of bicephalic felines and small human figures (cat. no. 227). There is also a serpent–effigy bowl; supported by two felines (cat. no. 238).

Far less common are the so–called *chacmools*, reclining figures with a shallow bowl in the belly. True chacmools are Mesoamerican human–shaped sculptures of the Early Postclassic Toltec and Toltec–Maya. In Costa Rica, they are composite figures. The one included in this exhibition (cat. no. 203) is a fierce–looking monkey; Mason (1945: pl. 35c) illustrates one with feline fangs, a raptorial beak, and rattlesnakes crawling over the body. The chacmool probably retained its Mesoamerican function as a receptacle for sacrificial offerings, but was decorated with new tropical–forest imagery: monkeys and raptors, which were used earlier as support images on flying–panel metates.

Among the technical masterworks of Costa Rican stone carving are thin, figure–decorated slabs, thought to be grave markers. The one exhibited here (cat. no. 202), is from Guayabo de Turrialba; Mason (1945: pls. 30–34) illustrates others from Las Mercedes in the Línea Vieja. These typically have a row of figures in low relief along each side, with openwork figures at the top. The slabs were made to stand vertically, with the base set in a cobble foundation. A local prototype may be metates or metate plates placed on end in graves of Periods IV and V (Snarskis 1978: 237).

Independent figural sculpture of this period includes a variety of types emphasizing human fertility and sacrifice. Fertility and sexuality are the themes of female breast display (cat. nos. 220, 221), while male potency is expressed in masturbation or penis–display figures (Ferrero 1977a: pl. XXVI). The explicit fertility and sacrificial imagery has prototypes in the Barriles tradition, which produced realistic male and female figures, with prominent sexual features, used as supports for a gigantic "metate" (Torres de Aráuz 1972: pls. 88–90).

The cycle of human sacrifice begins with prisoner figures (cat. no. 204), and the completed act is represented by sacrificers bearing axes and human heads (cat. nos. 193, 205, 206). Independent heads showing a variety of facial features and hair motifs are numerous, and may represent slain ancestors or trophies taken in battle (cat. nos. 212–216). Independent feline heads are also known (cat. no. 211), but some may have been broken from effigy "metates." Some figures are holding unidentifiable objects (cat. nos. 222, 223); other figures, with eyes closed, may be memorial effigies (cat. nos. 194, 224). The so-called *sukia* or shaman figures show men in attitudes of contemplation (cat. nos. 218, 219) and smoking a cigar or playing a flute during ritual activity (cat. no. 217).

The technical expertise developed in the early tradition for carving flying–

panel metates was clearly the basis for the refined and expanded production of stone sculpture in the late tradition. From c. 400–500 A.D. on, Costa Rica was the center of perhaps the most advanced figural stone–carving tradition in Nuclear America. At this time, independent figural sculpture represents stages and themes of ritual activity, including human fertility and sexuality, religious contemplation and curing, and acts of human sacrifice. The chacmools, atlantean platforms, and stone bowls appear to be related to sacrifice and consumption of special foodstuffs. Effigy "metates" were probably thrones for rulers and the elite, whose graves were marked by the thin stone slabs. Most of these objects were installed in semi–architectural ritual contexts at centers such as Las Mercedes, where debris from a stone–carving workshop was found by Hartman (1901).

The relative downgrading of agricultural symbols, such as metates, with the corresponding emphasis on individual figures of cult activity, suggests a more hierarchical and centralized organization of ritual, removed from the earlier emphasis on individual mortuary ritual. Late–period religion appears to have been more concerned with group activity directed by officials (priest–lords?) of larger polities. These lords would have controlled art production, supported by people in surrounding villages who went to the chiefly centers for major rituals, for example, rites of passage, planting and harvest celebrations, war preparation, and accession and funerary rituals of the aristocracy. On these occasions, the public display of stone sculpture would have been prominent.

DIQUÍS AND NICOYA

In the Diquís region, there were few innovations during this period. Most types from the early tradition probably continued. Tetrapod effigy platforms and bowls were made, the local variants of a late general style that extended from the Atlantic Watershed through western Panama.

The biconical effigy seats of the Nicoya region probably date from middle Period V and later (cat. nos. 99, 100). Their prototype is obscure, but they may be based on wooden mortars. The saurian motifs resemble those of the probably coeval independent figures of this period in the Atlantic Watershed (see cat. nos. 196–198). There is little secure archaeological evidence yet for the dating of the few known examples of independent figural sculpture in the Nicoya region. For the most part, these seem to be isolated southern examples of the style Haberland (1973: 144) has reported from Nicaragua, where they have been known since the 19th century in the lake region (Hartman 1901). Similar "alter–ego" sculptures from Nacascolo, at Bahía Culebra, in Nicoya (Stone 1977: fig. 61), have been assigned to the Middle Polychrome period (800–1200/1350 A.D.), on the basis of vague but probably correct ceramic associations. Baudez (1959) has reported on a nearby site, Papagayo, with cruder and smaller but apparently similar stone figures, also associated with Middle Polychrome ceramics. All these Nicoyan figures are so poorly documented that little can be said about them beyond their probable northern origin and their dissimilarity to other Costa Rican traditions.

1. Brian Dillon, director of the 1980 UCLA excavations at Nacascolo, reports finding a metate very similar to MNCR 24192 with a mano in an Early Polychrome grave, and a small plain tripod metate and mano in another grave of the same period (personal communication).

Plate 64. Feline, Diquís zone, stone (cat. no. 246).

Plate 65. Armadillo, Diquís zone, stone (cat. no. 247).

Plate 63. Bound prisoner, Línea Vieja, Atlantic Watershed, stone (cat. no. 204).

Plate 62. Standing figure, Azul de Turrialba, Atlantic Watershed, stone (cat. no. 194).

2. See, for example, Lange (in press), who stresses the probable use of Nicoyan metates as ceremonial stools. However, as I suggested in a recent paper, this function is not incompatible with a derivation from maize metates; see Graham 1979.

3. A conceivable local prototype for the rim feature of Atlantic Watershed metates may be the rimmed ceramic griddles, or *budares*, found by Snarskis in a Middle Formative site in the Turrialba Valley (Snarskis 1978: 86 ff.). The griddles are thought by Snarskis to have been used in manioc preparation, but he strongly counters arguments that the rimmed metates could have been so used (Snarskis, in press).

4. The Barriles site was discovered in 1947, and Matthew Stirling worked there briefly for the National Geographic Society, which published his only report on the site (Stirling 1950: 227–246). Most of the sculptures are illustrated by Torres de Araúz (1972: figs. 81–91).

5. Stone (1977: 105–106) assigns the stone spheres to her early Aguas Buenas phase, 1–300 A.D., apparently in accord with an early dating of the Barriles sculptures, which I have not accepted.

6. Chronological data for the late tradition in the Atlantic Watershed are based on Snarskis (1978: 277 ff.). Virtually all types of this tradition are illustrated by Mason (1945).

JADE

Elizabeth Kennedy Easby

The word "jade" has to be understood in context. To jewelers, it means jadeite or nephrite, two minerals of different composition but similar properties, which are unique. Mineralogists add chloromelanite and some mixtures of jadeite with such minerals as diopside or albite. Archaeologists speaking of "jades" usually mean lapidary work, the carving of hard stones generally. In Middle America, the stones selected by ancient peoples were predominantly green and not always very hard.

In addition to being rare and often beautiful, jade (mineralogically speaking) is much harder than obsidian, slightly less hard than quartz, and, because of its structure, the toughest and most durable of stones. It cannot be worked by the flaking and chipping procedures that are effective on flint and other quartz minerals, so its superiority could have become evident only at the neolithic level of technology, when stone could be worked by abrasion. This happened in prehistoric times in most parts of the world where jade was to be found—in the Americas, Europe, Asia, and certain islands of the Pacific.

Axes and blade forms seem to have been universal. In many cultures, blades of various shapes and materials appear as emblems. In Olmec Mexico, for example, ceremonial celts retained the utiliarian form, but their symbolic role is evident. They appear in nearly every offering at La Venta, Tabasco, sometimes in large numbers and arranged in patterns. Even though many show signs of use, some are decorated or made of stones too soft to hold an edge, while others are unsharpened models or blanks (Drucker *et al.* 1959: 132-187). Since weapons and cutting tools of jade greatly excel those of other stones, they became symbols of authority and ceremony. In elaborate Olmec burials and offerings, a high proportion of the surviving objects are of jade—seemingly an indication that the material itself had assumed mystical qualities.

Jade objects have been found in quantity from Mexico to Costa Rica, and rarely in the Greater Antilles, Venezuela, and Colombia, and even in Peru. By their style of carving, a surprising number are identifiable with distant places (Olmec and early Maya jades in Costa Rica, for example), and remarkable quantities have been discovered at sites far from any geologic zone where jadeite

Plate 66. Avian axe pendant, Atlantic Watershed zone, jade (cat. no. 150).

Plate 67. Avian pendant, Atlantic Watershed zone, jade (cat. no. 155).

Plate 68. Avian axe-god pendant, Guanacaste–Nicoya zone, jade (cat. no. 25).

could possibly occur (La Venta, Chichén Itzá). The known sources lie in the mountains above Guatemala's Motagua valley—all essentially a single deposit. So rare are the conditions under which jadeite is formed and brought to the surface that only five other deposits are known in the world (Coleman 1980: 9). Geological evidence is thus against the existence of another deposit in Middle America, yet archaeological evidence leaves much to be explained. Motagua valley sites, even Quiriguá, present no sign of disproportionate prosperity nor any unusual wealth of carved jadeite. Certain other sites have yielded much more (La Venta, Kaminaljuyú, Nebaj, Altun Ha, Chichén Itzá)—enough to show a probable local style and a distinctive type of jadeite among unidentifiable or obviously foreign pieces. Sophisticated mineralogical studies such as the Boston/ Brookhaven project reported upon (this volume) by Lange, Bishop, and van Zelst hold great promise of enabling identification of a worked object with a jade source.

The 18th century gave the names "imperial" and "jewel" jade to the translucent, intense–green jadeite of Burma. Indistinguishable to the eye from the Burmese stone is the dark, brilliantly green jadeite that was, by at least 600 B.C., the most precious of stones in Mexico. Found with jewel jade at La Venta were objects of the "blue jade" characteristic of fine Olmec work, as well as other varieties of jadeite, ranging from mottled bright green and white through pale to dark greenish gray, and softer materials, such as serpentine. The green jadeites of Middle America continued to be sought out, transported long distances (both as raw material and worked), reworked, and imitated until the European conquest.

Jewel jade occurs as veins and spots in blue jade (Foshag 1957: 21–22; Proskouriakoff 1974: 6, pl. IIIh; Lange *et al.*, this volume). These two rare types of translucent, nearly pure jadeite (which have not yet appeared in samples from the Motagua source) are really only one. Their combination is seen in a few Olmec carvings and in many more of Costa Rican workmanship, but not in other styles. A single source has seemed probable, with Costa Rica the most likely location. Blue jade, with and without inclusions of the jewel type, seems to have been relatively plentiful there. The pieces are very large, as jades go, and shaped with little regard to the form of the raw material or to the distribution of color. The most spectacular carving in combined blue/jewel jade is the Kunz Axe, one of several enormous Olmec effigy celts discovered in the last century, reportedly in Oaxaca (Joralemon 1976: figs. 10n, 12). Shaped from a heavy boulder, it weighs over seven kilograms, even though a large wedge was sawed out of the back of the head—probably in Olmec times—to get at the large veins of jewel jade that appear on the cut surfaces.

It is clear that the source of blue/jewel jade was being exploited during the time of strong beliefs embodied in the effigy–celt form. These beliefs reappeared in Costa Rica in characteristic axe–gods(essentially effigy–celt pendants), carved sometimes of the same distinctive material used by the Olmec. Its source must have been worked out or lost (in a volcanic cataclysm?) before jade working developed at other centers that might otherwise have had access to it.

Costa Rican lapidary work is tied to that of the Olmec not only by a special material and a special theme, but also by stylistic and technical parallels, and by the many Olmec objects that have turned up in Costa Rica, some of them exceptionally fine, and one of them documented. Yet discontinuity is evident. Olmec effigy celts, and nearly all Olmec figurines, lack major perforations, and so must have been used ceremonially; Costa Rican axe–gods were uniformly perforated to be worn as symbols or insignia.

Although Costa Rica was a major lapidary center, the examples found in recorded excavations would scarcely fill a hatbox. The two directly associated C–14 dates, 144 and 345±65 A.D. (Stirling 1969: 240; Snarskis 1975: 8), are both from the Atlantic region (Línea Vieja) and apply to blue jade and to a carving mode generally considered late. Also datable, with varying degrees of certainty, to the Zoned Bichrome and Early Polychrome periods are eight other, at least partially published, finds of lapidary work (Hartman 1907a: figs. 6, 9, 15, 23, 25–27; Stone and Balser 1965: 313; Stirling 1969: 240, 243, 245–246; Lange 1975: fig. 1i; Stone 1977: 33–34; Snarskis 1978: figs. 126f, 126Ai [here, cat. no. 156], 127Ac, 146B; 1979a: fig. 7 [here, cat. no. 26]). Excavated pieces from sites in the Atlantic, Central, and Nicoya regions represent a wide range of jade and other stones, and nearly all the well-known Costa Rican forms, as well as the celebrated Olmec clamshell pendant from Tibás (Snarskis 1979a: fig. 6). No jades have yet appeared, to my knowledge, in officially excavated contexts later than Early Polychrome (Period V). Archaeologists who have long been gleaning all possible information from unofficial digging by *huaqueros* report jade found with gold (Stone and Balser 1965: 317–318), but rarely. A few presumably late forms occur in both materials (Lothrop 1955: 46).

The primary Costa Rican jade form is the axe–god (a somewhat quaint name, but short, time-honored, and, no doubt, fairly accurate). The anthropomorphic type (cat. no. 32) is often lumped together with what can be called the bird celt (cat. no. 26); together, they formed a large proportion of Costa Rican lapidary production—30 per cent in Nicoya and 7 per cent in the Línea Vieja region by Lothrop's estimate of 25 years ago, figures that may have changed with the surge of digging that began about that time. If uncarved celt, half–celt, and quarter–celt pendants are added, the proportion is even greater.

Many examples are composite human/bird representations (cat. nos. 161, 162)—a few by reason of being carved both front and back. The bird aspect, marked by harpy–eagle traits, seems to replace the jaguar aspect seen in some Olmec celts. Elements of both are present in the fanged bird–monster, a creature of Olmec and later times, carved at one end of certain shell–like spoons or palettes; five of the eleven examples I know are from Costa Rica (Balser 1968: fig. 6a–b; Easby 1968: figs. 64, 66; Joralemon 1976: fig. 20). Appearing within the bird–celt category only is a tall, narrow type with blocky head and a crest greatly elaborated or stylized in purely rectilinear forms (cat. nos. 19, 20, 27–29), which might be of different age or origin.

Outside the country, axe–gods are dispersed more widely than any other form, although few come from controlled excavations. Not often found in adjoining Panama or Nicaragua, they are encountered more frequently in north-western Honduras, along with other indications of early contacts, and also northward along the Pacific coast in El Salvador, the Guatemalan highlands, and in Mexico at least as far as Guerrero. A large, unusual bird celt of blue jade discovered in the famous cache at Cerro de las Mesas, Veracruz (Drucker 1955: pl. 36f) resembled an ornament in this exhibition (cat. no. 150) in having a strongly projecting beak and a second transverse perforation in the lower part. The Cerro de las Mesas cache, a mixed collection of nearly 800 jades—including perhaps a dozen that may be Costa Rican—was contemporaneous with the latter part of the El Bosque phase.

A number of elaborate axe–gods, many unique and exceptional in material and workmanship, are Olmecoid in appearance, since they retain the overall celt

OVERLEAF:
Plate 69. Avian pendant, Atlantic Watershed zone, jade (cat. no. 154).

Plate 70. Two anthropomorphic–avian pendants, Atlantic Watershed zone, jade (cat. no. 164).

shape, broad noses and mouths, pits drilled where Olmec faces have them, and sometimes serpent tongues (in jade, probably a late or post–Olmec feature). These elements sometimes appear on axe–gods that have the entire body represented above the blade (cat. nos. 33–35), rather than only the head and arms or wings. Although some Olmec effigy celts also show the whole figure, it is incorporated into the celt, not perched upon it. Whether early or late among Costa Rican jades, Olmecoid pieces have a flavor of archaism. A number are enriched by incised and low–relief patterns, especially the guilloche and braid bands seen on stone sculpture, as well as on Guinea Incised and later pottery. An Olmecoid axe–god with bifurcated tongue and incising, but no band pattern, was found in a Las Huacas, Nicoya, burial with a plain, short–legged metate and a Zoned Bichrome ocarina (Hartman 1907a: 20–21, fig. 15; Fonseca and Scaglion 1978: 297); a reportedly similar axe–god was found with Early Polychrome pottery at Pangola, in the Atlantic region (Stirling 1969: 245; personal communication, 1965).

Even when Olmecoid, figure pendants (cat. no. 169) bear little resemblance to Olmec figurines. The majority are essentially axe–gods with feet and legs defined by incising and notches or slits (cat. no. 162). Often the arms were sawed free of the body, and other openings were produced by drilling and string sawing, a technique common in the Atlantic region. Mercocha yielded the previously mentioned 144 A.D. date from charcoal found with a blue–jade figure pendant much like one in the present exhibition (cat. no. 161), but about a third smaller and with L–shaped slits between arms and body (Stirling 1969: 239–40, 246 lower left; personal communication, 1965; Stone 1977: 152).

Eastern lapidaries seem to have improved the string–sawing process (Lothrop 1955) by using a special saw frame or a new abrasive or cord material that transformed the style, producing a variety of ornaments notable for their open-work and elaborate contours (cat. nos. 174–176, 179). Many, although quite flat and depicting a profile figure, are carved and polished on both sides and perforated to hang facing forward. These jades parallel stone sculpture in style and motifs. The motifs also appear as appliqué decorations on El Bosque pottery.

Two well–known Costa Rican motifs, the beak–bird and the curly–tailed animal, have a distinctive way of hanging when worn, with the strongly projecting beak or tail seeming to dwarf the rest of the body. Both categories range from flat silhouette figures to three–dimensional carvings (cat. nos. 154, 155). Flat examples have been found in El Bosque contexts, carved of blue jade (Stirling 1969: 240, 246 upper and lower right; personal communication, 1965), and of russet chalcedony (cat. no. 156). A white marble bird with long beak—probably a Costa Rican import—was found at Coclé, Panama, in a grave from the end of the Conte phase (500–700 A.D.); slightly earlier was a three–dimensional curly–tailed animal, also popular in Panama, both in stone and in gold (Lothrop 1937–42, I: fig. 175a, b; Cooke 1976: 129–131).

Among other animals in the repertoire, the frog, cayman or alligator, and bat are notable because they appear in the art of other cultures. The bat was perhaps implied iconographically in all varieties of winged pendants, the second largest formal category (Balser 1974: 22, 63, pls. IX, XXIX). Most are plain or simply decorated rectangles, perforated to hang horizontally. Sometimes the animal is portrayed explicitly, occasionally with a human face, recalling Olmec and Mezcala winged pendants with a face at the center (M. Coe and Diehl 1980, I: figs. 247–249). With or without a bat body, the ends may bear geometric decoration, a cayman or other head at each end (cat. nos. 36, 37), or a head at one end and tail at the other.

Large tubular beads may be carved with similar decoration (cat. no. 159). Some are reported to reach 52 centimeters (Stone 1977: 162), the longest drilling accomplished in jade in Precolumbian America. Very long ones and those that are tapered or carved asymmetrically—especially with vertical orientation (cat. no. 158)—suggest use as snuff tubes. Some plain tubes were undoubtedly bar pendants; others may have served as ear rods or in bracelets, strung parallel. Short tubular or barrel beads were strung end–to–end, and sets of small pendants were used as beads, but necklaces were predominantly made of disk beads. Conspicuously missing are the quantities of globular beads that, along with ear flares, were a major part of lapidary production at centers farther north. Conversely, disk beads of stone are rare elsewhere—and generally early—but are common in Costa Rica and Panama, where some 5,500 came from two graves dated 450–500 A.D. (Lothrup 1937–42, I: fig. 134b–d; Cooke 1976: 129). Ear ornaments, rare in Costa Rica, are usually spool–shaped (cat. no. 41) with open ends.

The lapidary schools of Costa Rica and Panama seem to have had contact only briefly, at the beginning of the gold–working era. Documented finds, principally of jade and greenstone tubes, and the repertoire of symbolic creatures in the same styles in gold, green stones, chalcedony, and shell, connect the beginning of the Conte phase in central Panama with the end of the El Bosque and beginning of the La Selva phases in eastern Costa Rica, c. 500 A.D. Only in Costa Rica was this complex associated with the axe–god tradition.

The latest imported jades that survive in any number are Early Classic Maya (Proskouriakoff 1974: 11–12). A few are carved in low relief (Hartman 1907a: pl. XLV, 10; Stone 1977: fig. 78a). Seemingly more numerous are flat pieces, incised with figures or glyphs, apparently of lowland style. In the Maya highlands, axe–gods are found occasionally, one an Early Classic copy (Easby 1963), but there is little trace of stylistic or technical influence in either direction.

The only other well–defined styles that developed in Late Preclassic times are far to the north: Mezcala and Teotihuacán. An axe–god from Mercocha was made of metadiorite, a stone typical of Guerrero (Foshag 1957: 26–27). Both these Mexican styles shared with Costa Rica the very un–Maya traits of three–dimensional composition and unornamented surfaces.

Found all over Middle America are numbers of pendants remarkable for having been made in such small size, but often notable also for their exceptionally fine bright–green material (Proskouriakoff 1974: 36, pl. 37f, nos. 2–5). Several shapes that resemble and grade into each other are described variously. Excluding fangs and claws, and those that are round in horizontal section and pointed, the rest seem to be related in motif and form—celt–shaped and drilled across the thicker end, which may be worked as the head of a duck or the upper part of a beaked bird or human figure, or simply marked by a groove or change of plane. Although some of these pendants occur, as early jades often do, in late archaeological contexts, some are Middle Preclassic and earlier. At Playa de Los Muertos, Honduras, eight examples—including two small axe–gods or bird celts of jewel jade—were found in burials of c. 500 B.C. (Easby 1968: fig. 62). At Chiapa de Corzo, Mexico, the earliest of several jades was an approximately coeval jade duck head (Lee 1969: fig. 97i). At La Venta, "tab" pendants were among the hundred or so small jadeite ornaments in an offering (Drucker 1952:

Plate 71. Two alligator pendants, Guápiles, Atlantic Watershed, jade (cat. no. 159).

Plate 72. Pendant, figure with alligator mask, Línea Vieja, Atlantic Watershed, jade (cat. no. 176).

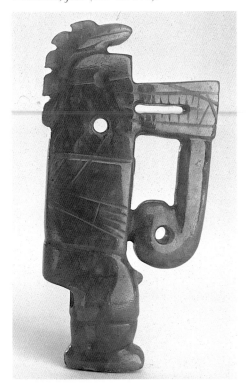

Plate 75. Anthropomorphic pendant with trophy heads, Hakiuv, Talamanca, jade (cat. no. 177).

Plate 73. Figure with ceremonial staff, Atlantic Watershed zone, jade (cat. no. 174).

Plate 74. Figure with ceremonial staff, Línea Vieja, Atlantic Watershed, jade (cat. no. 175).

Plate 76. Monkey–effigy pendant,
Atlantic Watershed zone, jade (cat.
no. 168).

FAR RIGHT:
Plate 77. Pendant, Guanacaste–
Nicoya zone, jade (cat. no. 181).

Plate 78. Two masked–figure
pendants, Atlantic Watershed zone,
jade (cat. no. 157).

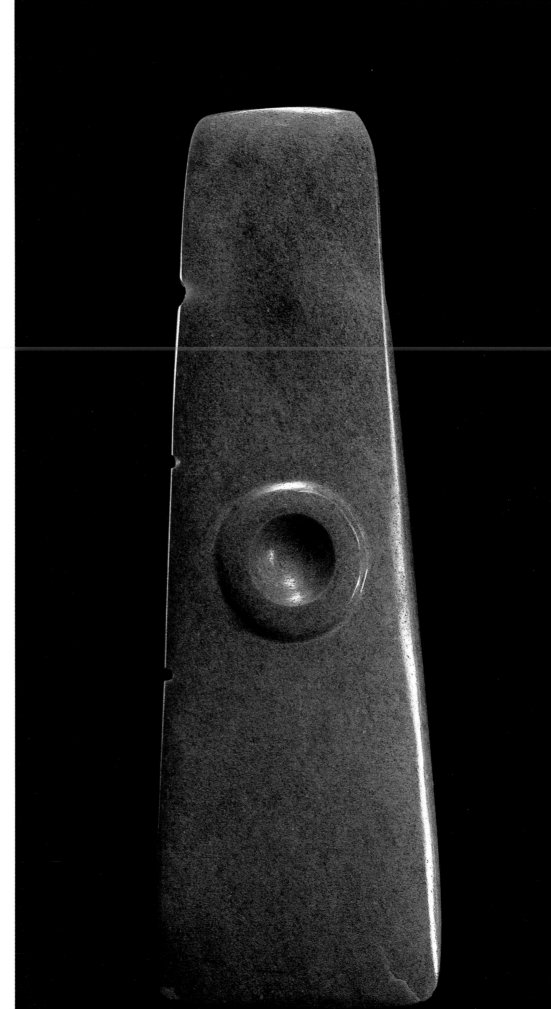

Plate 79. Pendant, Atlantic Watershed zone, jade (cat. no. 167).

CENTER:
Plate 80. Avian axe-god pendant,
Guanacaste–Nicoya zone, jade (cat.
no. 24).

FAR RIGHT:
Plate 81. Avian axe–god pendant,
Guanacaste–Nicoya zone, jade (cat.
no. 29).

Plate 82. Avian axe–god pendant,
Atlantic Watershed, jade (cat. no.
19).

Plate 83. Avian axe–god pendant,
Guanacaste–Nicoya zone, jade (cat.
no. 28).

OVERLEAF:
Plate 84. Anthropomorphic pendant,
Atlantic Watershed zone, jade (cat.
no. 165).

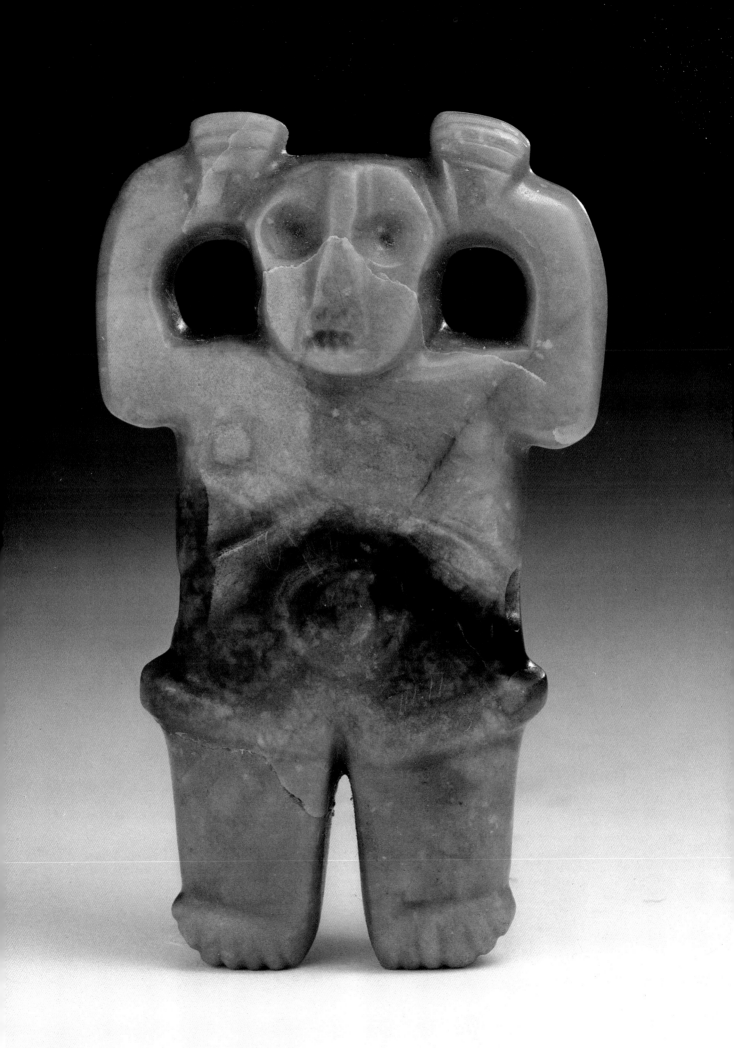

Plate 85. Bat pendant with sharks, Guanacaste–Nicoya zone, jade (cat. no. 36).

Plate 86. Bat pendant with alligators, Guanacaste–Nicoya zone, jade (cat. no. 37).

pl. 58). At Chalchuapa, El Salvador, two small "tab" pendants and two of axe–god type in black and red–brown stone occurred in levels dated c. 800–600 B.C. (Sharer, ed. 1978: fig. 8c, nos. 2–5). At Cuello, Belize, a grave of the Swasey phase contained the top centimeter of a brilliant green jadeite pendant resembling a bird celt; its lower part was broken off when it was buried c. 1200 B.C. (Norman Hammond, personal communication, 1980).

Unlike a full-sized axe-god found elsewhere, a miniature is thus not to be assumed an export from Costa Rica, nor, if dated early, any proof that jade was being worked there. The wide distribution—geographic and chronological—of miniature axe–gods and related objects suggests that the form did not originate in Costa Rica, although it flourished there as nowhere else. The axe–god complex, the predilection for disk beads, and the knowledge of jade working, were probably not direct offshoots from Olmec culture; they may have arisen instead, almost certainly with Olmec stimulus, from an ancient tradition widespread in Middle America.

GOLD WORK

Warwick Bray

As its name implies, Costa Rica has been famous for its gold since the moment of European discovery. Enthusiastic reports by Columbus and successive 16th–century conquistadors are fully confirmed by the abundance of archaeological finds. The two main national collections, in the Banco Central and the Museo Nacional, between them contain over 2,000 metal items, and this number doubles when private collections and those of foreign museums are added. Only a handful of pieces come from scientific excavations. The rest— accidental discoveries or purchases from treasure hunters, amateur and professional—have lost all their archaeological background information. There are many gaps in our knowledge of Costa Rican metallurgy, but, as new archaeological excavations are published, an outline is beginning to emerge.

Within the New World, gold metallurgy spread gradually from south to north. In Peru, the first objects of hammered gold can be dated c. 2000–1500 B.C.; there was then a long period of local experimentation, during which techniques of casting and the use of various alloys of gold, copper, and silver were developed. In contrast, metallurgy was introduced into Mexico suddenly, and already fully developed, between 700 and 900 A.D. In time, as well as in space, the Isthmian metal industries fall midway between those of Peru and Mexico, playing an important role in the northward transmission of techniques.

With neighboring Colombia, the Central American republics form a single metalworking province, with a series of closely related art styles, and a technology characterized by a preference for lost–wax casting and gold–copper alloys (*tumbaga*), false–filigree ornament, and depletion gilding. Spanish chronicles note that, throughout the whole of this province, objects of precious metal had a special role in aboriginal society. Chiefs competed among themselves for power of all kinds–for ritual and supernatural power, but also for power in the form of wealth and of trade goods from distant lands. To advertise their riches and prestige, chiefs and others of the elite wore distinctive insignia and gold ornaments as a mark of rank and status, and local rulers showed their generosity by giving presents to their allies and political supporters (Helms 1979). Exchanges of this kind served to maintain wide-ranging contacts between different regions. Within the Isthmus, regional gold styles ignore modern national frontiers; Costa

Plate 87. Feline pendant, Puerto González Viquéz, Diquís, gold (cat. no. 260).

Plate 88. Peccary ornaments, Palmar Sur, Diquís, gold (cat. no. 255).

153

Rican gold cannot be understood without some reference to Nicaragua in the north, and Panama to the south.

Gold Work Before 1000 A.D.

The case for early metalwork in Costa Rica relies on comparisons with better–dated material from central Panama, where the sites of Las Huacas (Casimir de Brizuela 1971), El Cafetal (Ichon 1980), and La India (Mitchell and Heidenreich 1965) are dated 200–500 A.D. By c. 450 A.D. the first corpses were being interred at Sitio Conte, in Coclé province, with rich offerings of gold; this cemetery continued in use until c. 900 A.D. (Lothrop 1937–42). Combining material from these sites, we can put together an inventory of early metal forms, many of which are found also in Costa Rica. The list includes double–spiral ornaments of a type popular in Caribbean Colombia (Bray 1978: 174), together with pendants made up of several animals side by side, double eagles of rather simple form, animals or birds with curved tails (cat. no. 183), frog effigies, and fairly naturalistic human figures, which have sleepy, half-closed eyes, and are usually nude except for their jewelry: spiral headdresses, multistrand necklaces, and ligatures bound around the arms and legs. These Isthmian figures are closely allied with those of the Quimbaya style from the Colombian Andes, independently dated to c. 400–1000 A.D. (Balser 1966; Bray 1978: 51).

Imports and local copies of such Colombian–Panamanian forms are fairly numerous in Costa Rica, where the scanty archaeological evidence tends to confirm the early date. At Tatiscú, near Cartago, Carlos Aguilar excavated part of a Coclé human figure with pottery of the period 500–800 A.D.; the beautiful tumbaga head from Hakiuv may be of similar age, or slightly earlier (Stone 1977: fig 228). The contemporaneity of all these forms is proved by the contents of two tombs at Guácimo, in the Línea Vieja region. Tomb 1 produced a gold frog, a Colombian double–spiral pendant and a Coclé curly–tailed bird. The second burial yielded a human figure very close in style to its Quimbaya proto-type, two frogs, a double-headed bird, and the heads of two curly–tailed animals (Stone and Balser 1965).

Plotted on a map, these early categories show an overwhelming concentration in the Atlantic Watershed region, particularly around Guápiles and the Línea Vieja, with an extension into the plains of San Carlos. Most of the copies of Colombian "Darién" pendants (Balser 1966; Falchetti de Sáenz 1979) also come from this area. It looks as if sea trade along the Caribbean coast played a key role in the introduction and spread of metallurgy from Colombia and Panama into Costa Rica.

Atlantic Watershed/1000 A.D. to the Conquest

Spanish chronicles suggest that the Atlantic coast retained its commercial domi-nance right up to the Conquest. In 1502, during his fourth voyage, Columbus dropped anchor in Almirante Bay, just inside the Panamanian side of the frontier. Here, more than 80 canoes came to exchange gold for Spanish hawk bells and grade goods. Accounts of this voyage speak of five great trading towns. At the principal one, where the chief resided, gold was collected from the rivers,

Plate 89. Pendant, two–headed figure, Palmar Sur, Diquís, gold (cat. no. 284).

and breastplates (*patenas*) of hammered sheet metal were manufactured for distribution all along the coast as far as Cariai–Puerto Limón, Costa Rica (Helms 1979: 63).

Another document, now in the archives of Cartago, describes Diego de Sojo's expedition of 1587 to this same region (MacCurdy 1911: 190–191):

> The quality of gold that abounds here is very great, and of good karat, as can be seen from the plates of gold the Indians beat out, it not being alloyed with other metals. The rivers abound with gold...and the Indians extract gold with calabashes in very large grains.... From these same hills Captain Muñoz...took from the tombs of the dead ...such a great quantity of gold as to swell two large chests of the kind in which shoes and nails for the cavalry are brought over from Castile.

A 1610 account by Fray Agustín de Zevallos refers to the Talamancan area of present–day Costa Rica. Marveling at the abundance of gold, Zevallos remarks that it was used in barter, worked into jewelry, and buried with the dead. He describes the beating out of patenas of pure gold, and the process of casting, by the lost–wax method, of tumbaga eagles, lizards, frogs, and spiders (Helms 1979: 149, 200). This description—especially the spider effigies—fits the Diquís style, from the Pacific southwest of Costa Rica. Gold disks, frogs, and eagles of Diquís type have been found along the Río Ururi, just inland from Columbus' landfall in Almirante Bay and close to the frontier with Costa Rica (Mitchell 1961). The few items recorded from the Talamancan region of Costa Rica are also in Diquís style.

The greatest concentration of archaeological finds on the Atlantic slope comes from farther north, from the Reventazón valley, the plains of San Carlos, and along the Línea Vieja. Here, too, Spanish chroniclers describe the manufacture and exchange of gold objects, including breastplates, bracelets, and trumpets three palms long.

The Línea Vieja region seems to have been a great commercial center, with trading contacts stretching from Panama to the Maya sites of Yucatán and Guatemala (Bray 1977). Costa Rican metalsmiths received, copied, and passed on items in every known Isthmian style. Archaeological finds include local versions of Darién pendants and Muisca votive figurines from Colombia, false–filigree lizards in the style of Venado Beach (Panama), as well as figure pendants and monkey bells imported from Diquís. It is not always easy to decide which items were locally made, but the strongest candidates are certain rather plain eagle pendants and the "cacique" figures—small, naturalistic human effigies with hair pulled up into a topknot or decorated with feathers. These "caciques" were exported as far away as El Salvador and Panama. Another regional specialty, linked primarily with the Reventazón valley, is a group of small but heavy figurines cast in copper.

Although discoveries of isolated objects are numerous, few are reliably dated. At Guayabo de Turrialba, two tumbaga frog pendants came from mounds dated 1000–1300 A.D. (Aguilar 1972b: 127). A similar, or even later, date is probable for the bells, gilded copper sheet, and beads of rolled strip from the stone–cist graves of Orosí (Hartman 1901). Recent excavations by Snarskis add a few more items to the list: a small, solid gold eagle from Heredia, near San José (900–1100 A.D.); a broken human figure in copper from a cemetery of stone–cist tombs near Cartago (100–1300 A.D.); and a little gold frog and some copper figure pendants from a similar burial site at San Carlos.

Plate 90. Bell pendant, Cabecera de Chánguina, Diquís, gold (cat. no. 259).

156

Guanacaste—Nicoya

By comparison with the Atlantic Watershed and Diquís, northwest Costa Rica has produced little archaeological metalwork, although a Spanish expedition of 1522 collected some 30,000 pesos of gold from the Gulf of Nicoya. Guanacaste has sources of copper and gold, and the discovery, in 1976, at the Ruíz site (a shell midden near the Bay of Culebra), of a lost—wax casting mold for a flange—footed frog pendant proves that this area supported local metallurgical work-shops in the centuries just before the Conquest (Lange and Accola 1979). By that time, the Nicoya region had been infiltrated by Nicarao settlers from Mexico, and these northern connections are seen in both metalwork and pottery. Heavy copper effigy bells were imported from Honduras, and a simpler form of bell from Nacascolo (1000–1200 A.D.) can be matched by specimens from Maya territory (*ibid.*). A set of openwork copper ear spools from La Plaza de Filadelfia has its counterpart even farther away, in northwest Mexico (Ferrero 1977a: fig. I–110; Bray 1977: 378). From the other direction, a gold ornament in the style of Veraguas (Panama) was taken from a grave at Potrero El Burro, Filadelfia, with pottery of the kind used at the time of European contact (Lothrop 1950: 87).

Otherwise, the metalwork of Nicoya and Guanacaste is entirely eclectic: small gold frog pendants, eagles, and crocodiles in the style of Diquís, human figures of copper like those from San Carlos and the Atlantic Watershed, and the so—called "Guanacaste eagles" (Aguilar 1972a: 31) found all over Costa Rica. For the Nicoya area, a gold frog was collected from the surface of a Late Polychrome shell midden at Guacamaya (1200–1550 A.D.), a Quimbaya-style figurine is reported from a site on the Bay of Culebra, and a small tumbaga eagle comes from San Lucas Island in the Gulf of Nicoya (Creamer 1980; Frederick Lange, personal communication). In general, however, there was little contact between Pacific Nicoya and the rich metallurgical provinces of the Atlantic slope. The northwest seems to have no regional style of its own, and no dated archaeological specimen older than c. 1000 A.D., although this is probably a result of inade-quate investigation and small samples.

Diquís

The Diquís zone of Pacific Costa Rica, on the frontier with Panama, has yielded more metal objects than any other part of the country, possibly due to availability of the raw material, since the Osa Peninsula is a major gold source. The conquis-tadors noted that each community in Diquís owned a stretch of river, where the inhabitants panned for gold, and that, in Coctu, one of the chiefs was himself a goldsmith who manufactured animal figurines and breastplates (Stone 1977: 127–128).

The richness described in the chronicles is corroborated by the quantity and diversity of archaeological finds. The inventory includes bells, needles, fish hooks, buttons, tweezers, earrings, beads, tooth sheathing, diadems, crescentic collars of sheet metal, masks, embossed plaques for sewing onto clothing, and the categories listed by the Spaniards—cast pendants in the shape of human or animal figures, and circular breastplates of hammered metal with raised bosses, geometric designs, or human faces and alligators in embossed relief.

Plate 91. Lobster pendant, Puerto González Viquéz, Diquís, gold (cat. no. 289).

158

Early in this century, several pounds of gold and tumbaga ornaments were unearthed at the Huacal de Los Reyes (MacCurdy 1911: 218–219). In 1956, three rich tombs were opened on Farm 4 at Palmar Sur (Lothrop 1963: 94). Grave Number 2 at this cemetery contained eighty-eight metal objects: thirty-four cast pendants, five bells, five discs with embossed decoration, thirty plain discs, two crescents, two sheet metal cuffs, and ten head bands. Several items from this grave are displayed in the exhibition (cat. nos. 269, 272, 280, 284, 287, 288).

Discoveries of this kind, with different forms associated in a single tomb, demonstrate the homogeneity of the Diquís style, and show that most categories of Diquís metalwork were in fashion at the same time. They also suggest that some objects were made specially for the grave. In the Palmar Sur treasure there were several defective pieces, with casting flaws not yet repaired and surfaces incompletely polished. Most items were fresh, with no signs of wear on the suspension loops. Elsewhere in Diquís, gold objects were ceremonially "killed" or mutilated before being placed in the tomb.

The most distinctive items in the Diquís repertoire are the pendants shaped like human beings or animals, some inlaid with colored stones or made, like puppets, from several articulated parts. Subject matter was strictly controlled; of the total range of animals, only a restricted group appears in the jewelry. The major food animals—the tapirs, deer, wild hogs, and river fish observed by Vásquez de Coronado in the 1560s, domestic dogs, or the many edible rodents that were essential sources of meat—are hardly ever represented in gold; a group of miniature peccaries (cat. no. 255) provides a rare exception to this rule. Goldsmiths depicted frogs, alligators (or perhaps iguanas), jaguars, turtles, lobsters, crabs, armadillos, scorpions, and spiders. The birds are almost exclusively eagles, hawks, or owls, although some appear to be hummingbirds; the fish, when identifiable, are sharks. The same range of creatures is portrayed also in pottery, stone, and carved bone.

Olga Linares (1976, 1977) has recognized a similar pattern of selection in the Coclé art of Panama, noting that, if we look at the behavioral qualities of these animals, a certain consistency appears. Many of the creatures have hard body parts or, like the eight-legged arachnids, stand apart from the common range of animals and insects. Most of the subjects depicted in gold are fierce, noxious, or dangerous: they nip, sting, bite, or are poisonous. Their predatory habits are emphasized. Some jaguars and alligators carry human bodies or limbs in their jaws (cat. no. 262), and birds of prey may hold animals in their beaks. It becomes clear that Diquís pendants are not simply "representations of nature," but the outward sign of a complex world of symbolism with its own system of beliefs, no longer accessible to us except, in a much attenuated form, through the mythology of present–day Indians (Helms 1977).

This conviction is reinforced by the series of pendants that incorporate human elements. There are a few naturalistic figures (notably musicians with drums or flutes). More common are creatures of fantasy and strange composite beings: jaguar–headed birds, and human torsos with the heads of jaguars, eagles, alligators, or vampire bats. Sometimes, as in the so-called Carbonera pendants (cat. no. 269), the central creature is surrounded by attendant figures, and the whole composition enclosed in a square frame. The preoccupation with supernatural forms suggests that Diquís pendants may have served as indicators of rank and family status, or perhaps as amulets (the Indian equivalent of, say, a Saint Christopher medallion or a zodiacal charm), and should not be considered merely as ornamental jewelry.

160

Plate 92. Bell pendant with bat effigy, Palmar Sur, Diquís, gold (cat. no. 263).

Plate 93. Masked–figure pendant, Palmar Sur, Diquís, gold (cat. no. 272).

Plate 94. Masked–figure pendant, Buenos Aires, Diquís, gold (cat. no. 273).

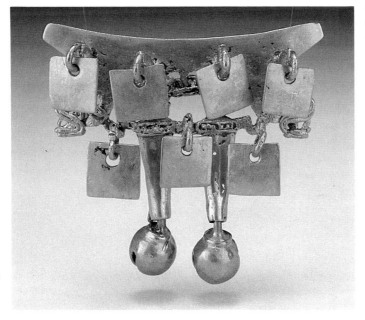

Plate 95. Bell pendant, two figures with danglers, Palmar Sur, Diquís, gold (cat. no. 276).

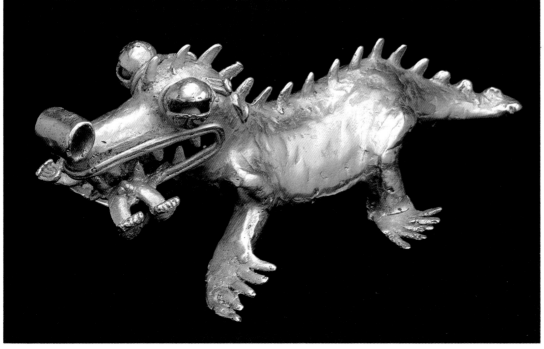

Plate 96. Frog pendant,
Palmar Sur, Diquís, gold
(cat. no. 288).

Plate 97. Alligator pendant,
Cabagra, Diquís, gold
(cat. no. 262).

Plate 98. Bell pendant,
framed jaguar–man figure,
Palmar Sur, Diquís, gold
(cat. no. 269).

OVERLEAF:
Plate 99. Bell pendant with
deer and snake motifs,
Palmar Sur, Diquís, gold
(cat. no. 270).

Plate 100. Alligator–man
pendant, Puerto González
Viquéz, Diquís, gold (cat.
no. 293).

Although many of the themes are found in other parts of the Isthmus, Diquís goldsmiths developed a distinctive local treatment. Human figures have splayed, trapezoidal feet; hands are made by the false–filigree technique, which gives the appearance of bent wire; spirals proliferate; and there is a marked liking for "braided–rope" elements in costume, as pure decoration, and for the frames of Carbonera figurines. Diquís metalwork, compared with other Costa Rican styles, is ornate and almost baroque in the exuberance of its decoration. Two subsidiary motifs were especially popular: serpents with triangular or diamond–shaped heads, and a stylized animal, conventionally called an alligator, with open mouth, long teeth, and curling snout. These two devices sprout, quite inappropriately, from heads, knees, arms, and wings of both human and composite figures.

Such items were made in Diquís or in adjacent Chiriquí, across the Panamanian frontier, but the Diquís region also received trade pieces: curly–tailed animals from Panama or Atlantic Costa Rica, "cacique" figurines from the Línea Vieja, false–filigree ear ornaments from the Sinú region of Colombia (Aguilar 1972a: fig. 85), and Colombian "Darién" pendants, which were copied by Diquís jewellers (Aguilar 1972a: fig. 39; Falchetti de Sáenz 1979).

The date of the Diquís style is not easy to establish. Most of the diagnostic early forms seem to be absent, though a few items show the influence of the Coclé style of Panama. The bulk of Diquís metalwork probably falls within the final centuries before the Spanish Conquest, an attribution supported by the few objects with reliable dates. A slab–roofed grave in a tumulus near Buenos Aires yielded a little gold animal with pottery of the period 1200–1500 A.D. (Haberland 1959: pl. XXIV); of roughly the same age are the hammered disks, cast frog, and bird fragment from Cemetery A at El Zoncho, near San Vito de Java (Laurencich de Minelli and Minelli 1966). In tombs at Finca Puntarenas, Jalaca, eagles and bells of Diquís style were excavated with pottery of the kind still in vogue at the time of European contact (Stone 1963). The most recent specimens are little beads made of rolled metal strips found in an Indian grave near the Río Chánguina along with iron tools and millefiori glass beads from the first Spanish settlements (Stone 1954).

Technical Appendix

PERSPECTIVES ON COSTA RICAN JADE: COMPOSITIONAL ANALYSES AND CULTURAL IMPLICATIONS

Frederick W. Lange, Ronald L. Bishop, and Lambertus van Zelst

The number and location of Precolumbian jade sources and the stylistic similarity between jade artifacts from different areas have been problems of long–standing interest. The Precolumbian quest for this luxury resource frequently forced contacts beyond narrowly defined cultural borders or culture areas. Where this happened, ideas diffused, often to be adopted intact or syncretized by the recipient group. A natural–resource area for jade exploitation was of particular importance in aboriginal economies; the rarity of the material provided partial stimulus for the development of long–distance exchange. As anthropologists have come to realize the role of exchange in the growth and maintenance of cultural systems, their need to know the sources of traded objects has intensified. In addition, if, as in the case of jade, the traded material is susceptible to stylistic modification, a study of the distribution of styles will provide essential information about contacts between different groups.

This paper reports on a project that attempts to use analyses of chemical trace–element concentration to characterize jade–source areas and to reconstruct trade and economic networks. Successful projects of this type have been conducted previously, involving such varying materials as ceramics (Bishop and Rands 1980), glass (Sayre and Smith 1974), silver (Meyers, van Zelst, and Sayre 1974), turquoise (Weigand, Harbottle, and Sayre 1977), and steatite (Allen and Penmell 1977). The results of this investigation, as reported here, are still preliminary, and analyses are continuing. In recognition of the archaeological and artistic value of the jade objects in this exhibition, we felt, however, that an initial statement would be useful. In addition, it presents the opportunity to express our gratitude for the cooperation of several agencies and institutions of Costa Rica, as well as specific individuals mentioned in the acknowledgements. Without their assistance, the Costa Rican focus of the jade investigation would not have been possible.

The analytical techniques selected for the determination of the trace–element concentrations is instrumental neutron–activation analysis. The samples are exposed to a flux of thermal neutrons, which are infinitesimally small, electrically neutral, elemental particles, produced in nuclear reactors. Because of their nature, the neutrons tend to penetrate the sample completely. By interaction of a small fraction of these particles with the nuclei of the various chemical elements that constitute the sample material, a minute portion of these stable nuclei are converted into radioactive ones. These nuclear reactions will create different radioisotopes for each element, each decaying with its own half–life, emitting characteristic radiation. Of the various kinds of radiation emitted, the gamma rays are of special importance, because the energy spectrum of the gamma rays emitted by a particular radioisotope forms a characteristic "fingerprint." Thus, by measuring the compounded gamma–ray spectrum of a sample, one is able to identify the radioisotopes within it, and, hence, their parent chemical elements. By the same token, the intensity of the gamma rays of a certain energy emitted from the sample constitutes a measure of the amount of parent elements present. Following a sufficient decay period, the sample, or object, if the latter was activated in its entirety, is left in essentially its original condition. The technique affords the ability to determine minute concentrations of some elements, in an extremely small sample.

Previous efforts to characterize jadeite and related minerals by trace element analysis demonstrated that various minerals found in the Motagua Valley of Guatemala could be chemically distinguished from one another (Hammond *et al.* 1977). The project suffered from limited sampling of specific jadeite samples, but did provide an extremely useful tabulation of data, from which our work proceeded.

There are two rocks called jade: jadeite, a pyroxene, and nephrite, an amphibole, common in Oriental jade carvings. Jadeite is composed primarily of sodium, aluminum, silicon, and oxygen, and forms under special conditions of low temperature and very high pressure. The exact physio–chemical environment during the formation process is responsible for the frequent occurrence of additional minerals with jadeite: albite, diopside, and aegirine. The jadeite itself contains very low concentrations of elements other than its primary constituents.

Experiments were conducted to ascertain the optimum condition of neutron bombardment, taking into consideration: (1) the color stability of the object during bombardment; (2) minimal residual radioactivity after six–month decay; and (3) reliability of determination of several rare–earth elements. The rare–earth elements, or "lanthanides," form a group of chemically very closely related elements, which occur in trace amounts in rock–forming minerals. Since many rocks tend to have distinctive rare–earth concentration patterns, it was anticipated that they might prove to have a highly diagnostic value.

Other problems to be resolved related to the sampling procedure. While, in principle, activation analysis can be conducted on the whole object, there are practical difficulties. Whole–object activation is carried out when an artifact is too small for destructive sampling or when sampling would damage the artifact design or form. It is preferable, however, to use a hollow–core diamond drill to remove a sample of approximately 60 mgs. for analysis. This not only provides an easily handled sample but eliminates the problem of residual radioactivity in the artifact. In most jade artifacts, such as figurines, axe–gods, bars, and beads, there is an unfinished or secondary surface from which the sample may be removed. After sampling, the hole is filled and the surface restored. In no case is there damage to the potential viewing surface of a museum object. Given the size of the equipment necessary for drilling, sampling has necessitated the loan of jade specimens from museums or private collections and their transport to

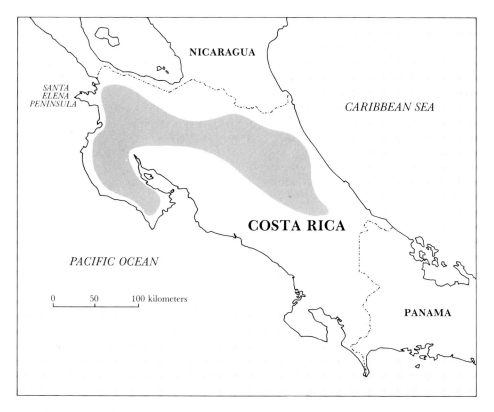

Figure 41. Map showing the Santa Elena Peninsula and the distribution and concentration of jade artifacts in Costa Rica.

Brookhaven National Laboratory for analysis. The willingness of different institutions and individuals to lend artifacts for sampling has been essential in the success of the project thus far.

Geological samples believed to be jade were brought to the United States during the late 1950s and early 1960s, initiating rumors that jade occurs naturally in Costa Rica. Speculation on the location of the source of these samples focused on the Santa Elena peninsula, in northwestern Costa Rica (fig. 41), a region subsequently thought to have been the source area for some jade objects found in southern Mesoamerica. Some scholars also speculated that local jade sources were an initial stimulus for the establishment of Olmec trade routes down the Pacific coast of Central America.

In late 1978, renewed geological interest in northwestern Costa Rica began generating jade–source rumors once again. A decision was made for a field excursion to Costa Rica to obtain geological samples from these reported sources. It was hoped that these new samples would provide comparative data for the limited number of geological jade samples already acquired from Guatemala and for those Precolumbian artifacts that had been analyzed.

The geological collecting trip to the Santa Elena peninsula was aided by satellite–photo interpretation and access to the results of geological mapping by CODESA (Corporation Costarricense de Desarollo S.A.). A week was spent sampling the suggested sources and surveying the surrounding area, while simultaneously carrying out an archaeological site survey. If the Santa Elena peninsula had been a source of Precolumbian jade, one should find cultural remains of those who had come to work the deposits, and possibly larger settlements that had sprung up to control this resource—a pattern seen in other Mesoamerican and Central American areas where luxury resources, such as obsidian, are centered.

169

The geological survey collected materials related to jadeite, but none were specifically jadeite. Among the materials identified in current analyses are diopside and actinolite (the latter is especially interesting where the actinolitic amphibole is also known as nephrite, the other form of jade).

The archaeological site survey also had limited results. Whereas jade had its principal importance between the beginnings of the Christian era and perhaps as late as 800 A.D., the cultural remains collected from looters' debris at the only site encountered in the backlands of the bay area near the lithic resources dated principally after 1100 A.D. Site density is higher on the northern side of the Santa Elena peninsula, surveyed and tested previously by M. Coe (1962b); cultural components dating from 300 B.C. to c. 1520 A.D. are present, but informant data and our own experience indicate that the traverse across the high backbone of the peninsula is of sufficient difficulty to rule out regular movement from one side to the other. This emphasizes the important point that, even if one identifies a source of raw material that may be used today, this does not imply that it was also used by Precolumbian people; to arrive at the latter conclusion, archaeological evidence of source utilization and associated cultural activities is required.

After completion of these geological and archaeological surveys, another short survey was made on the Nicoya peninsula. This area seemed a more likely source for jade, both because of the greater concentration of archaeological sites (including those of the appropriate date) and the large number of jade artifacts from this area that have been brought into the market over the last century. This survey was only superficial, but the search for suitable geological outcroppings did not yield positive results. Of course, much additional geological surveying will be necessary before Costa Rica can be excluded as an ancient source for jade, but the information obtained thus far is negative.

A second objective of the excursion to Costa Rica was the sampling of materials in the collections of the MNCR and the Instituto Nacional de Seguros. Both collections contain not only exquisite jade artifacts, but also blanks and sawn boulders of raw material periodically brought in, reportedly, from jade–workshop sites. The real origin of these samples has never been determined, however, because the portable drilling equipment was not adequate for the sampling, export permission was sought and was granted, enabling the transport of the objects to Brookhaven National Laboratory. There, most of the objects were quickly sampled; several others, too small or too fragile to be sampled, were held for a longer period in order to undergo whole–object activation. The selection of 126 objects from both institutions was based partially on whether the visual appearance of an artifact indicated that it was of jadeite. In addition, several non–jadeite comparative pieces were chosen.

Table 1 lists some of the analytical results. It illustrates some of the chemical differences between jadeite and jadeite–albite from areas under consideration. One cannot be sure whether Precolumbian artisans could distinguish, or even tried to, between jadeite and some of its near "relatives." Many analyses will be needed to establish whether, for instance, objects with certain forms or particular decorative motifs were exclusively, or with very high frequency, executed in real jadeite and others in "imitation" materials. For such analyses, one does not need the sophisticated, expensive techniques necessary for the work described here.

The problems surrounding intersource variation of chemical concentrations and the covariation to minute changes in mineralogy are still under investigation. Nonetheless, we are currently faced with some tantalizing possibilities regarding the analyzed Costa Rican jades. The analytical results suggest that at least some of the Costa Rican jade artifacts may not have been produced using material from local sources.

The detailed set of analytical data will not be reviewed here, but some aspects relative to Mesoamerican source data can be summarized. Within the data for Mesoamerica, we have been able to isolate groupings of chemically similar jadeite artifacts that have a common archaeological provenience: for example, there are groups of jades from Copán that are different from jades found at Chichén Itzá or at Holmul. Also, over 100 samples of jadeite and jadeite–albite source rock from the Middle Motagua region have been analyzed. The latter sample demonstrates a fair degree of chemical homogeneity, especially in the data for the rare–earth elements.

We are able, therefore, to form a Motagua "source group," against which to compare the artifactual analyses. Taking this Motagua group as a reference unit and considering its distribution around its centroid in multivariate space (i.e., the space in which the coordinates represent the concentrations of the chemical elements analyzed), we are now able to assess the probability that an object may be a member of the group, on the criterion of its distance in multivariate space to the group centroid. On the basis of statistical considerations, we cannot exclude the possibility that many of the analyzed Costa Rican jade artifacts were manufactured from materials the sources of which were located in the Motagua Valley of Guatemala. This is true for jades showing Maya glyphs (Balser 1974) as well as for "Olmecoid" spoons. Other chemically established groups of Costa Rican jade artifacts are observable, and, for the most part, are composed of objects containing diopside as a mineralogical accessory.

The presently limited quantity of analytical data does not allow for a detailed evaluation. For instance, the occurrence of groups of chemically similar jadeite artifacts in the Maya Lowlands may reflect little more than exploitations of particular subregions in a large resource area, rather than totally different sources. In other words, the variations in the chemical data might reflect only minute mineralogical differences. By the same token, the chemical similarity between the Costa Rican jade artifacts and the Motagua Valley source materials might reflect only the fact that both are composed of largely monomineralic jadeite. Presently, however, in archaeological perspective, the possibility of a Guatemalan jade source for Costa Rican artifacts has been strengthened.

One small group of artifacts from Costa Rica deserves special mention. Mineralogical analysis revealed that they are comprised only of jadeite. The elemental correlations within this group of five specimens suggest that they have a source different from that of other Motagua and Costa Rican samples currently analyzed. They are, nonetheless, more similar to the Costa Rican jadeite–diopside specimens than to the jadeite Motagua source samples or to Maya artifacts. This suggests the possibility of another source, of unknown location.

Many years ago Charles Balser (1974: 7) suggested that many Maya and Olmec jades found in Costa Rica may have been recycled from the north after Costa Rican sources were exhausted, reflecting traditional ideas that jade sources in Costa Rica were boulders off the Pacific coast, which had been lost or had become more difficult to reach because of changes in the sea level. He may well have been on the right track, but we may need to revise the part of his idea that suggests there were originally jade resources in Costa Rica. Given the frequent problems in visually discriminating real jadeite from similar–looking related materials available in Costa Rica, we need to await tests on specific artifacts interpreted as recycled from Mesoamerica before we can comment more fully. That jade artifacts sometimes do show reworking suggests that the material was highly valued and scarce, and could indicate that it was procured from external sources. It is significant that we find very little raw jade, or working debris, in archaeological sites in Costa Rica, and that jade artifacts are not found scattered amongst debris and refuse in habitation sites, as is apparently the case in some Maya sites (D. Freidel, personal communications; Garber 1980). The Costa Rican jade and jadelike materials available to us for study and analysis come almost entirely from cemetery/mortuary contexts.

The social, political, and economic implications are equally intriguing, whether we entertain the idea of the possible lack of Costa Rican resources and the use of Guatemalan ones, or continue to entertain the idea of possible Costa Rican sources. Relevant to either scenario is the virtually total absence of jade artifacts from Nicaragua and Panama. Some evidence of a Guatemalan–based trade network should have left its mark in Nicaragua, while, on the other hand, if the sources were in northwestern Costa Rica, it would have been even easier to trade into Nicaragua, a pattern that would be in accord with distributions of other types of artifacts in the Greater Nicoya area from the same time period (Norweb 1964; Lange 1980). Moreover, only very small amounts of jade have been found in Panama, which was also linked by Precolumbian trade routes to northwestern Costa Rica. Costa Rica is, then, the only one of the three countries with a considerable presence of jade.

It is not difficult to visualize quantities of material moving through a trade network from Guatemala to Costa Rica. Looking at avenues of natural communication and contact, it is fairly easy to trace possible routes southward from a Guatemalan source area into Costa Rica (fig. 42). If jade was arriving in Costa Rica via long–distance contacts, a number of testable hypotheses regarding the social and economic relationships that facilitated movement of the raw material southward from its source can be postulated. Consideration of a Guatemalan–Costa Rican jade route requires, however, a better understanding of how changes in the presence of jade in Costa Rica can be articulated with evidence of changes in Maya society in the possible source area.

Another interesting aspect remaining to be assessed and evaluated is the aesthetic–functional–social relationship between jadeite and jadelike materials, on one hand, and on the other, the somewhat different materials that were used to produce the same forms with many of the same decorative motifs. Such a group of artifacts is shown in figure 43. Possible interpretations of imitative behavior or adaptation can be suggested. The jade artifacts are usually found in what, based on limited, controlled excavations, we might refer to as higher–class cemetery remains. It is, therefore, tempting to propose that these jade artifacts might have come into Costa Rica as a result of exchanges of exotic goods between upper–class elites in various parts of lower Central America and southern Mesoamerica. These social interpretations would fit with earlier ideas of Charles Balser (1974) that split jades (fig. 44), usually found with one half in one grave and one half in another grave or other disassociated location, may indicate specific relationships. Stylistically similar jade or jadelike artifacts are found in both the Atlantic and Pacific parts of Costa Rica, indicating social and economic ties transcending the distinct ecological differences between the two regions.

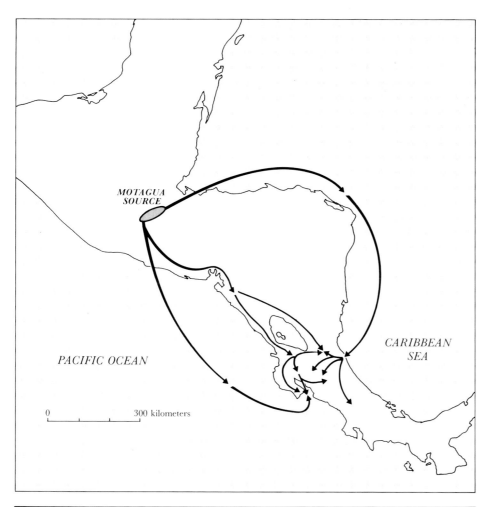

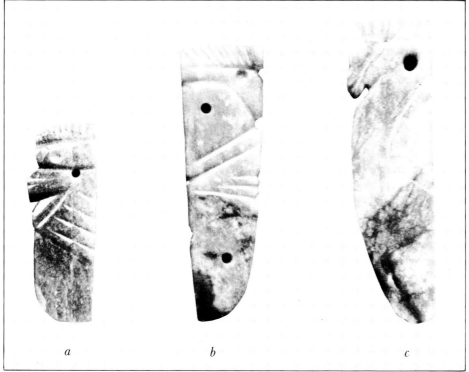

Figure 42. Possible jade routes from Guatemala to Costa Rica.

Figure 43. Stylistically similar jade and non–jade objects from different parts of Costa Rica. (a) Nosara. (b) Canas. (c) Guacimo. Photo: Ronald L. Bishop.

Figure 44. Split jade. Instituto Nacional de Seguros. Photo: Ronald L. Bishop.

Jadeite shells, spoons, and related artifacts (fig. 45) form another significant category. This whole complex of artifacts was brought into focus by a significant discovery, in the fall of 1977, at the site of Tibás in the Central Valley of Costa Rica. A MNCR research crew, under the direction of Hector Gamboa and Michael Snarskis, discovered the largest jade or jadeite–like artifact yet to be found in Costa Rica (Snarskis 1979). This shell–shaped jade artifact is one component of the ceremonial stool/jade/mace head ritual complex described elsewhere (Lange 1979). The chemical and mineralogical composition of this artifact and the associated large Guanacaste–style axe–god are as yet unknown. (These were the only two artifacts for which the Board of Directors of the MNCR expressly forbade export for the testing described in this paper.) For present purposes, a great deal of interpretive speculation can be derived from the visual inspection of these two artifacts. Based on analyses of visually similar material, it is quite feasible to suggest that the two objects were produced from almost monomineralic jadeite. The really intriguing question, of course, is whether or not the clam shell is actually of Guatemalan origin or could possibly be of Costa Rican material.

Another research direction that needs to be followed is to study more precisely areas in Costa Rica where jade artifacts have been found in concentration. Well–known areas already documented include the Bagaces region and the Nicoya–Nosara regions; there also appear to have been relatively heavy concen-

Figure 45. Jade spoon. Instituto Nacional de Seguros. Photo: Ronald L. Bishop.

trations of jade artifacts in the Línea Vieja region. Further delineation of such concentrations of artifacts may help in interpreting the mechanisms and patterns of Precolumbian jade trade routes. The whole problem of whether particular forms of jade artifacts, or particular stylistic distributions, are related to geographical–temporal factors, cannot be solved without an opportunity to study larger quantities of artifacts and, most importantly, artifacts with much better provenances than the current body of jade data. Only when analysis is

Table 1 Examples of Mean Elemental Concentrations*			
	Maya apple green jadeite	Motagua jadeite/jadeite-albite	Costa Rican divergent jadeite
Na	10.0%	11.5%	13.8%
Rb	3.76	2.31	ND
Cs	.350	.206	ND
Ba	190.	57.0	21.0
Sc	4.68	1.30	4.13
La	.107	.457	.575
Ce	2.88	.488	1.93
Eu	.155	.026	.237
Lu	.108	.019	.236
Hf	.34	1.29	4.03
Cr	2080.	8.10	2.44
Fe	1.30%	1.29%	1.64%
Co	7.13	3.68	4.53
Sm	.954	.087	.413
Yb	.575	.097	1.04

*All concentrations expressed as oxides.

Table 1. Comparative analytical results: Apple–green jadeite from Maya lowlands; jadeite/jadeite–albite from Motagua Valley of Guatemala; nonidentified–source Costa Rican jadeite. Data are reported here as oxides in parts per million, except for sodium and iron, which are reported as per cent concentrations. ND = not determined.

based on a large collection, rather than on a small number of visually selected samples, will we be able to determine how much is jadeite and how much is a different material; we may find that only a very small percentage of that material commonly identified in Costa Rica as jade is really jadeite.

The investigation reported in this paper reflects activities of the Maya Jade and Ceramics Project, a joint venture of the Research Laboratory, Museum of Fine Arts, Boston, and the Department of Chemistry, Brookhaven National Laboratory. Funding for the program is partially provided by Landon T. Clay, Boston. Logistical assistance and archaeological survey support in Costa Rica were provided by the MNCR. Aspects of the investigation were carried out under the auspices of the U.S. Department of Energy. In addition, we are pleased to recognize the assistance of the following: Board of Directors, MNCR; Luis Diego Gómez Pignataro, Hector Gamboa Paniagua, and José A. Patiño, MNCR; German Serrano P., Executive President, and Ricardo Monge O., Instituto Nacional de Seguros de Costa Rica; and Zulay Soto de Andrade, Museo del Jade; and Raul Castallanos. Frederick and Jan Mayer, Denver, have supported Lange's research in various ways. A December 1980 meeting at Dumbarton Oaks, Washington, D.C., brought together many persons interested in jade research in Mesoamerica and Central America, and helped to clarify and focus some of the ideas summarized in this chapter. We would like to thank Elizabeth Boone, Dumbarton Oaks, for making that meeting possible.

1
Globular jar
Ceramic; h. 31.2 cm, w. 33.7 cm
Guanacaste–Nicoya zone
Middle Period IV, c. 500–100 B.C.
Instituto Nacional de Seguros 3864
See pl. 1
The earliest whole pottery vessels known from
Guanacaste–Nicoya are of the Toya Zoned
Incised ceramic type, to which this piece
belongs. Similar pottery is also referred to as
Palmar Ware, an earlier, more general
appellation. The elegant, yet entirely functional,
form of this jar is typical of middle Period IV
pottery. Although the red–on–buff–or–brown
zoning is not especially apparent in this piece,
zoning is typical of pottery of this time in
northwestern Costa Rica, suggesting
participation in the ceramic tradition of
Mesoamerica, to the north.

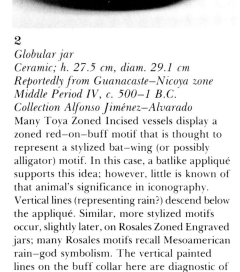

2
Globular jar
Ceramic; h. 27.5 cm, diam. 29.1 cm
Reportedly from Guanacaste–Nicoya zone
Middle Period IV, c. 500–1 B.C.
Collection Alfonso Jiménez–Alvarado
Many Toya Zoned Incised vessels display a
zoned red–on–buff motif that is thought to
represent a stylized bat–wing (or possibly
alligator) motif. In this case, a batlike appliqué
supports this idea; however, little is known of
that animal's significance in iconography.
Vertical lines (representing rain?) descend below
the appliqué. Similar, more stylized motifs
occur, slightly later, on Rosales Zoned Engraved
jars; many Rosales motifs recall Mesoamerican
rain–god symbolism. The vertical painted
lines on the buff collar here are diagnostic of
early pottery in both Guanacaste–Nicoya and
the Central Highlands–Atlantic Watershed.

3
Two avimorph ocarinas
Ceramic; h. 7.5 cm, w. 5 cm; h. 9.5. cm,
w. 5.5 cm
Guanacaste–Nicoya zone
Middle–late Period IV, 300 B.C.–300 A.D.
Museo Nacional de Costa Rica 10557, 15314
Bird–effigy ocarinas come in a variety of sizes,
producing tones ranging from that of a tenor
recorder to that of a shrill whistle. They are
decorated in the early Zoned Bichrome–period
style with wide–incised lines, sometimes
surrounding areas of fine, dentate rocker
stamping. Although quite stylized, the avian
models may have been of the family
Caprimulgidae, perhaps whippoorwills (Luis
Diego Gómez Pignataro, personal
communication).

4
Collared jar
Ceramic; h. 14.5 cm, w. 14.5 cm
From Hacienda Tempisque, Guanacaste
Late Period IV, c. 1–300 A.D.
Collection Carmen de Gillen
The clean–lined design of this small Rosales
Zoned Engraved jar is typical of pottery
manufactured during the first few centuries of
the Christian era in most of Costa Rica. Its
extremely high collar and wide mouth, however,
suggest a function different from that of most
Rosales jars, whose large bodies, small mouths,
and typical incised motif—possibly symbolic of
rain—would seem to indicate use as containers
for liquids. The very simple design on this
example offers no clue as to function.

5
Avian–effigy vessel
Ceramic; h. 17 cm, l. 19 cm
Guanacaste–Nicoya zone
Late Period IV, 1–300 A.D.
Museo Nacional de Costa Rica 20949
See pl. 3
6
Monkey–effigy vessel
Ceramic; h. 20 cm, l. 16 cm
From Tomb C, Talamanca de Tibás, Central
Highlands; trade piece from Guanacaste–
Nicoya
Late Period IV, 1–300 A.D.
Museo Nacional de Costa Rica 1.5 (26)
See pl. 4
A variety of Rosales Zoned Engraved,
incorporating red and brown slip on buff,
instead of the usual black on red, frequently
takes the form of realistic animal–effigy
vessels, the majority of which are "bridge–
and–spout" designs like the two shown here.
Such vessels were typical of late Preclassic
Mesoamerican ceramic complexes. The avian
effigy (no. 5), with an apparently inflated
breast pouch, could have been modeled after

the king vulture (*Sarcorhampus papa*), while the other effigy looks like a howler monkey (*Alouata palliata*) (Luis Diego Gómez Pignataro, personal communication). Monkeys seem to have been the most frequent subjects for such zoomorphic effigy vessels, the best of which are among the most aesthetically pleasing ceramic sculptures of Precolumbian Costa Rica. Both mouth and spout are directly connected to the hollow body of these vessels, which could have been used as pitchers.

7
Hunchback–effigy vessel
Ceramic; h. 8.1 cm, w. 6.1 cm
Guanacaste–Nicoya zone
Late Period IV, 1–300 A.D.
Instituto Nacional de Seguros 2499

8
Hunchback figure
Ceramic; h. 14.9 cm, w. 13 cm
Reportedly from La Guinea, Filadelfia,
Guanacaste
Late Period IV, c. 1–300 A.D.
Collection Juan and Ligia Dada

Hunchbacks were objects of fascination in most Precolumbian cultures. Although of a solid black–brown color, this tiny human hunchback vessel with a conical hat belongs to the late Period IV Zoned Bichrome style, with characteristic subtle, but realistic, modeling and careful, fine–line engraving. The larger figurine has a similar pose, and, like the tiny effigy vessel (and others of its kind), it shows a bearded personage, with two hornlike protuberances. The repetition of bearded hunchback figures may indicate a mythological being or characterize a certain societal role, i.e., that of shaman or diviner. The maroon–orange painted decoration of number 8 is unusual for this time period.

9
Zoomorphic–effigy vessel
Ceramic; h. 10.5 cm, w. 8 cm
Guanacaste–Nicoya zone
Late Period IV, c. 1–300 A.D.
Museo Nacional de Costa Rica 20950

In Rosales Zoned Engraved effigy jars, modeled zoomorphic heads are combined with engraved humanlike features, or, at least, human postures. This suggests that masked or transformed human beings are portrayed. The smaller jar (no. 9) apparently shows a duck, of the family Anatidae, while the head on the larger vessel (no. 10) is that of an armadillo (family Dasypodidae). The iconographic significance of the animals is unknown. The duck effigy has a necklace and an object hanging from the left wrist; it has a composite insect–wing silhouette seen on certain Olmec and Izapan stelae in Mexico.

10
Zoomorphic–effigy vessel
Ceramic; h. 24 cm, w. 16 cm
Guanacaste–Nicoya zone
Late Period IV, c. 1–300 A.D.
Museo Nacional de Costa Rica 24059

11
Human–effigy vessel
Ceramic; h. 24.5 cm, w. 21.5 cm
Guanacaste–Nicoya zone
Late Period IV, 1–300 A.D.
Collection María Eugenia de Roy

12
Human–effigy vessel
Ceramic; h. 23.5 cm, w. 20 cm
Guanacaste–Nicoya zone
Late Period IV, 1–300 A.D.
Museo Nacional de Costa Rica 9518
These figures have a lustrous red slip decorated
with zones of black and/or white paint, outlined
by engraving. The zones may represent body
painting, tattooing, or, in some cases, articles
of clothing or jewelry. A sense of dignity and
sculptural monumentality is conveyed by the
proportions and by the Buddhalike pose,
which may be a ceremonial posture, or perhaps
one of sexual receptivity.

13
Anthropomorphic–effigy vessel
Ceramic; h. 41 cm, w. 23 cm
Guanacaste–Nicoya zone
Late Period IV, c. 1–300 A.D.
Instituto Nacional de Seguros 6512
See pl. 2
This effigy vessel of the Rosales Zoned Engraved
type has unusual features. Apparently female,
it seems to be hunchback; its raised shoulders
and bulbous mouth configuration create a
surprised or agitated expression. The white
area around the chin may depict only body
painting, but swelling and distortion of the
mouth suggest two other possibilities: a mask
representing a pouched bird, or an infirmity
such as a tumor, a goiter, or some congenital
defect. A helmetlike coiffure, ear spools, and
body painting or tattooing are also shown.

14
Relief–decorated metate
Volcanic stone; h. 16 cm, w. 26.8 cm,
l. 44.5 cm
Reportedly from Santa Cruz, Guanacaste
Late Period IV, 1–500 A.D.
Collection Dr. Hernán Paéz U. and
Dr. Carlos Roberto Paéz S.
See pl. 48

15
Relief–decorated metate
Volcanic stone; h. 34.5 cm, w. 41.9 cm,
l. 69.8 cm
Guanacaste–Nicoya zone
Late Period IV, 1–500 A.D.
Instituto Nacional de Seguros 4136
Curved–plate stone tables with three cylindrical
legs were made in northern Costa Rica during
the first several centuries after Christ, and
perhaps slightly earlier. They usually have
little decoration on the upper surface,
suggesting the quotidian food–processing
metate as a model. While many are worn from
grinding on the concave plate, their thinness
and the elaborately carved low–relief decoration
on the bottom of the plate suggest occasional
or ceremonial use. The unusual position of the
designs may simply mean that metates were
stored with the underside visible, perhaps
leaning against a wall. Such elaborate carving
argues against a casual explanation, however.
The placing of the design may indicate a
cosmographic representation of mythological
beings as part of the underworld, as opposed
to the middle (earthly) or upper (celestial)
realms. Undoubtedly, a complex mythological
symbolism is depicted, which is, unfortunately,
not yet clear. The metate morphology is
certainly not accidental. While such objects
may have been used as "thrones" for elite
personages, it is likely that their principal use
was in rituals dealing with agriculture or the
processing and redistribution of foodstuffs.

16
Relief–decorated metate
Volcanic stone; h. 26 cm, w. 33 cm, l. 52 cm
Guanacaste–Nicoya zone
Late Period IV, c. 1–500 A.D.
Instituto Nacional de Seguros 3493
See pl. 47

17
Relief–decorated metate
Volcanic stone; h. 31.8 cm, w. 47 cm, l. 81.5 cm
Reportedly from Nosara, Nicoya Peninsula
Late Period IV, c. 1–500 A.D.
Collection Dr. Hernán Paéz U. and
Dr. Carlos Roberto Paéz S.
Like other examples of curved–plate,
cylindrical–legged tripod metates, these two
display low–relief carving on the underside.
Number 16 shows a realistic alligator, the head
of which is incorporated into one of the
supports; the style is elegantly simple and
direct. Number 17 shows a human figure
wearing a headdress and/or cape in the form
of a feline head and pelt; the sharp teeth and
eyes are emphasized, and the hind legs and tail
hang alongside and between the human figure's
legs. Large plumes adorn the top of the
headdress, and long feathers (probably from
the quetzal) dangle from it, as well as what
appears to be a broad–bladed weapon, like
those seen on certain Olmec stelae. As in some
contemporary jade pendants, small birds hang
over the human figure's ears, and he appears
to be playing a long flute. Obviously, this is a
special personage, probably a shaman–chieftain.

Such metates have not yet been excavated by
archaeologists in controlled circumstances, but
surface collections in looted cemeteries suggest
that they were associated with pottery like
Rosales Zoned Engraved, usually dated
c. 1–300 A.D.

18
Ceremonial metate
Volcanic stone; h. 47 cm, w. 55 cm, l. 98 cm
Guanacaste–Nicoya zone
Middle–late Period IV, c. 300 B.C.–
  300 A.D.
Museo Nacional de Costa Rica 23065
Whereas most metates of this type are decorated
in low–relief carving on the underside, this
example displays openwork at one end. A
central human figure is flanked by two
perforated circular elements, which have been
called "mushrooms" (Ferrero 1977a: 279), but
may also be stylized reptilian figures whose
tails curl around their exaggerated headdresses
or crests, as in the later alligator *incensarios*
(nos. 89–92). Stylized alligator scutes outline
the upper surface of this object, which shows
no wear from grinding.

19
Avian axe–god pendant
Jade; h. 14 cm, w. 2.1 cm
Reportedly from Atlantic Watershed
Late Period IV, c. 1–500 A.D.
Instituto Nacional de Seguros 5929
See pl. 82

20
Avian axe-god pendant
Jade; h. 15.2 cm, w. 2.5 cm
Probably Guanacaste–Nicoya zone
Late Period IV, c. 1–500 A.D.
Museo Nacional de Costa Rica 23268
One of the most typical forms of Precolumbian
lapidary work from Costa Rica is the so-called
"axe–god" in which an animal, human, or
composite effigy surmounts a celtlike polished
blade; such objects were drilled for suspension.
Axe–god effigies are frequently avian; these
two pendants probably show a quetzal, to
judge by the dominant centerline crest (Fonseca
and Scaglion 1978).

Functional polished celts were forest–clearing
tools, usually associated with agricultural,
sedentary societies. Their representation in an
obviously symbolic, high–status object (the
large jade pendants were highly valued)
suggests that their owners may have been
influential in decisions involving land use or
redistribution of foodstuffs. Such effigies were
probably important in rituals, or they may
have been clan symbols; their precise meaning
is as yet unclear. Axe–gods are known as early
as 800–500 B.C. in the Olmec culture of
Mexico and at Playa de los Muertos, Honduras.

21
Anthropomorphic axe–god pendant
Jade; h. 13 cm, w. 4.5 cm
Guanacaste–Nicoya zone
Period IV, c. 200–600 A.D.
Instituto Nacional de Seguros 6223

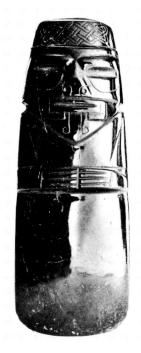

22
Anthropomorphic axe–god pendant
Jade; h. 13.7 cm, w. 5.2 cm
Guanacaste–Nicoya zone
Period IV, c. 200–600 A.D.
Instituto Nacional de Seguros 6244
Human figures are portrayed on some axe–god
pendants, almost always in a formal, rather

stiff pose, seen from the waist up. Hands meet or cross at the belly, and the faces are sometimes serene, but more often severe or masklike. A ritual pose, perhaps that of a shaman–chieftain, is indicated. Number 21, made of light green–blue jade of high quality, is typical of such carvings. Number 22, probably of chloromelanite, is more sinister and more complex. The figure's cap is incised with a matlike pattern, similar to patterns on Carrillo and Galo Polychrome pottery, a motif indicative of high status in Mesoamerica. The incised spirals above and below the mouth are probably "speech scrolls"; the personage (or office) depicted on such objects was obviously important, probably politically and religiously.

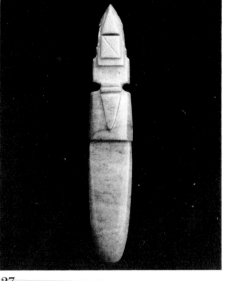

23
Avian axe–god pendant
Jade; h. 16.8 cm, w. 4.6 cm
Reportedly from Atlantic Watershed
Middle–late Period IV, c. 300 B.C.–
*   500 A.D.*
Instituto Nacional de Seguros 1798
See pl. 6
24
Avian axe–god pendant
Jade; h. 11 cm, w. 4.7 cm
Guanacaste–Nicoya zone
Middle–late Period IV, c. 300 B.C.–
*   500 A.D.*
Instituto Nacional de Seguros 6433
See pl. 80
25
Avian axe–god pendant
Jade; h. 8.4 cm, w. 4.1 cm
Guanacaste–Nicoya zone
Middle–late Period IV, c. 300 B.C.–
*   500 A.D.*
Instituto Nacional de Seguros 6186
See pl. 68
In this series of avimorph pendants, there is a transition to fully avian features. Arms and hands become stylized wings. The heads have a masklike quality, accentuated by tiny bird effigies leaning over what would be human ears. Number 25 is entirely avian, with wings and feet realistically rendered in a birdlike posture, which makes the celt–form base seem almost like a tail with spread feathers. This sequence is entirely stylistic, with no chronological significance implied. It may have spatial importance, however, for more human pieces with string–sawed legs (nos. 160–163) are more typical of the Atlantic Watershed; but the almost total lack of contextual control prevents the testing of even that hypothesis.

26
Avian axe–god pendant
Jade; h. 20.3 cm, w. 5.1 cm
From Talamanca de Tibás, Central
*   Highlands; trade piece from Guanacaste–*
*   Nicoya*
Middle–late Period IV, c. 300 B.C.–500 A.D.
Museo Nacional de Costa Rica 1.5 (34)
This pendant is similar in style to number 23; it is a masklike head, but with naturalistic tufts. It was excavated by the MNCR from a Central Highlands tomb that included a large Olmec heirloom jade in the form of a clamshell. Like some other objects (no. 6) from that cemetery, it is considered to be a trade piece from Guanacaste–Nicoya.

27
Avian axe–god pendant
Jade; h. 18.2 cm, w. 3.3 cm
Guanacaste–Nicoya zone
Late Period IV, 1–500 A.D.
Instituto Nacional de Seguros 1711
28
Avian axe–god pendant
Jade; h. 15.5 cm, w. 1.7 cm
Guanacaste–Nicoya zone
Late Period IV, 1–500 A.D.
Instituto Nacional de Seguros 4457
See pl. 83
29
Avian axe–god pendant
Jade; h. 18.4 cm, w. 2.4 cm
Guanacaste–Nicoya zone
Late Period IV, 1–500 A.D.
Instituto Nacional de Seguros 5932
See pl. 81
Among the avian axe–god pendants is a class defined by crisp, angular carving that looks almost machine–tooled. This stylized geometricity is seen only in pieces from Guanacaste–Nicoya. The bird portrayed is usually the quetzal, with a tiered headdress. Number 27 has a high crest, which incorporates nonrealistic traits, like the frontal box with crossed lines. The box and the position of the eyes suggest that this is either a person wearing a mask and headdress or a bird with at least one human trait. Design elements emphasizing the four corners of a square often had cosmographic significance, for the concept of the four corners or directions of the world was important in Precolumbian cultures. Number 28 has squared–off lines, even in the axe blade. The impression of a tiered, totem–polelike headdress is strong; the uppermost figure may not be avian. Number 29 exhibits a more rounded style of carving, but the tiered headdress is unmistakable. Only the uppermost of the three figures shows the cephalic morphology of a real bird.

30
Avian axe pendant
Jade; h. 9.5 cm, w. 3.7 cm
Guanacaste–Nicoya zone
Late Period IV, 1–500 A.D.
Instituto Nacional de Seguros 2023

31
Avian axe pendant
Slate; h. 14 cm, w. 3.7 cm
Guanacaste–Nicoya zone
Late Period IV, 1–500 A.D.
Instituto Nacional de Seguros 1800
Number 30 is a skillful modification of the
axe–god form, in which the rounded lines of a
whippoorwill are effectively characterized in
jade. This bird is the most common effigy
portrayed in contemporary Guanacaste–Nicoya
ocarinas (no. 3). Number 31 is one of the rare
slate pendants found in Costa Rica (they are
also known in the Olmec lapidary tradition).
The sequence of totem–polelike effigies is not
typical; the bottom, or main, figure seems to
be entirely avian, while the upper one looks
like a human being in avian costume.

32
Anthropomorphic axe pendant
Jade; h. 12.9 cm, w. 5.2 cm
Guanacaste–Nicoya zone
Late Period IV, 1–500 A.D.
Instituto Nacional de Seguros 6432
This is another in the large class of anthropomorphic pendants with small birds (avian
allies) perched over the head. The pendant
is distinguished by skillful carving and
drilling techniques. It has an unusual, lobed
projection beneath the mouth, possibly part of
a mask or collar.

33
Effigy axe–god pendant
Jade; h. 10.3 cm, w. 4 cm
Reportedly from Vereh, Alta Talamanca region,
*   Atlantic Watershed*
Late Period IV, 1–500 A.D.
Instituto Nacional de Seguros 4508
See pl. 5

34
Effigy axe–god pendant
Jade; h. 7.9 cm, w. 4.1 cm
Guanacaste–Nicoya zone
Late Period IV, 1–500 A.D.
Instituto Nacional de Seguros 5945

35
Effigy axe–god pendant
Jade; h. 9.3 cm, w. 5.8 cm
Reportedly from Línea Vieja, Atlantic Watershed
Late Period IV, 1–500 A.D.
Instituto Nacional de Seguros 5915
Pendants like these have been called bat
effigies, perhaps accurately. That identification

was probably suggested by the thin, bent legs drawn up under the torso, as on a bat or bird in flight. Of greater interest is the humanoid aspect of certain pendants in this style. Number 33 is a superb example: it is probably a human being in bat guise; speech scrolls emanate from the corners of the mouth. The crosshatched decoration on the headdress, the band below the eyes, and the panel descending from the mouth could be construed as a symbol of maize, a crop with which the shaman–bat may have been associated. The pendant with a grimacing face, number 34, has a crosshatched headdress, incised extremities, and parallel V's descending from the mouth— the last might be either a variant speech scroll or a beard. As a group, these pendants resemble wrinkled old men. Small birds or alligators incised on the cheeks of number 35 look almost like feline whiskers. The coiffure resembles that of monkey pendants, and is somewhat similar to that of anthropomorphic pendants with birds perched over the ears.

36

Bat pendant with sharks
Jade; h. 3 cm, w. 15.5 cm
Guanacaste–Nicoya zone
Late Period IV, 1–500 A.D.
Instituto Nacional de Seguros 6494
See pl. 85

37

Bat pendant with alligators
Jade; h. 2.2 cm, w. 15.8 cm
Guanacaste–Nicoya zone
Late Period IV, 1–500 A.D.
Instituto Nacional de Seguros 1931
See pl. 86

Both of these horizontally hung pendants depict bats, with distinctly different animal effigies incorporated into their outspread wings. Number 36 is an especially felicitous combination of forms; the pointed elements of the bat wings become the dorsal fins of two giant sharks. Number 37 relies on engraved detail to create a similar composition; the extremities are alligator heads, preceded by a matlike pattern, possibly representing corrugated hide. The two outlined drilled pits near either end give the piece a potential double aspect: hung vertically, it bears a passing resemblance to the avian axe–pendants. Horizontal bat–wing pendants, usually very stylized, are also known from northern South America along the Caribbean.

38

Man–alligator pendant
Jade; h. 2 cm, w. 6.7 cm
Reportedly from Nicoya Peninsula
Late Period IV, c. 1–500 A.D.
Museo Nacional de Costa Rica 8387

Carved from light blue, translucent jade, this piece appears at first glance to be a winged head. The lateral elements are alligators, however, and the central human head has the tiniest of birds at each corner. The style is basically like other horizontally hung bat pendants with alligator heads at either end (no. 37).

39

Crab pendant
Jade; h. 2.5 cm, w. 8.3 cm
Guanacaste–Nicoya zone
Late Period IV, 1–500 A.D.
Instituto Nacional de Seguros 5925

Of a form that recalls the longer, horizontal bat pendants (nos. 36–37), this piece may have been reworked or the theme may have been altered during manufacture. The center section is a fairly realistic crab, a rare motif in jade; the end elements also look crablike, but it is probable that they represent stylized "beak–birds," with tiny legs, formed by notches, and large, down–thrusting beaks.

40

Tubular bead, alligator head
Jade; h. 2.5 cm, l. 12.7 cm
Reportedly from Nicoya Peninsula
Late Period IV, 1–500 A.D.
Museo Nacional de Costa Rica 7711

The guilloche pattern usually indicated serpents or woven mats in Costa Rican Precolumbian sculpture, but has been used here to represent the body of an alligator, whose head is at one end. The sparkly stone used for this piece is virtually unknown in other Costa Rican lapidary work, and may have been imported.

41

Ear spools
Jade; h. 1.8 cm, w. 2.6 cm
Guanacaste–Nicoya zone
Late Period IV, 1–500 A.D.
Instituto Nacional de Seguros 6450a, 6450b

Jade ear spools or flares are found only rarely in Costa Rica—ceramic, bone, and other materials were apparently used more often for these ornaments. This pair, in translucent jade, is of exceptionally fine workmanship. The original cylindrical blank was made with a tubular drill; the spool shape was then produced, and another, smaller tubular drill was employed to hollow out the spool. The string–sawn openwork was the last step.

42
Articulated avian ornament
Whale bone; h. 11 cm, w. 2.5 cm
Reportedly from Nicoya Peninsula
Late Period IV, 1–500 A.D.
Museo Nacional de Costa Rica 25654
Bone carvings, rarely preserved in Costa Rica, sometimes survive in the shell middens of the Pacific coast. This splendid piece, probably of whalebone (Luis Diego Gómez Pignataro, personal communication), depicts the "eagle" (probably a king vulture) that appears often in Period IV sculpture throughout the country. The head was carved to be attached to the body, but is movable. It is not known how this piece was worn or used.

43
Ceremonial mace head
Stone; h. 6.4 cm, w. 9.4 cm
Guanacaste–Nicoya zone
Late Period IV, c. 1–500 A.D.
Instituto Nacional de Seguros 541
See pl. 8

44
Ceremonial mace head
Jade; h. 8.5 cm, w. 7.7 cm
Guanacaste–Nicoya zone
Late Period IV, c. 1–500 A.D.
Collection Alfonso Jiménez-Alvarado
The ceremonial mace heads characteristic of late Period IV (and perhaps early Period V) in both Guanacaste–Nicoya and the Central Highlands–Atlantic Watershed zones appear— along with the carved stone metates and the jade pendants of the same period—to have been of considerable symbolic importance, probably associated with elevated rank. The three kinds of objects have been found together in obviously elite funerary contexts.

Formerly referred to as war clubs, many mace heads could have had that function, in view of their solidity and weight, but others are delicately carved and too fragile to have been weapons. All seem to have been mounted on staffs, probably wooden: a large central perforation (usually biconical and made with a tubular drill) is always a salient feature. It is probably more correct to interpret these mace heads as badges of office or of a clan or moiety affiliation—like a bishop's miter or a king's mace. The nature of the handle and hafting might resolve the question, but it is not known. In at least one case, the principal burial at Talamanca de Tibás, which included a large Olmec clamshell jade and three metates, the two associated mace heads were almost certainly not on staffs when interred.

The two mace heads here are monkey effigies, the first of the genus *Cebus* (the capuchins) and the second the squirrel monkey, genus *Saimiri* (Luis Diego Gómez Pignataro, personal communication). The latter displays a strange conical projection on the forehead and smaller ones on the jowls. Also seen on some effigies of human trophy heads, these projections may have had to do with the process of preparing shrunken heads.

45
Ceremonial mace head
Stone; h. 6.6 cm, w. 7.1 cm
Guanacaste–Nicoya zone
Late Period IV, c. 1–500 A.D.
Instituto Nacional de Seguros 509

46
Ceremonial mace head
Stone; h. 8.5 cm, w. 8 cm
Reportedly from Nicoya Peninsula
Late Period IV, c. 1–500 A.D.
Museo Nacional de Costa Rica 9094
See pl. 7
These two mace heads seem to portray human heads. Number 45 has a shield or band around the face, which recalls the feathered facial disk of the harpy eagle. Number 46 may represent a flayed head, from which most of the tissue has been removed; the temporal lines on the top of the skull are visible, and the teeth are bared in a lipless grimace. The accentuated treatment of the auditory meatus, however, allows the object to be interpreted as a fantastic animallike head. This double meaning may have been purposeful, as it was in the case of many jade pendants.

47
Ceremonial mace head
Stone; h. 8.4 cm, l. 14.7 cm
Reportedly from Nosara, Nicoya Peninsula
Late Period IV, c. 1–500 A.D.
Instituto Nacional de Seguros 6163

48
Ceremonial mace head
Volcanic stone; h. 8 cm, w. 8.5 cm
Guanacaste–Nicoya zone
Late Period IV, c. 1–500 A.D.
Instituto Nacional de Seguros 3082
Number 47 depicts a stylized avian effigy,
probably a quetzal; the central crest has been
rendered in the form of another small bird.
The pointed projection that forms the tail
seems distinctly weaponlike, although that
aspect may be symbolic only of domination or
prowess in warfare. Number 48, of light,
porous volcanic stone, appears to portray a
member of the family Canidae, probably
Urocyon, a small quadruped known as a "little
tiger" in Costa Rica (Luis Diego Gómez
Pignataro, personal communication). This
mace head was almost certainly not a weapon.

49
Ceremonial mace head
Stone; h. 6.8 cm, w. 8.1 cm
Reportedly from Línea Vieja, Atlantic Watershed
Late Period IV, 1–500 A.D.
Instituto Nacional de Seguros 6032
See pl. 9

50
Ceremonial mace head
Stone; h. 3.5 cm, l. 9.5 cm
Reportedly from Chilamate de Sarapiquí,
* Atlantic Watershed*
Late Period IV, 1–500 A.D.
Museo Nacional de Costa Rica 22303
Ceremonial mace heads are also found in late
Period IV in the Central Highlands–Atlantic
Watershed. Many are virtually identical to
Guanacaste–Nicoya examples, suggesting
limited centers of manufacture and a well-
established, elite–oriented trade network. Most
are zoomorphic. Number 49 seems to be a
harpy eagle (or an owl), with facial disk and
hornlike feather tufts; the eyes were emphasized
by repecking the polished stone. Number 50
seems to be a stylized feline, or perhaps an
alligator.

51
Mace head
Stone; h. 5.3 cm, w. 7.4 cm
Guanacaste–Nicoya zone
Late Period IV, c. 1–500 A.D.
Instituto Nacional de Seguros 498
See pl. 10
This mace head has a simple spherical form,
whose very lack of representational carving
suggests that it may have been used as a
weapon.

52
Axe facsimile
Stone; h. 27.8 cm, w. 19 cm
Probably Guanacaste–Nicoya zone
Probably late Period IV, c. 200–500 A.D.
Collection María Eugenia de Roy

53
Axe facsimile
Stone; h. approx. 29 cm
Probably Guanacaste–Nicoya zone
Probably late Period IV, c. 200–500 A.D.
Collection María Eugenia de Roy
Not illustrated
Axes were represented by nonfunctional
sculptures in stone and ceramic in greatest
quantity near the end of Period IV. They may
have played a part in rituals (the first example
here is perforated, as if for suspension or
attachment), or they may have been made as
symbolic burial furniture. Note the hafting
technique depicted in the stone carving.

54
Pedestal bowl
Ceramic; h. 19.3 cm, w. 22.8 cm
Guanacaste–Nicoya zone
Late Period IV, c. 300–500 A.D.
Instituto Nacional de Seguros 4870

58

Composite–effigy whistle
Ceramic; h. 23.8 cm, w. 21.8 cm
Reportedly from San Juan de Santa Cruz,
    Guanacaste
Late Period IV, c. 300–500 A.D.
Collection Oduber
See pl. 11

In this musical instrument, a human figure is masked and caped to imitate a bat, with wings outspread over his shoulders and feet dangling on his chest. The costume also includes three alligator masks, with the conical headdress often associated with representations of that reptile. Both the bat and the alligator were of considerable mythological importance during late Period IV in northwestern Costa Rica, but in contexts not yet fully understood. Figurines like this one are often shown seated on tetrapod benches somewhat similar in form to the contemporary stone metates.

56

Peccary–effigy vessel
Ceramic; h. 18 cm, w. 20 cm
Guanacaste–Nicoya zone
Late Period IV, c. 300–500 A.D.
Museo Nacional de Costa Rica 23139

The Guinea Incised ceramic type includes many zoomorphic effigy vessels, as well as humans masked as animals. A peccary, a member of the family Tayassuidae, is shown here; its features are not distinctive enough to make a definite identification of genus; it may be either *Tayassu* or *Pecari* (Luis Diego Gómez Pignataro, personal communication).

55

Pedestal bowl
Ceramic; h. 23 cm, w. 21.5 cm
Guanacaste–Nicoya zone
Late Period IV, c. 300–500 A.D.
Museo Nacional de Costa Rica 23083

Guinea Incised, the ceramic type to which these two vessels belong, has analogues in the Atlantic Watershed and, with its modeled, appliqué, and incised techniques, seems to be part of the southern and eastern Central American tradition of plastic decoration. The best examples, however, have a highly burnished, waxy brown–orange finish reminiscent of Usulután pottery in Mesoamerica, to the north.

Number 54 displays a human figure arrayed as a bat, complete with mask, in what might be a flying pose, with the scalloped rim of the vessel representing wings. Number 55 appears to be similar, but close examination shows that the human figure is costumed as an alligator, although apparently retaining wings; the chest cavity is open, possibly implying ritual sacrifice. Both bats and alligators were important deity images during the period 300–700 A.D.

57

Male and female effigy bowls
Ceramic; h. 14.8 cm, l. 36 cm; h. 13 cm,
    l. 31 cm
Guanacaste–Nicoya zone
Late Period IV, c. 300–500 A.D.
Museo Nacional de Costa Rica
    23090, 23827

Paired ceramic figurines, male and female, are encountered with some frequency in the Costa Rican archaeological sequence. These two Guinea Incised examples are more bowls than figurines. Their facial features and coiffures presage those of the slightly later Galo Polychrome figures.

59

Effigy vessel with lid
Ceramic; h. 6.8 cm, w. 4.9 cm
Guanacaste–Nicoya zone
Late Period IV, c. 200–500 A.D.
Instituto Nacional de Seguros 2794

61
Two tapir—effigy ocarinas
Ceramic; h. 9.4 cm, l. 21.2 cm; h. 9.7 cm, l. 18.2 cm
Reportedly from Chira, Filadelfia, Guanacaste
Late Period IV, c. 200–500 A.D.
Collection Dr. Hernán Paéz U. and Dr. Carlos Roberto Paéz S.

60
Effigy vessel with lid
Ceramic; h. 9 cm, w. 8.5 cm
Guanacaste—Nicoya zone
Late Period IV, c. 200–500 A.D.
Museo Nacional de Costa Rica 15164
During the last part of Period IV in
Guanacaste—Nicoya, tiny effigy vessels, ocarinas,
whistles, stamps, spindle whorls, and ear spools
were manufactured, almost all with incised,
punctate, and appliqué motifs. In these two
examples, the head forms a lid. The uses of
such small vessels are unknown.

We see here imagery typical of late
Period IV: a person costumed as a bat in
number 59 and as an alligator in number 60.
The latter image is less clear, but the rectangular
eyes, nobby crests, and two–tiered cylindrical
headdress all suggest an alligator.

62
Armadillo—effigy whistle
Ceramic; h. 8 cm, l. 11.7 cm
Guanacaste—Nicoya zone
Late Period IV, c. 200–500 A.D.
Museo Nacional de Costa Rica 23906

Zoomorphic effigies are commonly seen in
late Period IV ocarinas and whistles. The
largest examples sound like tenor recorders,
somewhat less resonant than a low–register
flute. The incised and modeled techniques in
these four examples are typical. The two
largest ocarinas (no. 61)—each with a ring for
suspension around the neck—are modeled
after Baird's tapir (*Tapirus bairdii*), with realistic
head features (Luis Diego Gómez Pignataro,
personal communication). The whistle is in the
form of an armadillo, probably *Cabassous
centralis*, while the copiously incised amphibian–
effigy ocarina represents *Bufo* sp.

64
Two masks
Ceramic; h. 19 cm, w. 15 cm; h. 17 cm,
* w. 14 cm*
Reportedly from Playas de Sámara, Nicoya
Probably late Period IV, 1–500 A.D.
Museo Nacional de Costa Rica 24053, 24054
See pl. 13; 24054 not illustrated
Masks like these, virtually *sui generis* in the
Costa Rican archaeological corpus, almost
certainly symbolize death heads. The series of
small perforations around the perimeters
suggests that they were sewn onto something,
either large effigy figures or, more likely,
funerary bundles.

63
Toad—effigy ocarina
Ceramic; h. 8 cm, l. 11.8 cm
Reportedly from Cerro Negro, Nicoya
Late Period IV, c. 200–500 A.D.
Collection Dr. Hernán Paéz U. and
* Dr. Carlos Roberto Paéz S.*

65
Effigy head
Ceramic; h. 11.7 cm, w. 16.5 cm
Probably Guanacaste–Nicoya zone
Probably late Period IV–early Period V,
  300–700 A.D.
Collection Oduber
Hollowed out in the back like a mask, this piece nevertheless shares attributes of size and facial expression with Atlantic Watershed effigies that depict shrunken trophy heads.

66
Standing–effigy vessel
Ceramic; h. 30.9 cm, w. 17.5 cm
Guanacaste–Nicoya zone
Late Period IV, c. 200–500 A.D.
Museo Nacional de Costa Rica 24174

67
Seated–effigy vessel
Ceramic; h. 21.5 cm, w. 15 cm
Guanacaste–Nicoya zone
Late Period IV, c. 200–500 A.D.
Instituto Nacional de Seguros 4858
These fairly realistic human effigy vessels, with voluptuously inflated bodies and expressive postures, are intermediate in style between the realistic bi– and trichrome ceramic sculptures of Rosales Zoned Engraved (nos. 5, 6, 9, 10, 12, 13) and the considerably more stylized effigy vessels of Tola Trichrome (nos. 70, 71). The standing female (no. 66) shows a carefully made skirt, body painting or tattooing, bracelets, and solid ear spools. The hunchback seated figure (no. 67) has a preoccupied expression, but shows few other surface details; emphasis is placed on the massive haunch and back.

68
Seated–effigy vessel
Ceramic; h. 47 cm, w. 30.5 cm
Reportedly from Chira, Filadelfia, Guanacaste
Late Period IV, c. 200–500 A.D.
Collection Dr. Hernán Paéz U. and
  Dr. Carlos Roberto Paéz S.
Also stylistically intermediate between Rosales Zoned Engraved and Tola Trichrome, this large, expressive, hunchback figure was obviously a special male personage. He wears what looks like a tunic, a headdress, and hollow ear spools. His face is accentuated by dark paint around the eyes.

69
Effigy vessel
Ceramic; h. 49.4 cm, w. 26.5 cm
Reportedly from Cañas, Guanacaste
Late Period IV, c. 200–500 A.D.
Instituto Nacional de Seguros 241
See pl. 12
Large effigy vessels portraying human beings costumed as alligators or bats are a common Costa Rican type. The very large size of most vessels suggests that they were containers for a (liquid?) substance utilized in a situation where mythological figures symbolized by bats and alligators were important. This vessel is quite realistic; a man arrayed as a bat, with a distinctive pendant around his neck, .strikes a bellicose pose. The two objects he holds in his hands may be paraphernalia for a drug–taking ritual.

70
Effigy vessel
Ceramic; h. 51 cm, w. 45 cm
From Hacienda Tempisque, Guanacaste
Late Period IV, c. 200–500 A.D.
Collection Carmen de Gillen

71
Effigy vessel
Ceramic; h. 30.8 cm, w. 29.5 cm
Guanacaste–Nicoya zone
Late Period IV, c. 200–500 A.D.
Instituto Nacional de Seguros 4761
Tola Trichrome is a ceramic type that combines modeled and appliqué decoration with

black–and–white painting on a zoned red slip. Number 70 is an effigy vessel of Tola Trichrome, and is a more stylized image than number 69, but it is still recognizable as a human being, this time costumed as an alligator. The painted motifs on the body also appear on other Tola vessels with less detailed modeling. Number 71 displays a human face with a poignant expression, accentuated by facial paint. The appliqué pellets above it are almost certainly symbolic of an alligator, and the whole composition probably signifies combined human and alligator traits in a transmogrification characteristic of shamanistic practices in many primitive cultures.

72
Decorated metate with mano
Volcanic stone; h. 23 cm, w. 22 cm, l. 40 cm;
  l. 34 cm, w. 4 cm
Guanacaste–Nicoya zone
Late Period IV–Period V, c. 300–700 A.D.
Museo Nacional de Costa Rica 24182, 24205
See pl. 50
Closely related to the Guanacaste–Nicoya metates that are decorated with a large, zoomorphic head at one end, this simpler version is copiously embellished with low–relief carving, openwork legs, and two tiny feline heads. In 1980, the MNCR excavated two very similar metates, both with heavy grinding wear and one with an associated "overhang" mano or muller. Both these decorated pieces were accompanied by small, tripod metates, one with limited use polish and the other with no grinding wear. The tombs in which they were found (at the Nacascolo site, Bay of Culebra), although not radiocarbon dated, probably are from 300–600 A.D.; they contained Tola Trichrome, Los Hermanos Beige, Chávez Red on White, and Carrillo Polychrome ceramics.

73
Alligator–effigy metate
Volcanic stone; h. 22.9 cm, w. 16.5 cm,
  l. 47 cm
Reportedly from Naranjal de Nicoya,
  Guanacaste
Late Period IV–Period V, c. 300–700 A.D.
Collection Dr. Hernán Paéz U. and
  Dr. Carlos Roberto Paéz S.

74
Zoomorphic–effigy metate
Volcanic stone; h. 42 cm, w. 30 cm, l. 77 cm
Guanacaste–Nicoya zone
Late Period IV–Period V, c. 300–700 A.D.
Instituto Nacional de Seguros 6383
The zoomorphic–effigy metates manufactured in Guanacaste–Nicoya from about 300 to 700 A.D. rank among the most extraordinary examples of stone sculpture in prehistoric America. Carved from a single piece of volcanic rock with only stone, wooden, or other perishable tools, plus abrasive, they exhibit remarkably graceful lines and proportions; the sweeping curve of the plain metate plate is set off by intricate low–relief volutes and open fretwork on the tripod legs. Number 73, lower and more solid than number 74, takes the form of an alligator; number 74 may depict a feline, but its unusually boxy head sets it apart from other feline effigies.

75
Avian–effigy metate
Volcanic stone; h. 29.5 cm, w. 23 cm, l. 50 cm
Guanacaste–Nicoya zone
Late Period IV–Period V, c. 300–700 A.D.
Instituto Nacional de Seguros 4119
See pl. 49

76
Avian–effigy metate
Volcanic stone; h. 34 cm, w. 31 cm, l. 76 cm
Reportedly from Upala (northern Atlantic
  Watershed), although of Guanacaste–
  Nicoya style
Late Period IV–Period V, c. 300–700 A.D.
Banco Nacional de Costa Rica 1661

Many metates show considerable wear from the grinding of a substance, probably maize, on their upper surface. Their use, however, was most likely restricted to ritual occasions. These objects are considered by some archaeologists to have been seats or "thrones," because of their frequent presence, unaccompanied by manos, in high–ranking burials, and because of the representation, in ceramic figurines, of personages seated on similar artifacts. The ceramic seats, however, are almost always tetrapod, and probably depict wooden seats made for that purpose. Certain elite males might well have possessed metates for ritual food preparation; the metates would have been interred with them, along with other status items, such as jade pendants and ceremonial mace heads. The zoomorphic effigies on these metates may have been clan symbols or deity representations, or may have had other symbolic significance, but all seem to be animals; no humans, masked or otherwise, are portrayed. The examples shown here are apparently a macaw (no. 75) and a harpy eagle (no. 76).

These two northern Costa Rican effigy metates are notable for detail and delicacy of carving. Number 77 may depict a feline, although it could be interpreted as a coyote (coyotes are still numerous in Guanacaste–Nicoya). Number 78, probably a feline, shows exceptional openwork carving in the head and legs.

80
Pedestal bowl with reclining figure
Ceramic; h. 16.2 cm, l. 31.5 cm
Reportedly from Nicoya Peninsula
Late Period IV–Period V, c. 300–700 A.D.
Collection María Eugenia de Roy
Carrillo Polychrome, named by Baudez (1967), is characterized by somewhat rough–hewn geometric patterns in red, maroon, and black paint on light–brown or cream slip. The type shares many motifs with Tola Trichrome, including big geometric patterns that probably symbolize bats and alligators. Like Tola, Carrillo displays modeled motifs, with anthropomorphic effigy vessels predominating, as in this example of a reclining figure. The production of Tola, although overlapping in time with Carrillo, is thought to have begun earlier.

77
Zoomorphic–effigy metate
Volcanic stone; h. 29 cm, w. 24.5 cm, l. 66 cm
Reportedly from Upala (northern Atlantic Watershed), although of Guanacaste–Nicoya style
Late Period IV–Period V, c. 300–700 A.D.
Banco Nacional de Costa Rica 1660

78
Feline–effigy metate
Volcanic stone; h. 42.3 cm, w. 34 cm, l. 89.5 cm
Guanacaste–Nicoya zone
Late Period IV–Period V, c. 300–700 A.D.
Collection Oduber

79
Seated figure
Ceramic; h. 19 cm, w. 15.5 cm
Reportedly from Nicoya Peninsula
Probably Period V, 500–1000 A.D.
Collection María Eugenia de Roy
This female figure, perhaps pregnant, is seated on a tetrapod bench with dual alligator–effigy heads. Although the maize–grinding metates of Periods IV and V sometimes have zoomorphic effigy heads and are similar in style to those shown here (nos. 73, 74), the heads are always single and the metates always tripods. It is possible that the Precolumbian potters who made sculptures like this took artistic liberties, adding a head and a leg, but it is more likely that a homomorphous wooden bench is portrayed here. Painted designs on the figure are probably alligator motifs and the hands–on–knees pose recalls the reflective attitudes of certain shaman figures in stone from the Atlantic Watershed (nos. 218, 219).

81
Anthropomorphic–effigy vessel
Ceramic; h. 15.2 cm, w. 21.5 cm
Guanacaste–Nicoya zone
Early Period V, c. 500–800 A.D.
Museo Nacional de Costa Rica 20489

82
Anthropomorphic–effigy vessel
Ceramic; h. 18.8 cm, w. 20 cm
Reportedly from Bagaces, Guanacaste
Early Period V, c. 500–800 A.D.
Collection Oduber
See pl. 14
Effigy–head vessels appear in both Carrillo and Galo Polychrome ceramic types, but are more frequent in the latter. Number 81 falls between the two types, tending more toward Galo. The agonized expression and rigidly drawn mouth suggest that this is a prisoner or a sacrificial victim; the facial–paint motifs recall alligator symbols. A similar aspect is observed in number 82; the black–masked eyes and grimacing mouth convey suffering or duress. In this piece, the alligator motif is clearer, placed horizontally on the vessel collar above parallel, wavy lines, which may symbolize water.

83
Anthropomorphic–effigy vessel
Ceramic; h. 24.5 cm, w. 22.5 cm
Guanacaste–Nicoya zone
Early Period V, c. 500–800 A.D.
Museo Nacional de Costa Rica 14505
See front cover
The lustrous, brilliantly colored ceramic type archaeologists call Galo Polychrome includes examples of human heads and full–figure effigies, which represent the best of the prehistoric Costa Rican potter's craft. A splendid example of a Galo Polychrome effigy vessel, this piece probably depicts an aged male; the posture is different from those seen in Galo female figurines (nos. 84–86), which are more numerous. Cream–colored disks on shoulders, knees, and abdomen may symbolize costuming as an animal. The body painting— dark zones with lobed designs—could be construed as avian or, more probably, alligator motifs.

84
Female figure with child
Ceramic; h. 36 cm, w. 16 cm
From Hacienda Tempisque, Guanacaste
Early Period V, 500–800 A.D.
Collection Carmen de Gillen
See pl. 15

85
Seated female figure
Ceramic; h 25.8 cm, w. 18.3 cm
Guanacaste–Nicoya zone
Early Period V, 500–800 A.D.
Collection Molinos de Costa Rica
Galo Polychrome figures provide a wealth of ethnographic detail because of their realistic style. Coiffures, clothing, and careful body painting or tattooing are all clearly shown. The vertical geometric bands passing through the eyes of number 84 probably represent patterns made with a roller stamp like that shown in number 133. Like most realistic, uncostumed, or simply dressed clay figures in Precolumbian Costa Rica, the Galo effigies are almost all female (no. 83 being one exception).

86
Female figure
Ceramic; h. 68 cm, w. 25.2 cm
Reportedly from Filadelfia vicinity,
  Guanacaste
Early Period V, c. 500–800 A.D.
Instituto Nacional de Seguros 3921
This extraordinary Galo Polychrome figure is one of the largest ceramic sculptures known from Costa Rica. Its arms–akimbo stance is frequently seen in female effigies. The coiffure is drawn back from the forehead in a halolike shape, and ear spools are prominent. A pubic cover, or *tanga*, is depicted. The extensive asymmetrical body painting is striking, but no zoomorphic symbolism is immediately apparent. Patterns acceptable for female body decoration were probably different from those for males, for whom mythologically important animal traits predominate.

87
Polychrome bowl
Ceramic; h. 9.2 cm, diam. 24 cm
Guanacaste–Nicoya zone
Period V, 500–800 A.D.
Museo Nacional de Costa Rica 14506

88
Polychrome jar
Ceramic; h. 20.7 cm, w. 19.3 cm
Guanacaste–Nicoya zone
Period V, 500–800 A.D.
Museo Nacional de Costa Rica 23967
Galo Polychrome has strong stylistic affinities with a Maya pottery group from Honduras known as Ulua Polychrome. Many Galo vessels are cylindrical, slab–footed forms, much more typical of the Maya area than of Costa Rica. The series of bands or panels in which the painted decoration occurs also constitutes a Mesoamerican trait, and undoubtedly had cosmographic significance, i.e., a celestial symbol uppermost, followed by terrestrial and underworld symbols below. Both vessels shown here display jaguar motifs, possibly representing a Mesoamerican deity (Luis Ferrero A., personal communication).

89
Incensario
Ceramic; h. 42.5 cm, w. 35 cm
From Hacienda Tempisque, Guanacaste
Period V–Period VI, c. 600–1100 A.D.
Collection Carmen de Gillen

90
Incensario
Ceramic; h. 57 cm, w. 41.5 cm
Guanacaste–Nicoya zone
Period V–Period VI, c. 600–1100 A.D.
Museo Nacional de Costa Rica 23069

91
Incensario
Ceramic; h. 45 cm, w. 30.4 cm
Guanacaste–Nicoya zone
Period V–Period VI, c. 600–1100 A.D.
Collection Juan and Ligia Dada

92
Incensario, jaguar base
Ceramic; h. 45 cm, w. 30.4 cm
From Hacienda Tempisque, Guanacaste
Period V–Period VI, c. 600–1100 A.D.
Collection Carmen de Gillen
Composed of a hemispherical bottom half and an elaborately decorated, vented lid, each of

these vessels seems designed to allow for limited combustion, hence their designation as incensarios, or censers. As in the case of the later stone seats from Guanacaste–Nicoya (nos. 99, 100), the crocodile or alligator (both species are found in Costa Rica) is the predominant motif; the rough–textured bands of appliqué pellets are almost certainly symbolic of the scutes on an alligator's hide. These alligators are fantastic creatures, sometimes two–headed, with explosions of spiky crests surrounding the head and snout like a nimbus. This image may represent a mythological animal, or may spring from drug–induced visions; the symbolism is still unclear. Other zoomorphic effigies, like the felines in two of these examples, appear more rarely as modeled decoration.

93

Figure seated on bench
Ceramic; h. 32 cm, w. 22.8 cm
Reportedly from Nosara, Nicoya Peninsula
Late Period V–early Period VI,
*   c. 800–1100 A.D.*
Collection Dr. Hernán Paéz U. and
*   Dr. Carlos Roberto Paéz S.*
See pl. 16.

94

Two seated figures
Ceramic; h. 34.5 cm, w. 23 cm; h. 31.2 cm,
*   w. 16.8 cm*
Reportedly from Nosara, Nicoya Peninsula
Late Period V–Period VI,
*   c. 800–1100 A.D.*
Collection Dr. Hernán Paéz U. and
*   Dr. Carlos Roberto Paéz S.*

As the Guanacaste–Nicoya polychrome tradition came into full flower during Period V, the long tradition of seated female figurines (seen in Costa Rica, since at least the time of Christ, in the form of Usulután ceramics, imported from Mesoamerica, and locally made Rosales Zoned Engraved examples) continued. The striking realism that was the hallmark of certain Galo Polychrome pieces, however, did not carry over into later types.

Archaeologists call these three colorful sculptures Guabal Polychrome, and they can be dated two to four centuries after Galo figurines. Apparently, the custom of almost allover body painting continued—unless the crosshatched patterns indicate garments or matting. The first figure (no. 93), seated on a tetrapod bench (which does not resemble a metate), has a tall, flattened headdress and large ear spools. Physical features are stylized, but the figure is probably a female, with accentuated breasts and possibly a pelvic girdle. The pair (no. 94), seated on small stools, may be male and female. Their funnel-like headgear is different from that of most Guabal figurines.

95

Bowl
Ceramic; h. 10.5 cm, diam. 24.5 cm
From Hacienda Tempisque, Guanacaste
Probably early Period VI, 1000–1200 A.D.
Collection Carmen de Gillen

Its brilliant red, orange, and black motifs painted on a cream–to–white slip make Papagayo Polychrome the most recognized pottery in (and, for many, synonymous with) the so–called Nicoya Polychrome style. The eye–catching designs stress Mesoamerican–derived, especially Mayoid, symbolism.

Number 95 shows a seated human figure with an elaborate headdress trailing three large plumes; he holds a small object in his hand. Two large eyelike forms fill the alternating panel. Lothrop (1926: 131–133) noted the similarity of this design to that on some Late Classic Maya pottery, speculating that the eyelike panel might represent bat wings. However, these standardized Papagayo bowls probably symbolize the confrontation between a man and a jaguar, with the surrounding panels depicting feline eyes (*ibid.*: 137–139, pl. XLVIIIc). The man may be seated on a jaguar skin, wearing a jaguar headdress, with symbolic spears behind him.

96

Pedestal jar
Ceramic; h. 23.2 cm, w. 15.6 cm
Guanacaste–Nicoya zone
Probably early Period VI, 1000–1200 A.D.
Instituto Nacional de Seguros 2919
See pl. 43

This pedestal jar shows basically the same theme as the preceding vessel. The main panel presents an elaborate jaguar form, with tail raised and mouth agape, ready to swallow the sun, symbolized here by a solid red circle with concentric arcs on two sides. The smaller panel above the jaguar may be either a stylized version of the anthropomorphic morning–star god or a conventionalized plumed–serpent motif, also associated with Venus. Pear–shaped jars with an annular base are a frequent form in this ceramic type.

97
Female figure
Ceramic; h. 17.8 cm, w. 8.7 cm
Guanacaste–Nicoya zone
Middle Period VI, c. 1100–1300 A.D.
Instituto Nacional de Seguros 4062
See pl. 17
Brightly painted figures like this one are
usually female, in a typical pose, with caplike
coiffure and simple skirt. Several show a
wealth of detail, and, although considerably
stylized, have an appealing, rather saucy air
about them. Facial painting is limited to lines
through the eyes, but the complex designs on
arms and breasts recall the stylized plumed–
serpent motifs seen on contemporary vessels.
A necklace worn by the figure apparently
includes a central pendantlike object whose
hourglass shape recalls spindle whorls or lip or
ear plugs; it may be a small container.

98
Male figure
Ceramic; h. 22 cm, w. 13.5 cm
Guanacaste–Nicoya zone
Middle Period VI, c. 1100–1300 A.D.
Collection María Eugenia de Roy
Not illustrated
One of the few male figures of this
type, number 98 is, like the previous
female figure, related to Pataky Polychrome.
They share the crosshatched band around
the head, but the upper part of the
coiffure here has nubbins like those seen
on many stone figures of warriors from
the Atlantic Watershed zone. The body paint
on this figure is less extensive than that
of the female, and he has prominent ear
spools and a necklace.

99
Seat
Volcanic stone; h. 30 cm, w. 32 cm
Guanacaste–Nicoya zone
Period VI, 1000–1550 A.D.
Museo Nacional de Costa Rica 23030

100
Seat
Volcanic stone; h. 44 cm, w. 44 cm
Guanacaste–Nicoya zone
Period VI, 1000–1550 A.D.
Instituto Nacional de Seguros 3923
These hourglass–shaped stone carvings are
probably seats. Similar artifacts were found by
Baudez (1967) at the coastal site of Papagayo,
which also had unusual circular house
foundations made from field stone. The
form depicted is a crocodile or alligator head,
the only effigy seen on such seats. Fantastically
realized, with an elaborate crest over the more
realistic snout, it resembles the modeled reptilian
features on slightly earlier ceramic incensarios
(nos. 89–92). The actual models for these seats
may have been masks which incorporated a
mythologized alligator image.

101
Zoomorphic–effigy vessel
Ceramic; h. 25 cm, w. 12 cm
Reportedly from Nosara, Nicoya Peninsula
Early Period VI, 1000–1350 A.D.
Instituto Nacional de Seguros 300
102
Zoomorphic–effigy vessel
Ceramic; h. 24.2 cm, w. 12.5 cm
Guanacaste–Nicoya zone
Early Period VI, 1000–1350 A.D.
Instituto Nacional de Seguros 4037
See pl. 18
These dark–brown, or black–slipped vessels,
usually characterized by modeled zoomorphic
features and white–filled engraved lines, seem
to represent standing human figures with
zoomorphic masks and other animal features,
perhaps cloaks or skins. Number 101 is a
feline, while number 102 is a crocodile with
feline headdress and supports. Incomplete
iconographic knowledge prevents further
interpretation of the roles of these animals
in the prevailing mythological framework,
although they also appear before and through
Period VI in central and eastern Costa Rican
settings, where modeled and appliqué
decoration was more common.

103
Tripod jar
Ceramic; h. 33.4 cm, w. 20 cm
Guanacaste–Nicoya zone
Late Period VI, c. 1200–1550 A.D.
Instituto Nacional de Seguros 4045

104
Globular vessel
Ceramic; h. 35 cm, w. 36.3 cm
Reportedly from Filadelfia vicinity,
*   Guanacaste*
Late Period VI, c. 1200–1550 A.D.
Instituto Nacional de Seguros 99
Increased production of white–slipped
polychrome during Period VI in the northern

part of the Greater Nicoya Subarea seems to
have stimulated the manufacture of similar,
but somewhat inferior, pottery in the vicinity
of the lower Tempisque River (Day and Abel–
Vidor 1980). This cream– or yellow–slipped
pottery was called by Baudez (1967) Jicote
Polychrome. While Jicote painting is generally
not as brilliant as that of Papagayo, Pataky, and
other types, its designs are often striking.
  Number 103 has the pear, or chimney,
shape popular in Period VI, with conical
tripod supports rather than the usual annular
base. The band around the collar contains
stylized plumed–serpent motifs. The face
painted on the body, with tiny ears
and ear spools, probably represents a mask.
Such round–eyed faces may depict the
Mesoamerican rain god (Luis Ferrero A.,
personal communication). Similar large eyes in
other painted designs, however, suggest that
this face may signify a feline (no. 95), an
interpretation supported by the whiskerlike
motif painted in red.
  Number 104, a large globular jar with an
annular base, has appliqué jaguars, but the
designs between them are difficult to interpret.
Composed of incised lines and fragmented
red–painted zones, they may represent a
plumed–serpent motif or an element associated
with a jaguar or stylized alligator. The dentate
black band around the middle of the jar recalls
a common alligator symbol.

106
Bowl, feline base
Ceramic; h. 13.5 cm, w. 10.5 cm
From Hacienda Tempisque, Guanacaste
Period VI, 1000–1550 A.D.
Collection Carmen de Gillen
A modeled jaguar is prominent in this late
Birmania Polychrome effigy vessel, in a stylized
but still naturalistic pose. The jaguar serves as
a base for a bowl, decorated in the style of the
plumed–serpent panels seen on number 105,
but here the panel incorporates unusual,
probably feline, motifs.

105
Death's head effigy vessel
Ceramic; h. 42 cm, w. 29 cm
From Hacienda Tempisque, Guanacaste ·
Late Period VI, c. 1200–1400 A.D.
Collection Carmen de Gillen
See pl. 20
This tripod effigy jar displays an especially
complex series of painted motifs. The modeled
figure seems to represent the Mesoamerican
ruler of the underworld and the dead.
The front legs are painted with silhouette
jaguar designs. On the unusual square collar
of the vessel, four panels are defined by
stepped frets, apparently showing different
manifestations of the plumed serpent and
sometimes incorporating elements of the
Mesoamerican wind god (Luis Ferrero A.,
personal communication). The panels around
the vessel body have similar, even more
elaborate, motifs.

107
Feline–effigy vessel
Ceramic; h. 34.5 cm, w. 25.5 cm
Guanacaste–Nicoya zone
Late Period VI, c. 1200–1400 A.D.
Instituto Nacional de Seguros 4036

108
Feline–effigy vessel
Ceramic; h. 32.5 cm, w. 24.5 cm
Guanacaste–Nicoya zone
Late Period VI, c. 1200–1400 A.D.
Instituto Nacional de Seguros 4039
See pl. 19

Jaguar-effigy jars have long been considered classic examples of Nicoya Polychrome. They belong to the Pataky Polychrome type, originally associated by Norweb (1964) with Rivas, Nicaragua. The realistic modeling of the feline head is combined with a humanlike pose of paws on legs. The hollow front legs often contain clay balls that make them into rattles. The supports and extremities of number 107 are covered with "silhouette–jaguar" motifs, which also occur in the first band of decoration under the lip; on number 108, they appear in red on the legs. Since the jaguar motif probably represents a sun–devouring Mesoamerican god, the smaller "silhouette–jaguars" have been thought to depict the stars revealed by approaching darkness (Luis Ferrero A., personal communication). These motifs, although rendered by positive painting in black, resemble resist-painted designs, in which the primary motif is formed through a batiklike process. On both vessels here, the wide panel around the jar neck seems to be composed of stylized plumed–serpent motifs, although jaguar elements are also present.

109
Zoomorphic–effigy vessel
Ceramic; h. 26.2 cm, w. 19.5 cm
Guanacaste–Nicoya zone
Late Period VI, c. 1200–1400 A.D.
Collection María Eugenia de Roy

This Pataky effigy vessel probably depicts a squirrel (family Sciuridae; Luis Diego Gómez Pignataro, personal communication). The plumed–serpent band is present around the vessel collar, but jaguar elements are absent; the black–line design on the body appears to be a continuation of the modeled features, perhaps a tail.

110
Celt
Stone; h. 18.8 cm, w. 6.3 cm
From San Vicente site, Guanacaste
Late Period VI, Bebedero phase, 1200–
  1550 A.D.
Museo Nacional de Costa Rica 191–1(15)

This elegant flared-end celt recalls similar objects made of metal (gold and copper) during this period. It was excavated by archaeologists of the MNCR from a funerary context containing the remains of at least three individuals. Other associated grave goods included vessels of Las Marías, Jicote, and Vallejo Polychromes, and Castillo Engraved, as well as other petaloid celts and a chipped–chert axe of similar shape.

111
Pedestal bowl
Ceramic; h. 20.8 cm, w. 21.8 cm
Guanacaste–Nicoya zone
Late Period VI, 1200–1550 A.D.
Instituto Nacional de Seguros 3999

112
Pedestal bowl
Ceramic; h. 18 cm, w. 20 cm
Guanacaste–Nicoya zone
Late Period VI, 1200–1550 A.D.
Museo Nacional de Costa Rica 15001
See pl. 44

The motif on these white-slipped vessels, formed by incision and gray, black, and orange paint, represents the insatiable "earth monster," supposedly a fantastic, clawed, toadlike creature, with mouth agape, complete with teeth. This Central Mexican deity, embodying the earth, received the human dead, as well as the heavenly bodies (gods) as they slipped daily below the horizon line into the nether world. The Costa Rican version of this motif appears more alligator– or dragonlike than the Mexican one; it is usually framed by what seem to be elaborate shields trimmed with feathers. There is little doubt, however, that the image derives from Mexican–highland mythology. Mexican iconography can be seen in many polychrome vessels from Guanacaste–Nicoya during Period VI.

113
Bridged double vessel
Ceramic; h. 18.2 cm, w. 26.7 cm
Guanacaste–Nicoya zone
Late Period VI, 1350–1550 A.D.
Museo Nacional de Costa Rica 15097

Lustrous black, gray, or red pottery like this double vessel of the Murillo Appliqué type may be that praised highly by the 16th–century historian Fernández de Oviedo: "They make very handsome earthenware . . . very well molded . . . with a glaze like that of highly polished jet . . . which, for their beauty, might be a gift for a prince. . . ." (Lothrop 1926: 40). Oviedo was describing pottery from the island of Chira, in the Gulf of Nicoya. Murillo has no obvious antecedents in Guanacaste–Nicoya. Current excavations by Winifred Creamer on Chira and nearby islands may assist in clarifying the Murillo enigma.

114
Bowl
Ceramic; h. 7.5 cm, w. 17.3 cm
Guanacaste–Nicoya zone
Late Period VI, c. 1350–1550
Collection Oduber
See pl. 22

115
Tripod bowl
Ceramic; h. 14.6 cm, w. 26.5 cm
Reportedly from Filadelfia vicinity, Guanacaste
Late Period VI, c. 1350–1550 A.D.
Collection Molinos de Costa Rica
See pl. 21

These two vessels belong to the type known as Luna Polychrome, which was recognized even by the earliest investigators (Lothrop 1926: 194) as coming from southwestern Nicaragua, perhaps from the Zapatero and Ometepe islands in Lake Nicaragua. Although not plentiful, it is found with some frequency in late Period VI contexts in Guanacaste–Nicoya, often associated with Murillo Appliqué.

The several varieties of Luna Polychrome decoration range from extremely stylized and subtle designs to very busy, *horror vacui* styles; this bowl and tripod tend toward the latter. The use of space in some Luna designs is remarkably similar to that found on painted pottery of

protohistoric and historic times from Marajó Island, at the mouth of the Amazon in Brazil. This may be coincidental, for the iconography of Luna motifs (plumed serpent, jaguar, monkey, human face) places the pottery squarely in the Greater Nicoya Polychrome tradition. "Lunoid" painted motifs derive from the esteemed Luna style, but true Luna is always distinguishable by its pearly cream slip and delicate, fine–line decoration. Luna has been found with Spanish artifacts in Nicaragua (Stone 1977: 82).

CENTRAL HIGHLANDS– ATLANTIC WATERSHED Nos. 116–229

116
Bowl
Ceramic; h. 17 cm, diam. 31 cm
Reportedly from Línea Vieja, Atlantic Watershed
Late Period IV, El Bosque phase, c. 1–
*   500 A.D.*
Museo Nacional de Costa Rica 21287
See pl. 24

117
Plate
Ceramic; h. 8.5 cm, diam. 27.3 cm
Atlantic Watershed zone
Late Period IV, El Bosque phase, c. 1–
*   500 A.D.*
Museo Nacional de Costa Rica 24482
See pl. 23

These two vessels are good examples of the clean–lined, functional forms that make up the El Bosque ceramic complex from the central Atlantic Watershed. The El Bosque Red on Buff type is characterized by a vibrant, well–burnished red ocher slip that usually covers all but the zone around the exterior collar; this is left the natural buff color of the clay, and plastic and/or painted decoration is applied. Technologically, El Bosque–phase pottery is among the best in Precolumbian Costa Rica. Huge quantities of it were manufactured, yet its quality seemingly did not degenerate over several centuries. This culture esteemed beautiful, functional pottery, unlike the peoples who inhabited the same zone 500 to 1000 years later, whose ceramics were shoddy and inferior.

Number 116 has stylized appliqué monkeys in the buff panel, with a single row of appliqué pellets below. Number 117 has a simple but striking motif that probably represents alligator jaws; it incorporates reed and roller dentate stamping.

118
Bowl
Ceramic; h. 9.5 cm, diam. 17.5 cm
From Severo Ledesma site, Guácimo, Atlantic Watershed
Late Period IV, El Bosque phase, c. 1–500 A.D.
Museo Nacional de Costa Rica 7–M.4–T.4 (79)

119
Jar
Ceramic; h. 11.5 cm, w. 15.2 cm
Atlantic Watershed zone
Late Period IV, El Bosque phase, c. 1–500 A.D.
Collection Molinos de Costa Rica
Number 118 was excavated by MNCR archaeologists in an El Bosque cemetery zone at Severo Ledesma, Guácimo, where El Bosque–phase rectangular houses were discovered. In a corridor–shaped tomb made of river cobbles, part of a mortuary complex containing 13 such tombs, this bowl was accompanied by three other red–on–buff bowls, an El Bosque Red jar, a plain stone pestle, and a tiny perforated fragment of jade. The vertical red lines of the bowl were made with a three–point multiple brush, and the appliqué and reed–stamped motif below represent stylized faces. Number 119, like number 116, has a band of appliqué pellets. In contemporary Guanacaste–Nicoya pottery, appliqué pellets frequently symbolize the alligator; in this case, dentate stamping on the buff collar strengthens the impression of alligator symbolism.

120
Pot stand
Ceramic; h. 17.5 cm, w. 18 cm
Atlantic Watershed zone
Late Period IV, 1–500 A.D.
Museo Nacional de Costa Rica 23125
See pl. 25

121
Pot stand
Ceramic; h. 26 cm, w. 25 cm
Atlantic Watershed zone
Late Period IV, 1–500 A.D.
Museo Nacional de Costa Rica 23124
Not illustrated

122
Pot stand
Ceramic; h. 19 cm, w. 14.5 cm
Atlantic Watershed zone
Late Period IV, 1–500 A.D.
Instituto Nacional de Seguros 3248
See pl. 26
These unusual objects—of the Molino Channeled ceramic type in the Central Highlands Pavas phase, or the El Bosque Orange-Purple group in the Atlantic Watershed El Bosque phase—appear to have functioned as separate pedestal bases for round–bottomed jars or similar vessels. As in much central and eastern Costa Rican sculpture of this period, avian effigies form the topmost band of modeled adornos, supported by alternating male and female Atlantean figures in number 120, and by toads, with exaggerated, dorsal, psychotropic–drug–producing glands, in number 121; small, lizardlike appliqué figures adorn the solid, channeled body of number 122. Almost certainly, the vertical ordering of these zoomorphic effigies had mythological significance, which is still unknown, however.

123
Jar
Ceramic; h. 11.4 cm, diam. 8 cm
Atlantic Watershed zone
Late Period IV, 1–500 A.D.
Instituto Nacional de Seguros 3991
Vessels slipped in orange and painted zonally in maroon are typical of both the El Bosque and Pavas phases, being rather more frequent in the Central Highlands in the latter phase. The channeling or fluting on this small jar is a decorative technique seen often in such pottery, as are the appliqué adornos in highly stylized zoomorphic forms.

124
Effigy–leg bowl
Ceramic; h. 17.5 cm, w. 24 cm
Atlantic Watershed zone
Late Period IV, 1–500 A.D.
Museo Nacional de Costa Rica 23374
The style of this effigy–tripod vessel is unlike typical El Bosque–phase pottery from the central Atlantic Watershed. It looks more like northern Atlantic–lowland styles, from the subregion known as San Carlos, east of Guanacaste. The zoomorphic figures modeled on the legs resemble manatees, the giant seallike mammals still occasionally sighted near the mouth of the San Juan river, the border between Costa Rica and Nicaragua.

125
Tripod vessel
Ceramic; h. 27.5 cm, diam. 34.5 cm
From Severo Ledesma site, Guácimo, Atlantic Watershed
Late Period IV, El Bosque phase, c. 1–500 A.D.
Museo Nacional de Costa Rica 7.1–T.B. (205)
A variety of modeled animal effigies adorn the supports of vessels in the Ticaban Tripod group; those on number 125 are felines, but alligators, monkeys, toads, turtles, owls, and other birds are also seen. Dentate stamping, probably done with the modified edge of a shell, occurs frequently around the collar or on the modeled zoomorphic adornos. Ticaban Tripods are often soot–covered, and the legs may have been made long so that the vessel could be placed over a fire.

This vessel was found as part of a mortuary offering in Tomb B within 7.1–M.1, a large (25 x 15 meters), rectangular, El Bosque–phase structure with internal walls. In the same tomb were two El Bosque Red on Buff bowls, both very large; a petaloid celt; and a rectangular metate, its tripod feet broken from the plate and placed in the opposite end of the tomb, some four meters away.

126
Ocarina
Ceramic; h. 9.5 cm, l. 9.5 cm
Reportedly from Guácimo, Atlantic Watershed
Late Period IV, 1–500 A.D.
Museo Nacional de Costa Rica 25459
See pl. 27

127
Ocarina
Ceramic; h. 8.7 cm, l. 16 cm
Reportedly from Guácimo, Atlantic Watershed
Late Period IV, 1–500 A.D.
Museo Nacional de Costa Rica 25419
See pl. 28

128
Two ocarinas
Ceramic; both h. 4.3 cm, w. 5.6 cm
Atlantic Watershed zone
Late Period IV, 1–500 A.D.
Instituto Nacional de Seguros 1084, 1085

129
Three ocarinas
Ceramic; h. 9.4 cm, w. 5.5 cm; h. 10 cm, w. 6.5 cm; h. 9 cm, w. 9.5 cm
Atlantic Watershed zone
Late Period IV, 1–500 A.D.
Instituto Nacional de Seguros 842, 843, 1170
Not illustrated

130
Flute
Ceramic; h. 14.5 cm, w. 4.5 cm
Atlantic Watershed zone
Late Period IV, 1–500 A.D.
Instituto Nacional de Seguros 570
Not illustrated

131
Two rattles
Ceramic; h. 7.2 cm, w. 4.8 cm; h. 7.2 cm, w. 5 cm
Atlantic Watershed zone
Late Period IV, 1–500 A.D.
Instituto Nacional de Seguros 561, 714
Not illustrated
Ocarinas like numbers 126–129 were made from a delicate biscuitlike ceramic, only 2–3 millimeters thick, which was molded into shape, then carefully smoothed on the outer surface. The mouthpiece and the size of the resonance chamber were modified to produce different tones. Such instruments, and figurines of the same ceramic group, are seen primarily in El Bosque–phase contexts, but they probably continued into the La Selva phase. Typically, these ocarinas are decorated with modeled adornos portraying costumed human beings. This suggests use in a ritual context. Their presence in high–status tombs corroborates such an interpretation; they were not made to pass an idle hour or as toys for children.

The first two examples have often–repeated shapes. In number 126, the figure (shown from the torso up, as is typical) wears a broad, flaring headdress, the original of which may have been made of hide or feathers. The black

spot is a firing cloud. In number 127, a similar figure, with hands clasped at his chest and headdress folded back in a streamlined fashion, perches on a long snout; its length is not acoustically necessary, and it may represent a symbolically important shape or an animal facsimile. The pair of tiny ocarinas (no. 128) shows a headdress thought to represent cotton armor. All ocarinas of this kind, known as the Santa Clara group, have a perforation that allows them to be hung around the neck. They are often painted in white, yellow, and black linear patterns.

132
Two nasal snuffers
Ceramic; h. 8 cm, w. 4.5 cm; h. 8.5 cm, w. 5 cm
Reportedly from Guácimo, Atlantic Watershed
Late Period IV, 1–500 A.D.
Museo Nacional de Costa Rica 25391, 25392
Among the figurines, rattles, stamps, and other small–scale ceramic artifacts of the El Bosque phase, double–tubed nasal snuffers sometimes appear. Single–stemmed pipes are also known, but the double variety is more common. It is a reasonable assumption that they were used to inhale substances like *Piptadenia* sp. or tobacco for their psychotropic effects; as such, they may have been part of the gear of a shaman or whoever employed such substances regularly. This pair is adorned with a vulturelike beak–bird, obviously a mythological creature, whose long, recurved beak had unknown significance. The snuffers have been ceremonially punctured, or "killed," probably for burial.

133
Roller stamp
Ceramic; h. 8 cm, w. 4 cm
Reportedly from Guanacaste–Nicoya
Late Period IV–early Period V, 1–700 A.D.
Collection María Eugenia de Roy

134
Flat stamp with feline motif
Ceramic; h. 7.1 cm, w. 8.1 cm
Atlantic Watershed zone
Late Period IV–early Period V, 1–700 A.D.
Collection Alfonso Jiménez–Alvarado
Both flat and roller stamps of clay, with a large variety of motifs, ranging from simple, geometric ones to realistic examples, were manufactured in some quantity during the first six or seven centuries after Christ in both

Guanacaste–Nicoya and the Atlantic Watershed, with most perhaps coming from the latter zone. It is assumed that they were used in body painting and textile decoration, but because of poor preservation of organic materials, there is no direct evidence for this. They were not used to stamp pottery.

135
Pestle
Volcanic stone; h. 22 cm, w. 11 cm
Atlantic Watershed zone
Late Period IV, 1–500 A.D.
Instituto Nacional de Seguros 3152
See pl. 61

136
Pestle
Volcanic stone; h. 17 cm, w. 9.5 cm
Atlantic Watershed zone
Late Period IV, 1–500 A.D.
Museo Nacional de Costa Rica 11745
See pl. 60
Pestles like these two examples have a thick, flared head to endure hammerlike blows and to provide a larger working surface. The elegantly stylized, usually zoomorphic, carvings of the butt end provide a firm grip. Together, these features convert a functional tool into a clean–lined, freestanding stone sculpture. Many such pestles have been found recently in Period IV, El Bosque–phase sites. They may have been used to crush palm nuts, although many broken examples are encrusted with red ocher, suggesting pigment preparation as an alternative use.

138
Zoomorphic–effigy mano
Volcanic stone; h. 12 cm, l. 23 cm
Atlantic Watershed zone
Late Period IV, 1–500 A.D.
Instituto Nacional de Seguros 4219
Many functional stone tools of the El Bosque phase in the central Atlantic Watershed assumed simple yet eloquent shapes, which have unquestionable sculptural strength. This quality is apparent in the preceding pestles and in the stirrup–shaped tool here (no. 137), which was grasped with both hands and used to crush some substance; a supine human form is incorporated into the upper part. Number 138 is also a kind of muller or rubber, but of a more delicate type; almost certainly, it was not employed in everyday grinding tasks. Surmounting the working surface is one of the enigmatic "curly–tailed animals" seen also in contemporary lapidary work.

137
Stirrup–shaped mano
Volcanic stone; h. 17 cm, l. 15.5 cm
Atlantic Watershed zone
Late Period IV, 1–500 A.D.
Instituto Nacional de Seguros 3879

139
Ceremonial mace head
Volcanic stone; h. 9 cm, l. 12 cm
Atlantic Watershed zone
Late Period IV, 1–500 A.D.
Instituto Nacional de Seguros 477

140
Mace or staff head
Volcanic stone; h. 8.3 cm, diam. 20.4 cm
Atlantic Watershed zone
Late Period IV, 1–500 A.D.
Instituto Nacional de Seguros 6129
These mace heads, like those associated with
the Guanacaste–Nicoya zone, have a large
vertical perforation and were probably mounted
on wooden staffs. Thought to have been
symbolic of power or rank, they were probably
not weapons, but may have symbolized weapons,
or domination in general. Number 139, carved
from porous volcanic stone, represents a
beak–bird, with the human head it customarily
holds in its beak. Although made of andesite,
the stone most often used for grinding tools,
number 140 is not a tool. It appears to have
been mounted on a staff as a kind of banner
stone of unknown symbolic significance. Its
large spokes would have made it impractical as
a weapon.

141
Axe
Stone; h. 13.5 cm, w. 11.1 cm
Probably Atlantic Watershed zone
Probably late Period IV, c. 1–500 A.D.
Instituto Nacional de Seguros 3875

142
Dagger
Stone; h. 24.5 cm, w. 9.2 cm
Atlantic Watershed zone
Late Period IV, 1–500 A.D.
Instituto Nacional de Seguros 3160
Functional objects like this polished axe
(no. 141) often have an appealing purity of
form. Some examples, like this one, show little
or no use. It was hafted at the unpolished,
squared-off end. Daggers (no. 142) made of
slate or fine basalt are typical El Bosque–phase
artifacts from the Atlantic Watershed. They
were chipped into the approximate shape
desired, then finished by grinding; the handles
were always roughened for better purchase.

143
Two bark beaters
Fine–grained granitic stone; l. 7.2 cm,
*   w. 6.3 cm; l. 6.5 cm, w. 5.5 cm*
Provenance unknown
Probably late Period IV, 1–500 A.D.
Museo Nacional de Costa Rica 8957, 9085
Made of fine-grained stone ground into an
oval plaque, then scored with deep incisions on
one face, these tools were probably used in a
pounding motion to flatten and soften tree
bark to make a kind of cloth. The large groove
around the edge served to bind the tools into
their probable hafting, a forked stick.

144
Flying–panel metate
Volcanic stone; h. 75.5 cm, w. 77 cm, l. 79 cm
Atlantic Watershed zone
Late Period IV, 1–500 A.D.
Museo Nacional de Costa Rica 25679
See pl. 29

145
Flying–panel metate
Volcanic stone; h. 56 cm, w. 52 cm, l. 77 cm
Reportedly from Azul de Turrialba, Atlantic
*   Watershed*
Late Period IV, 1–500 A.D.
Museo Nacional de Costa Rica 20788
The so–called flying–panel metates of late
Period IV are among the best examples of
stone carving in the Central Highlands–Atlantic
Watershed zone. A raised–rim metate plate,
usually in the shape of a rounded square, is
perched upon a veritable panoply of zoomorphic
deity images, whose relative vertical and
horizontal positions may sometimes symbolize
a cosmogeny. As has been mentioned, the
extraordinarily delicate openwork on these
large sculptures was accomplished with only
stone and organic tools, plus abrasive; the
whole was carved from one boulder of
andesitic rock, the tensile strength of which is
not great. Some flying–panel metates show
wear on the plate, others do not. They were
probably used to process special foodstuffs
and/or drugs in ritual contexts, and many may
have been made as mortuary furniture.

Number 144 shows the beak–bird seen on
contemporary jade pendants. Number 145
also incorporates the beak–bird as the central
motif, but anthropomorphized; it might be a
person wearing a bird mask. The figure stands
upon two recumbent humans, possibly
representing the sacrificial victims required by
the bird. Human trophy heads line the exterior
rim of the metate plate (in the other
flying–panel metates shown here, these are
stylized with simple notches). Attendant monkey
figures form the tripod legs.

146

Flying–panel metate
Volcanic stone; h. 46 cm, w. 80 cm, l. 82 cm
Reportedly from La Unión de Guápiles,
  Atlantic Watershed
Late Period IV, 1–500 A.D.
Caja Costarricense del Seguro Social, on loan
  to Museo Nacional de Costa Rica
  73.981
See pl. 51

147

Flying–panel metate
Volcanic stone; h. 70 cm, w. 85 cm, l. 77 cm
Reportedly from San Rafael de Coronado,
  Central Highlands
Late Period IV, 1–500 A.D.
Museo Nacional de Costa Rica 15150

Relatively realistic zoomorphic sculpture is
present in these two flying–panel metates. In
number 146, the central figure is a human,
apparently masked to portray an alligator; he
is perched on the back of a feline. Vulturelike
birds, holding human heads, hang from the
outside of the tripod legs, a combination seen
often in late Period IV symbolism, suggesting
carrion birds stooping over battlefield dead or
sacrificial victims.

Extremely complex imagery is found on
number 147. The central figure is a human
being masked as an alligator, but with a
serpentiform tongue issuing from his mouth;
tiny feline effigies hanging from the bottom of
the plate complete his headdress. He stands on
a bicephalic alligator. On the legs of the metate,
monkeys hold their upswept tails in a form
that recalls the beak–birds of number 144;
below the monkeys are felines with tails
curling over their backs, again reminiscent of
the beak–bird in profile; the felines hold a
human trophy head in their front paws.

148

Figure on columnar base
Volcanic stone; h. 148 cm, w. c. 34 cm
Atlantic Watershed zone
Probably late Period IV–early Period V,
  300–700 A.D.
Collection Mr. and Mrs. Harry Mannil

149

Figure on columnar base
Volcanic stone; h. 84 cm, w. 22 cm
Atlantic Watershed zone
Probably late Period IV–early Period V,
  300–700 A.D.
Instituto Nacional de Seguros 3932

This pair of unusual sculptures shows the same
scene: a human figure emerges from the top of
what seems to be a hollow tree trunk, while a
four–legged creature descends head first
down the trunk behind him. A simple scene
from nature would not likely elicit such effort in
stone carving, and the repetition of the scene
in two or more sculptures strongly suggests
that it is an allegorical or mythical composition,
as are most of the compositions on flying–panel
metates (nos. 144–147), which are
contemporary.

150
Avian axe pendant
Jade; h. 9.1 cm, w. 2.9 cm
Atlantic Watershed zone
Middle Period IV, c. 500–1 B.C.
Instituto Nacional de Seguros 2069
See pl. 66

Many Olmec–style (early Mesoamerican) jades have supposedly been found in Costa Rica—at least 20 or 30 are reported in the literature—although recovery by archaeologists in controlled excavations has been rare (Snarskis 1979a). Most of these pieces appear to have been reworked; they are found associated with objects several centuries later in date, which suggests that they were heirlooms. There is disagreement on the role of the Olmec jade–carving tradition vis-à-vis that of Costa Rica, some specialists seeing no connection (Pohorilenko 1981), others postulating stylistic and iconographic linkages (Easby 1968; Snarskis, in press).

Number 150 might, therefore, be described either as an Olmec piece (perhaps reworked) found in Costa Rica or as a very early Costa Rican avian axe pendant, one that shares stylistic traits with certain Olmec jades. These traits include the flared central crest, downturned beak (like that of the Olmec bird–monster), and the style of engraving on the head. A very similar piece was found in the Cerro de las Mesas jade cache, in Mexico (Drucker 1955: pl. 36f). Like this one, it has a second transverse perforation in a thickened area on the celt blade, but the Cerro de las Mesas blade continues below the perforation. Number 150 may have been smoothed at the base after a longer celt blade broke off. The opposing triangles, possibly an alligator motif, may have been added at that time. The multiple perforations in such pieces may have served for the stringing of two or more strands of beads. The engraving and the beak of the Cerro de las Mesas pendant are much like those on the example here, which is definitely not typical of Costa Rican axe–god pendants. The Cerro de las Mesas cache, although late Preclassic or early Classic, contained several artifacts that are typically Olmec. Drucker (1955: 60) called the pendant found there "unquestionably Olmec, although . . . probably a trade object. . . ."

151
Pendant
Jade; h. 8.9 cm, w. 2.2 cm
Reportedly from Línea Vieja, Atlantic Watershed
Late Period IV, c. 1–500 A.D.
Instituto Nacional de Seguros 5954

152
Pendant
Jade; h. 10.2 cm, w. 2.9 cm
Atlantic Watershed zone
Late Period IV, c. 1–500 A.D.
Instituto Nacional de Seguros 5979

These pendants are almost certainly reworked; their original form was probably close to that of number 150. The most striking thing about them is their use of an open circle as a design element, which is very rare in Costa Rican lapidary work. Number 151 is a double–aspect pendant. The engraved horizontal line and faint eye pits drilled below the circle form a stylized face with the circle as a plumed headdress; stubby legs and feet are seen at the bottom of the pendant. Seen another way, the open circle is the tail of a curly–tailed animal, whose eyes and head are formed by the perforation and engraved motifs at the narrow end of the piece. Number 152 has been carved so that the empty circle corresponds to the head of a person, with small birds perched above and arms bent below; this is a sophisticated and striking use of the empty circle. Yet this piece may also possibly signify a crab as a second image.

153
Pendant
Jade; h. 11 cm, w. 4.8 cm
Atlantic Watershed zone
Late Period IV, 1–500 A.D.
Instituto Nacional de Seguros 5982

154
Avian pendant
Jade; h. 8.2 cm, w. 3.5 cm
Atlantic Watershed zone
Late Period IV, 1–500 A.D.
Instituto Nacional de Seguros 1642
See pl. 69

155
Avian pendant
Jade; h. 3.6 cm, w. 2 cm
Atlantic Watershed zone
Late Period IV, 1–500 A.D.
Instituto Nacional de Seguros 1827
See pl. 67
Numbers 154 and 155, as purely avian
sculptures in the round, are unusual in the
Costa Rican lapidary corpus. Number 154
seems to have been carved with a keen sense of
appreciation for the natural contours and hues
of the material; it appears to be a toucan
(family Ramphastidae; Luis Diego Gómez
Pignataro, personal communication). Number
155 could be a kingfisher (family Alcedinidae),
like those that flash up and down the rushing
streams of the upper Atlantic Watershed.

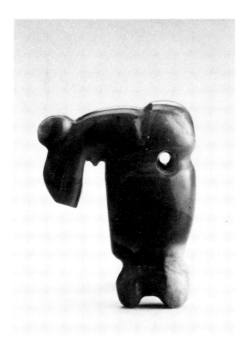

156
Avian pendant
Jade; h. 3.4 cm, w. 2.6 cm
From Severo Ledesma site, Guácimo, Atlantic
  Watershed
Late Period IV, El Bosque phase, 1–500 A.D.
Museo Nacional de Costa Rica 7.1–Pt.1–(4)
This tiny bird pendant was found by MNCR
archaeologists lying outside a river–cobble
tomb of the El Bosque phase. Other grave
goods included vessels of the El Bosque Red
on Buff group and a Ticaban Tripod. The
downturned beak and caruncle of the vulture
on this pendant have been emphasized to
accentuate its beak–bird aspect.

157
Two masked–figure pendants
Jade; h. 6.5 cm, w. 2.5 cm; h. 6.7 cm,
  w. 2.9 cm
Atlantic Watershed zone
Late Period IV, 1–500 A.D.
Instituto Nacional de Seguros 1922, 1923
See pl. 78
Perforated differently from most vertical
pendants—that is, obliquely from the back,
through what are the eyeholes of a large,
alligator headdress adorned with crouching
animals—this pair of jade sculptures depicts
human beings, costumed probably as alligators.
The grasping of ellipsoidal objects in both
hands is an interesting trait. The same pose is
known for cast–gold figures and for tiny
carved–stone figures (nos. 222, 223) that are
thought to be from Period VI. Archaeologists,
then, have a choice of placing these jade
figures late or the other figures early; lack of
contextual information prohibits a resolution
of this problem for the present.

158
Two alligator–effigy beads
Jade; h. 15 cm, w. 1.5 cm; h. 14.5 cm,
  w. 1.6 cm
Atlantic Watershed zone
Late Period IV, 1–500 A.D.
Instituto Nacional de Seguros 1928, 1929
See frontispiece
Human figures costumed as alligators/crocodiles
are important in Period IV symbolism
throughout Costa Rica. These two examples
are unusual in that they are tubular beads,
carved so as to hang vertically. The figures
wear truncated conical hats, one incised with
chevrons; the same headgear is seen on other
jade pendants in the form of monkeys. One of
these tubes has been perforated and
string–sawed through the jaws, perhaps for
hanging by a horizontal cord.

159
Two alligator pendants
Jade; h. 11.5 cm, w. 1.9 cm; h. 11.4 cm,
  w. 2.1 cm
Reportedly from Guápiles vicinity, Atlantic
  Watershed
Late Period IV, 1–500 A.D.
Instituto Nacional de Seguros 1916, 1917
See pl. 71
Alligator pendants were popular products of
Atlantic Watershed jade carvers. Some alligators
were carved on longitudinally perforated
tubes, while others, like this pair, were made to
hang vertically, with the snout uppermost.
These are quite realistic, except for a strangely
forked tail with two bands around it; there are
also bands around the neck, possibly indicative
of a tethered animal.

160
Anthropomorphic pendant
Slate; h. 16 cm, w. 5.1 cm
Reportedly from Guanacaste–Nicoya
Middle–late Period IV, c. 300 B.C.–
  500 A.D.
Instituto Nacional de Seguros 1799

161
Anthropomorphic/avian pendant
Jade; h. 9.5 cm, w. 4 cm
Reportedly from Línea Vieja, Atlantic Watershed
Middle–late Period IV, c. 300 B.C.–
    500 A.D.
Instituto Nacional de Seguros 5921

162
Anthropomorphic/avian pendant
Jade; h. 8.7 cm, w. 2.9 cm
Reportedly from Guanacaste–Nicoya
Middle–late Period IV, c. 300 B.C.–
    500 A.D.
Instituto Nacional de Seguros 5937

163
Anthropomorphic/avian pendant
Jade; h. 6 cm, w. 3.3 cm
Atlantic Watershed zone
Middle–late Period IV, c. 300 B.C.–
    500 A.D.
Instituto Nacional de Seguros 1745
Common in the Costa Rican lapidary corpus
(both in Guanacaste–Nicoya and the Atlantic
Watershed) are pendants portraying a human
figure arrayed as a bird, almost always a harpy
eagle (*Harpia harpyja*) (Fonseca and Scaglion
1978). The relative degree of "humanness" or
"birdness," however, is highly variable; some
pendants show an obviously masked human,
others are much more ambiguous, perhaps
purposefully. Such pendants probably depict
shamans, or chieftain–shamans, with high
political as well as religious status. The harpy
eagle may have been chosen as a symbol of
strength and nobility among birds; it is also
reclusive in nature, a dweller in the high forest
canopy, and a striking image when glimpsed,
with its facial disk (feathers which form circles
around the eyes) and two high tufts of feathers
like horns. On many pendants these tufted
projections are replaced by tiny images of
lesser birds, like kites and buzzards, bending
over the human ears of the masked figure
below. These birds are high–soaring species,
and it is possible that they were viewed as
emissaries, the all–seeing "eyes and ears" of
the shaman–eagle. This concept is more
clearly displayed in certain ceramic effigy
heads (no. 191).
    In this series of four pendants, human traits
gradually give way to avian ones. Number 160
is a resolutely human figure with a
suggestion of an eagle mask only above the

nose (there is a possible flattened facial disk
around the eyes, with tufts above). Numbers
161 and 162, while maintaining a string–sawed
separation of the legs and, in the former,
humanlike arms and hands, have full–face
masks that are more realistically avian; in each
case, tiny birds perch above the ears. Number
163 appears to be the reworked top half
of a larger pendant, with an added separation
of the stubby legs. The head seems to be
fully avian.

164
Two anthropomorphic/avian pendants
Jade; h. 7.1 cm, w. 2.4 cm; h. 6.9 cm,
    w. 2.9 cm
Atlantic Watershed zone
Late Period IV, 1–500 A.D.
Instituto Nacional de Seguros 1932, 1933
See pl. 70
This pair of pendants reiterates the bird/man
theme, depicting a quetzal in human posture,
or a costumed person. The carving shows
string–sawed details: grooves around beak and
forehead and between the legs. The eyes were
produced by a combination of large tubular
and small solid drills. The high–quality jade
bespeaks an early date.

165
Anthropomorphic pendant
Jade; h. 8.5 cm, w. 5.3 cm
Atlantic Watershed zone
Late Period IV, 1–500 A.D.
Instituto Nacional de Seguros 1924
See pl. 84

166
Anthropomorphic pendant
Jade; h. 2.5 cm, w. 2.4 cm
Reportedly from Línea Vieja, Atlantic Watershed
Late Period IV, 1–500 A.D.
Instituto Nacional de Seguros 5869
Pendants showing human figures in a relatively
realistic form are rare. Number 165 seems to
be holding two small birds over his ears, just
where they are seen on other anthropomorphic
pendants. This figure, wearing a kind of
girdle, is shown with an exaggerated navel, in

the form of a circular motif that is seen on other pendants. Its significance is unclear, but it is associated only with jades; hence, it must have been of politico–religious importance. The miniature figure (no. 166) strikes a similar pose, although without birds.

167
Pendant
Jade; h. 16.3 cm, w. 5.1 cm
Atlantic Watershed zone
Late Period IV, 1–500 A.D.
Instituto Nacional de Seguros 5978
See pl. 79
The simplicity and sculptural power of this pendant are quite impressive. The symbolism, however, is probably like that of number 165, in which a similar circular element represents an enlarged navel; perhaps the circle conveys a sense of focus or of "being at the center," arising from drug–induced trances.

168
Monkey–effigy pendant
Jade; h. 8.1 cm, w. 3.3 cm
Atlantic Watershed zone
Late Period IV, 1–500 A.D.
Instituto Nacional de Seguros 1705
See pl. 76

169
Monkey–effigy pendant
Jade; h. 5.4 cm, w. 3 cm
Reportedly from Línea Vieja, Atlantic Watershed
Late Period IV, 1–500 A.D.
Instituto Nacional de Seguros 5952
This pair of figurative pendants may represent monkeys with human postures and coiffure, or human beings costumed as monkeys. In

number 168, the carver may have originally had an avian pendant in mind; hence the hornlike elements on the head and the circles around the eyes. The snout and the elements on the side of the head, however, give a distinctly nonavian aspect. Number 169 is seated in a posture like that of a shaman, but facial features are monkeylike, in spite of the arranged coiffure.

170
Monkey pendant
Jade; h. 7.3 cm, w. 4 cm
Reportedly from Línea Vieja, Atlantic Watershed
Late Period IV, 1–500 A.D.
Instituto Nacional de Seguros 5953
Monkey figurines, whether in ceramic or stone, were usually shown in naturalistic postures. In number 170, a monkey with curling tail looks over his shoulder; fore and hind paws are posed as if grasping a tree trunk. The two perforations may have been made for different hanging positions, or to accommodate two strands of smaller beads passing through the pendant. Number 171, while suggesting a similar pose, has been anthropomorphized. Paws are held at the chest, and knees are drawn up in a direct, frontal posture that is characteristic of certain humanoid axe–god pendants. Nevertheless, its full–round carving style is the salient feature of this piece, setting it apart from the low–relief celt–form pendants.

171
Monkey pendant
Serpentine; h. 7 cm, w. 2.5 cm
Atlantic Watershed zone
Late Period IV, 1–500 A.D.
Museo Nacional de Costa Rica 8488

172
Avian pendant
Jade; h. 4.4 cm, w. 5.7 cm
Reportedly from Guanacaste–Nicoya
Late Period IV–Period V, c. 300–700 A.D.
Instituto Nacional de Seguros 5904
Very few avian pendants have outstretched wings. This piece may have been reworked from a larger horizontal bat pendant like numbers 36 and 37; the proportions of body and feet further support this interpretation.

Figures with staffs fit well into the symbolism of Period IV Costa Rica: ceremonial mace heads of jade and other materials, usually in avian forms, were important ritual articles, made to be placed on staffs. Jade figures like these, thought to come almost exclusively from the Atlantic Watershed, are characterized by many string–sawed details. Number 174 is typical; the staff is crowned with a beak–bird effigy. Number 175 has an especially complex design; the string sawing produced a lacy effect. The central human figure is almost lost in a welter of zoomorphic embellishments: his bicephalic headdress, hanging vertically down his back, seems to be composed of two alligator (or at least saurian) heads; the staff is crowned with a bird or alligator head, as well as an inverted human trophy head; another head is carved at the bottom of the staff; and the whole composition is perched on a running animal of indeterminate type.

173
Double–aspect pendant
Jade; h. 9.3 cm, w. 2.4 cm
Reportedly from Línea Vieja, Atlantic Watershed
Late Period IV–Period V, c. 300–700 A.D.
Instituto Nacional de Seguros 5917
The axe–god shape is discernible in this pendant, but it has been modified with a cut to form legs. The hands raised below the utterly blank face make a surrealistic impression. From the side, however, the piece becomes an alligator, with the perforation forming the eye.

174
Figure with ceremonial staff
Jade; h. 5.7 cm, w. 2.8 cm
Atlantic Watershed zone
Late Period IV–Period V, c. 300–700 A.D.
Instituto Nacional de Seguros 1708
See pl. 73
175
Figure with ceremonial staff
Jade; h. 5.8 cm, w. 2.6 cm
Reportedly from Línea Vieja, Atlantic Watershed
Late Period IV–Period V, c. 300–700 A.D.
Instituto Nacional de Seguros 5877
See pl. 74
Figures like these, holding a staff decorated with zoomorphic effigies, have long been described as "Tiahuanaco–like" (Balser 1974) because of their superficial similarity to panels of low–relief carving on the Gate of the Sun at Tiahuanaco in Bolivia. The connection is unlikely; the motifs are not really much alike, and the period of the "expansionist" Huari–Tiahuancoid culture occurred after the probable date of manufacture for these jades.

176
Pendant, figure with alligator mask
Jade; h. 7.4 cm, w. 3.8 cm
Reportedly from Línea Vieja, Atlantic Watershed
Late Period IV–Period V, c. 300–700 A.D.
Instituto Nacional de Seguros 5951
See pl. 72
A splendidly detailed carving, this pendant depicts a crouching (dancing?) man, costumed as an alligator/crocodile. His crested headdress is a tiny version of the same animal, and from his beak issues a long, curling tongue. This unnatural feature recalls the beak–birds, whose beaks are sometimes shown as curling. Whatever iconographic quality it implies, the curling tongue incidentally provides a perforation for suspending another object.

177
Anthropomorphic pendant with trophy heads
Jade; h. 11.6 cm, w. 5 cm
Reportedly from Hakiuv, Talamanca region
Late Period IV–early Period V, c. 300–
*   700 A.D.*
Instituto Nacional de Seguros 4507
See pl. 75

178
Anthropomorphic pendant
Jade; h. 9 cm, w. 5 cm
Atlantic Watershed zone
Late Period IV–early Period V, c. 300–
*   700 A.D.*
Instituto Nacional de Seguros 1930
Number 177, a splendidly carved jade, is a treasure trove of symbolism. It is one of the few jades that show a warrior or chieftain carrying trophy heads—here, he has one in each hand. This figure wears a waistband and what may be ligatures on his legs. String–sawed separations between arms and body are very clear, and the gap in his bow–legged stance was also produced by that technique. His allies in the animal world are depicted with a clarity rarely seen in Costa Rican jade carving: in addition to the ubiquitous birds over the ears, what appears to be a crab is perched at the crown of his conical hat. The significance of the crab is unknown, but it may not be accidental that it outlines a cross, a symbol of cosmographic importance in Period V. Two alligator heads are engraved on the feet of the figure, a position that probably reflects their level in the mythological universe vis–à–vis the other animals depicted. The figure's eyes are formed by incised scrolls (not unlike speech scrolls) instead of the usual drilled pits.

   Number 178 shows a more traditional treatment of the same theme, the shaman–warrior with emissary birds perched over his ears, but with considerable, delicately string–sawed detail. The beak–bird aspect of the avian allies is emphasized. These two pieces, while sharing a symbolic vocabulary, are of radically different styles, pointing up the probable existence of several jade–working centers in the Atlantic Watershed.

179
Monkey pendant
Jade; h. 3 cm, w. 7.3 cm
Atlantic Watershed zone
Late Period IV–Period V, c. 300–700 A.D.
Instituto Nacional de Seguros 2070
String sawing has produced an openwork plaque in which two monkeys are portrayed; if the plaque is placed horizontally, both are on their sides, with heads toward the ends. Each monkey holds his tail over his back; the tail is a long, curved element that ends, in each case, in a snake head. The monkeys' other forepaws are in their mouths. Identically posed monkey effigies form the tripod legs of certain flying–panel metates (nos. 145, 147), which were contemporary with this jade.

180
Pendant
Jade; h. 6.2 cm, w. 5.5 cm
Atlantic Watershed zone
Late Period IV–Period V, c. 300–700 A.D.
Instituto Nacional de Seguros 1938

181
Pendant
Jade; h. 7.4 cm, w. 3.8 cm
Reportedly from Guanacaste–Nicoya
Late Period IV–Period V, c. 300–700 A.D.
Instituto Nacional de Seguros 5924
See pl. 77
Another pendant that incorporates as a main motif a large perforation or low–relief circle, number 180 was probably reworked from a larger pendant that incorporated the circle, perforated or not (see no. 167). Number 180 looks like a vortex surrounded by stylized human trophy heads. A cartouche with a small circle within it was a Maya glyph for seed, while a small circle within a larger one was the Maya jade symbol, also associated with water. The sacrificial decapitation of prisoners (producing trophy heads) was related, directly or indirectly, to agricultural practices throughout Costa Rica.

In number 181, the large circle is the bottommost element in a tiered composition. Above it is what appears to be a two–headed snake, and above that is a rectangular area, engraved with interlocking ellipses; these are topped by two beak–birds in their standard position, as if the whole composition symbolized a standing figure. Again, the circle might be a jade or water symbol. The two–headed snake appears in late Period IV petroglyphs and ceramics (but also on Period VI southern gold work). The engraved linked element recalls the stylized alligator motifs of Carrillo Polychrome, although, in that case, they are at right angles; linked diagonally, as they are here (and on Galo Polychrome), the open spaces left by the links form a kind of Kan cross, a Maya symbol for yellow, blue–green, "precious," and water. The Kan cross appears extensively on Mora Polychrome (c. 800–1200 A.D.). Water symbolism, tied to agricultural fertility, seems to have been important to Costa Rican jade carvers.

182
Two tubular beads
Jade; l. 24.5 cm, w. 3 cm; l. 24.6 cm,
* w. 2.6 cm*
Atlantic Watershed zone
Late Period IV–Period V, c. 300–700 A.D.
Instituto Nacional de Seguros 6020, 6021
The incredible length of certain tubular beads found in Precolumbian Costa Rica has long astounded archaeologists. Lengths up to 50 centimeters are known; the biconical perforation of such objects (holes were drilled from both ends, meeting in the center) is, in itself, a formidable lapidary feat. It has been said (Balser 1974) that tubes in the 10–20–centimeter range might have been used as breast supports—the Spanish observed a similar use of gold tubes in certain Panamanian groups—but this seems unlikely. The larger tubes probably served as a horizontal bar in complex necklaces, while the smaller versions may have been hung either horizontally or vertically, as in the necklaces portrayed on freestanding stone sculptures of men wearing alligator masks and headdresses (nos. 196–198).

Tubular beads with bands, like this pair, are thought to have come into common use only in Late Classic times in Maya Mesoamerica (Proskouriakoff 1974: 55). Archaeologists of the MNCR excavated a smaller banded tube at the La Fábrica site, in the Central Highlands, among offerings in a burial that rested on three decorated metates, and was accompanied by polished black celts of a teardrop shape, a waisted axe of chipped stone, a ceremonial avimorph mace head, and other tubular beads of lesser stones, as well as a jadelike rectangular plaque.

183
Zoomorphic pendant
Gold; h. 4.8 cm, l. 8.5 cm
Reportedly from San Carlos, Atlantic Watershed
Early Period V, c. 500–800 A.D.
Banco Central de Costa Rica 28
This curly–tailed animal has a parrotlike head, but a quadruped body and a pose that is possibly feline. Atlantic Watershed jade carvers employed a similar motif at times, and a gold pendant not unlike number 183 was reportedly found with jade and early Period V pottery in the Atlantic Lowlands (Stone and Balser 1965), one of the few times that jade and gold pendants have been found associated. Metallurgy arrived in Costa Rica as the centers of lapidary production were disappearing, c. 500–700 A.D.; the style of this piece recalls the style of the Quimbaya region of Colombia, where lustrous, full volumes characterize most gold work.

184
Double avian pendant
Gold; h. 1.5 cm, w. 2.3 cm
Atlantic Watershed zone
Late Period V–Period VI, c. 800–1550 A.D.
Museo Nacional de Costa Rica 22929

185
Double avian pendant
Gold; h. 1.3 cm, w. 2 cm
Atlantic Watershed zone
Late Period V–Period VI, c. 800–1550 A.D.
Museo Nacional de Costa Rica 22933

186
Triple avian pendant
Gold; h. 1.7 cm, w. 3.7 cm
Reportedly from Aguacaliente de Cartago
*   vicinity, Central Highlands*
Late Period V–Period VI, c. 800–1550 A.D.
Museo Nacional de Costa Rica 28
Tiny "eagle" pendants are usually made of
pure, heavy gold, and are relatively simple in
form. They are found almost exclusively in the
Central Highlands–Atlantic Watershed, and
were probably manufactured there, using
uncomplicated casting and joining techniques.
A single *aguililla* ("little eagle") was found
beneath the largest quadrangular structure at
Barrial de Heredia by MNCR archaeologists. It
was unaccompanied, but other tombs or

caches beneath the same mound yielded many
polychrome vessels traded in from
Guanacaste–Nicoya, as well as local ceramics
(Snarskis and Blanco 1978).

187
Tripod vessel
Ceramic; h. 26.1 cm, w. 22.1 cm
Atlantic Watershed zone
Late Period IV–early Period V, c. 300–
*   700 A.D.*
Instituto Nacional de Seguros 2613
See pl. 34
Although graceful Africa Tripods like this one
succeeded the Ticaban group of the El Bosque
phase, they overlapped in time, and spatial (or
functional) variables may have been significant,
too. One group of potters may have made
these delicate, hollow–legged forms, while
another manufactured the more stolid Ticaban
variety; this is a question still to be determined
by stratigraphic excavations.

The small, flared–mouth cup of this tripod
vessel is supported by long, curved legs
bearing men in alligator array, with the
elongated snout and crested head so typical of
that animal in Costa Rican iconography.

188
Human–head–effigy vessel
Ceramic; h. 8.8 cm, w. 7.3 cm.
Atlantic Watershed zone
Probably Period V, 500–1000 A.D.
Collection Alfonso Jiménez–Alvarado

189
Human–head–effigy vessel
Ceramic; h. 4.8 cm, w. 5.5 cm
Atlantic Watershed zone
Probably Period V, 500–1000 A.D.
Museo Nacional de Costa Rica 24198
190
Trophy head
Ceramic; h. 9.3 cm, w. 10.7 cm
Atlantic Watershed zone
Probably Period V, 500–1000 A.D.
Instituto Nacional de Seguros 2997
See pl. 32
From the first few centuries after Christ until
the Spanish arrival, the taking of trophy heads
during warfare and the sacrificial beheading of
captives seem to have been of considerable
ritual importance. These three ceramic objects
appear to be representations (perhaps to scale)
of shrunken trophy heads; one may be mounted
on a pole (no. 188). The style of the first two
heads is unusual, almost Colombian; facial
scarification or painting is visible, and the
mouths are stretched open in unnatural
expressions. The third example (no. 190) is
made in a style typical of the Atlantic Watershed
during Period V; it apparently depicts a
trophy head with eyes sewn shut.

191
Anthropomorphic effigy vessel
Ceramic; h. 10 cm, w. 9.5 cm
From site 18–LM, Turrialba, Atlantic
*   Watershed*
Late Period IV–early Period V, c. 400–
*   700 A.D.*
Museo Nacional de Costa Rica 18–5(22)
See pl. 33
This head, which was found with a smaller,
similar effigy without embellishments, would
appear to be a portrait, not a shrunken trophy
head. The expression is alive, and the small
birds perched over the ears and the eyes
probably signify the far–reaching eyes and

ears of a shamanistic personality (i.e., bird emissaries), as described for historic Costa Rican Indians by María Eugenia Bozzolli (personal communication, 1975). Archaeologists of the MNCR excavated this vessel from a La Selva–phase cemetery at the La Montaña site near Turrialba. Other grave goods in the cemetery included ceramics of the types known as Roxana Shiny Maroon on Orange, Zoila Red, La Selva Brown, Africa Tripod, and La Selva Sandy Appliqué (Snarskis 1978).

192
Resist–painted urn
Ceramic; h. 25.3 cm, w. 26 cm
Atlantic Watershed zone
Period V, 500–1000 A.D.
Instituto Nacional de Seguros 3974
During Period V in the Central Highlands–Atlantic Watershed zone, important changes occurred in all aspects of culture, indicating a burgeoning "southern" (Colombian–Panamanian) influence. Among the changes was an increased emphasis on resist, or negative–painted, decoration for pottery. During late Period IV (1–500 A.D.), this technique was known most frequently from the Pacific coasts of Peru, Ecuador, and Colombia, with a subsequent broad distribution throughout Central America and western Mesoamerica.

The modified cylinder shape of this urn probably appeared in mid–Period V, but is most characteristic of Period VI, when it occurs in many ceramic types; the openwork annular base is known only from the earliest versions. The motif of both the modeled appliqué figures and the resist decoration is the alligator/crocodile, an important southern motif and one that predominates in the resist–decorated pottery known from Costa Rica.

193
Warrior with trophy head
Volcanic stone; h. 158 cm, w. 77 cm
Reportedly from Azul de Turrialba, Atlantic
  Watershed
Late Period V, c. 700–1000 A.D.
Collection Maritza Castro de Laurencich
The largest stone figures from central and eastern Costa Rica are warriors, usually brandishing an axe and carrying a shrunken trophy head. Because a few figures include details of physical deformities, they have been thought to represent specific individuals. They are known to come from only the largest of late Period V and Period VI sites—Las Mercedes, Guayabo, Anita Grande, and, in this case, Azul. Hartman (1901) encountered the remains of a stonemason's precinct at Las Mercedes; he also discovered the foot of one such large sculpture broken off and still in its mounting to one side of a staircase on the major mound of the site. These larges sculptures were apparently placed around plazas and principal mounds (residences) that defined the "ceremonial" sector of important sites characterized by earth–filled, cobble–faced architecture.

This sculpture is exceptional in its size and detail. The pointed, furrowed coiffure is rare, but the trophy head tied to an arm and the displayed axe are typical. Recently, archaeologists of the MNCR excavated (at Barrial de Heredia) a meter–long metate, upon which were placed five chipped–stone axes, one of which was identical in shape to that shown in this sculpture. Two of the original axe–handles were also preserved, the first such discovery in Costa Rica. The handles were made from human femurs. Other tokens of vanquished enemies adorn this sculpture; facsimiles of human heads appear at elbows, waist, and knees. The relief observed on arms, torso, and legs probably represents tattooing, but it is remarkably like certain images of the Mesoamerican deity Xipe Totec, who dressed in the flayed skins of his human victims.

194
Standing figure
Volcanic stone; h. 56 cm, w. 26.3 cm
Reportedly from Azul de Turrialba, Atlantic
  Watershed
Late Period V, c. 700–1000 A.D.
Collection Alfonso Jiménez–Alvarado
See pl. 62
As sculptures of warriors, armed with axes and carrying human trophy heads, began to be produced in late Period V, prisoner effigies also appeared. It is not certain that this figure represents a prisoner, yet it shows traits often associated with that class of sculpture. It carries no weapon or ritual object; it is apparently without clothing or other distinctive corporeal embellishment; its posture does not suggest participation in a definite activity, nor is it a recognizable "standard" pose. The figure seems to be "awaiting its fate," in an exceptionally eloquent attitude.

195
Figure with trophy head
Volcanic stone; h. 42.8 cm, w. 22.5 cm
Atlantic Watershed zone
Late Period V, c. 700–1000 A.D.
Collection Alfonso Jiménez–Alvarado
In a rare pose, this male figure displays a
shrunken trophy head, held in front of him
with both hands. He probably represents a
warrior, although he is not carrying an axe.
Such conical hairdos are seen on the earliest
examples of this kind of statuary.

196
Masked figure
Volcanic stone; h. 26 cm, w. 15.4 cm
Atlantic Watershed zone
Probably Period V–Period VI, c. 700–
*   1100 A.D.*
Collection Alfonso Jiménez–Alvarado

197
Masked figure
Volcanic stone; h. 28.1 cm, w. 14.5 cm
Atlantic Watershed zone
Probably Period V–Period VI, c. 700–
*   1100 A.D.*
Collection Alfonso Jiménez–Alvarado

198
Masked figure
Volcanic stone; h. 37 cm, w. 21 cm
Atlantic Watershed zone
Probably Period V–Period VI, c. 700–
*   1100 A.D.*
Instituto Nacional de Seguros 6399

These male figures are good examples of the
"standardized" poses that characterized
freestanding stone sculpture in central and
eastern Costa Rica during the last six or seven
centuries before the Spanish arrival. All wear
fantastic alligator masks, with crests above the
snout. The two– or even three–tiered
"wedding–cake" headdresses are also a
consistent feature. Their morphology recalls
the hourglass–shaped stone seats from
Guanacaste–Nicoya that are carved with very
similar alligator masks (nos. 99–100); the seats
may have assumed their shape to incorporate
the proper headdress style.

   The attitude of these standing figures is
always the same, with arms akimbo and hands
on hips or chest, as if in a ritualized
"presentation" posture. Invariably present is a
necklace, composed of a long horizontal bar
with hanging vertical elements, or sometimes
only the latter. These may represent the jade
tubes found in this part of Costa Rica, but in
general style, the figures seem to postdate
the period of intense lapidary work. There may
have been an overlap, however, for such figures
have not been recovered by archaeologists in
context, and their dating is, therefore,
ambiguous.

199

Ceremonial metate
Volcanic stone; h. 40 cm, diam. 75 cm
From Guayabo de Turrialba, Atlantic Watershed
Early Period VI, probably La Cabaña A phase,
  c. 1000 A.D.
Museo Nacional de Costa Rica 108
See pl. 53

This exquisitely proportioned stone piece
displays free–hanging feline motifs combined
with an interlocking geometric pattern around
the edge of a circular metate. The graceful
cut–out pedestal base forms one piece with the
metate plate, a tour de force in stone sculpture,
especially since it was accomplished with stone
and wooden tools. This piece and the decorated
slab monolith (no. 202), both found at Guayabo
de Turrialba early in this century, indicate the
importance of that site.

Like the flying–panel metates of earlier
cultures in central and eastern Costa Rica, this
potentially functional, yet obviously ceremonial
artifact, was probaby used only in very special
circumstances for preparation of a ritual
foodstuff or drug, or it may have been
manufactured only for interment and "use" in
the afterlife, since it shows no obvious wear.
Although its circular–pedestal–base form is
echoed in many other smaller pieces in both
the Central Highlands–Atlantic Watershed
region and the Pacific Southwest during this
period, none approaches it in size, state of
preservation, or aesthetic excellence.

200

Ceremonial metate
Volcanic stone; h. 31 cm, diam. 51 cm
From Guayabo de Turrialba, Atlantic
  Watershed
Early Period VI, La Cabaña A phase,
  c. 1000 A.D.
Museo Nacional de Costa Rica 6384

Like number 199, this smaller piece has realistic
feline heads hanging from the exterior of the
plate. Two look outward, not down, and
resemble human faces masked as felines.
Pieces like this and number 199 were

undoubtedly important ceremonial objects.
The presence of feline figures on each may be
significant, for the jaguar clan was one of
only two (the other being the monkey clan)
from which *caciques*, or chiefs, could be chosen
as late as the 19th century in the Talamanca
region of the Atlantic Watershed. A C–14 date
from a cache containing a wooden metate of
similar style found at Retes, Cartago, was
c. 960 A.D. (Stone 1977: 210).

201

Ceremonial metate
Volcanic stone; h. 27 cm, diam. 41 cm
Atlantic Watershed zone
Early Period VI, c. 1000 A.D.
Museo Nacional de Costa Rica 20446

The grace and proportions of this metate
make it one of the finer stone sculptures of its
kind. Atlantean monkey figures support a
circular metate plate decorated with a guilloche
pattern along the edge. Atlantean motifs are
found with some frequency in Periods V and
VI, in both the Central Highlands–Atlantic
Watershed and the Diquís region.

202

Decorated monolith
Volcanic stone; h. 184 cm, w. 63 cm
From Guayabo de Turrialba, Atlantic Watershed
Early Period VI, La Cabaña A phase,
  c. 1000 A.D.
Museo Nacional de Costa Rica 104

This heavy stone slab, decorated around
three–quarters of its border with both
freestanding and high–relief zoomorphic
effigies (feline and avian), was probably made
specifically for a mortuary context. Although
not recovered by archaeologists, its provenance
is reasonably secure; it was reportedly
found within a large stone–cist tomb, at what is
now the national park of Guayabo de Turrialba,
by Anastasio Alfaro during the first part of
this century. Since it is of human dimensions,
the monolith may have served as a funeral bier
for display of a mummified deceased personage,
as described by Christopher Columbus for a
locality near what is now Limón, Costa

Rica. This and similar monoliths, however, have a plain, tablike base, implying their eventual vertical placement, reportedly the position in which this was found. In historical, and even modern, times, the indigenous population of Costa Rica has been organized into matrilineal clans, and, in the absence of contradictory evidence, the zoomorphic effigies can be interpreted as clan symbols, or, alternatively, as individual "alter–egos." Monoliths were probably more frequently made of wood, no longer preserved; stone ones are extremely rare.

203
Effigy basin
Volcanic stone; w. 55 cm, l. 115 cm
Atlantic Watershed zone
Early Period VI, c. 1000–1200 A.D.
Collection Mr. and Mrs. Harry Mannil
Among the stone sculptures of Period VI are a few striking objects like this one. The reclining figure, incorporating a basin in its torso, recalls the so–called chacmool figures of Mexico's Toltec culture. The temporal correspondence is right, but little else in Atlantic cultures at this time suggests a strong Mesoamerican influence. Yet we know there was contact with the north, at least through Guanacaste–Nicoya, and it is certain that Aztec merchants were in the Atlantic Watershed when the Spanish arrived, so the possibility of a sculptural trait acquired from Mexico cannot be discarded. The figure itself is radically different from Toltec versions. This appears to be an ape–monster, but might be construed as a human with an ape–feline mask. Such objects have never been found in archaeological context.

204
Bound prisoner
Stone; h. 98 cm, w. 45 cm
Reportedly from Línea Vieja, Atlantic Watershed
Early Period VI, c. 1000 A.D.
Collection Alfonso Jiménez–Alvarado
See pl. 63
Obviously a prisoner, this figure, like number 194, has an accentuated rib cage, a detail seen more often on prisoners or seated figures than on warriors. Here, the elaborate coiffure and waist bindings suggest a captured warrior.

205
Warrior with trophy head
Volcanic stone; h. 61 cm, w. 38 cm
Atlantic Watershed zone
Early Period VI, c. 1000–1200 A.D.
Museo Nacional de Costa Rica 11697
See pl. 46
This figure, the MNCR logo, displays a pose often seen in the stone sculpture of the Atlantic Watershed during the last five or six centuries before the Spanish arrival: the warrior, with double–bitted axe in one raised arm, cradles a shrunken trophy head in the other. What may be bark or cloth armor is depicted wound about the waist; it is unclear if this material is also shown on the head, or if the segmented arrangement is a careful hairdo. Most examples of this kind of figure, including this one, have a stiff, formalized feeling; they are stereotyped warriors rather than portraits of specific individuals. Similar "standard" poses are also the rule for females (holding breasts), and probably shaman figures (seated with hands on knees). Although some figures are more naturalistic, and many must have portrayed actual personages, it is evident that certain role images were strictly perceived after 1000 A.D. in eastern Costa Rica.

206
Warrior with trophy head
Volcanic stone; h. 52.5 cm, w. 25 cm
Atlantic Watershed zone
Early Period VI, c. 1000–1200 A.D.
Museo Nacional de Costa Rica 14832
This warrior sculpture strikes a symmetrical pose, with axe laid on his left shoulder (its handle has been striated for a better grip), and a trophy head hanging from a rope that goes over the right shoulder. The diamond–pattern coiffure is a common alligator (and sometimes jaguar) symbol.

207
Tripod bowl
Ceramic; h. 11.5 cm, w. 25 cm
Atlantic Watershed zone
Period VI, c. 1000–1200 A.D.
Banco Nacional de Costa Rica 1582
Lothrop (1926: 226, 335) called pottery like this "Chocolate Ware," noting its occurrence in both Guanacaste–Nicoya and the Central Highlands–Atlantic Watershed. Since he lacked stratigraphic data, Lothrop's "Chocolate Ware" included several different brown–slipped ceramic types spanning a thousand years. Archaeologists now call this type Tayutic Incised. Its panels of geometric, incised motifs sometimes recall Mora Polychrome designs. Effigy supports are common; here, the seated human figure superficially resembles certain stone effigies of shamans.

208
Tripod urn
Ceramic; h. 29.7 cm, w. 25.8 cm
Reportedly from Línea Vieja, Atlantic Watershed
Period VI, 1000–1550 A.D.
Collection Molinos de Costa Rica

A diagnostic form for Period VI, these tripod urns appear in several ceramic types and many sizes. Their precise function is unknown, but they are found as grave goods in high–status burials. The form here is a typical large, modified cylindrical vessel with modeled, appliqué, human–trophy–head and zoomorphic–effigy–head supports; the latter are probably felines, but possibly coyotes or even alligators. Large urns like this, usually painted with white bands, were found in a series of tiny tombs or caches along a raised enclosure surrounding the main plaza at the La Cabaña site, Guácimo (Snarskis 1978: 248–249, figs. 181–183; Snarskis and Herra 1980).

209
Tripod urn containing other vessels
Ceramic; h. 17.5 cm, w. 18 cm
From La Zoila, Turrialba, Atlantic Watershed
Period VI, 1000–1550 A.D.
Museo Nacional de Costa Rica 5–T.21(1)–(5)
See pl. 45
This urn was found by MNCR archaeologists in a large stone–cist tomb, capped with flagstones, at the La Zoila site near Turrialba. Four other vessels had been placed inside it, and two small stone celts lay below. Adjoining tombs lacked flagstone lids and contained only a few soot–caked culinary pots. Skeletons, which could have told more about the owners of the large urns, were unfortunately not preserved.

210
Human–effigy vessel
Ceramic; h. 34.5 cm, w. 25 cm
Central Highlands–Atlantic Watershed zone
Period VI, 1000–1550 A.D.
Museo Nacional de Costa Rica 20611
See pl. 35
This vessel is one of the few large figurative ceramic sculptures known for Period VI, for stone figures took precedence. As is often the case with ceramic sculptures, it portrays an anomalous subject, here an obese male. His haughty bearing and elaborate coiffure, however, suggest a person of importance. He is seated on a round stool identical to pedestal–base pottery stands seen frequently in this period, apparently used as bases for separate round–bottomed jars.

211
Jaguar head
Volcanic stone; h. 19 cm, w. 25.7 cm
Atlantic Watershed zone
Period VI, c. 1000–1300 A.D.
Collection Alfonso Jiménez–Alvarado
See pl. 59
Zoomorphic heads, as individual pieces, are quite rare; they usually appear incorporated in metates or other larger carvings. Note the N–shaped incisors, whiskers, and diamond pattern, which probably represents the feline's spots.

213
Head
Volcanic stone; h. 15.3 cm, w. 14.8 cm
Atlantic Watershed zone
Period VI, 1000–1550 A.D.
Collection Alfonso Jiménez–Alvarado

212
Trophy head
Volcanic stone; h. 13.8 cm, w. 13.4 cm
Atlantic Watershed zone
Period VI, c. 1000–1300 A.D.
Collection Alfonso Jiménez–Alvarado
Freestanding heads represent some of the best stone carving in Period VI. This one is a trophy head, bound with rope, perhaps for carrying, as is seen on certain large warrior sculptures.

214
Head
Volcanic stone; h. 15.3 cm, w. 17 cm
Atlantic Watershed zone
Period VI, 1000–1550 A.D.
Collection Alfonso Jiménez–Alvarado
215
Head
Volcanic stone; h. 12.2 cm, w. 10.6 cm
Atlantic Watershed zone
Period VI, 1000–1550 A.D.
Collection Alfonso Jiménez–Alvarado
See pl. 58

216
Head
Volcanic stone; h. 15 cm, w. 13 cm
Atlantic Watershed zone
Period VI, 1000–1550 A.D.
Museo Nacional de Costa Rica 7701
See pl. 57
Some freestanding stone heads (no. 215) may be stone versions of the shrunken trophy heads realized more vividly in slightly earlier pottery (nos. 188–190), yet most have a dignity or alertness of expression that suggests living models, or at least a favorable, perhaps respectful, attitude on the part of the sculptor. The sculptures may be portrait heads of specific individuals. Note the differences in the carefully prepared coiffures.

217
Sukia figure
Volcanic stone; h. 26 cm, w. 12.5 cm
Atlantic Watershed zone
Period VI, 1000–1550 A.D.
Museo Nacional de Costa Rica 11689
Hunkered figures, known in Costa Rica as *sukias*, have been described as shamans playing a flute, smoking, or blowing and sucking through a tube. All of these activities were carried out by shamans in Precolumbian Central America, but the latter two probably best describe what these seated figures are doing, perhaps as part of a curing ritual (Ferrero 1977a: 201). This class of sculpture is perhaps the most frequently encountered type in Period VI central and eastern Costa Rica; MNCR archaeologists recently excavated an example from a stone–cist cemetery near Cartago. Although size may vary, the pose is virtually identical in hundreds, even thousands,

of examples, giving a sense of mass production. One might speculate that such sculpture was kept in indigenous domiciles for much the same reasons that a crucifix is hung on the walls of many modern Costa Rican homes.

218
Seated figure
Volcanic stone, h. 25.7 cm, w. 14.4 cm
Atlantic Watershed zone
Period VI, 1000–1550 A.D.
Instituto Nacional de Seguros 3251
219
Seated figure
Volcanic stone; h. 29.5 cm, w. 17.5 cm
Atlantic Watershed zone
Period VI, 1000–1550 A.D.
Banco Nacional de Costa Rica 971
See pl. 54
While displaying a repeated, standardized pose, this class of Period VI stone sculpture usually has more "humanity"—individualization or facial expressions that change from figure to figure—than the more generalized *sukia* (shaman) and warrior sculptures. The head slightly to one side and the gaze seemingly turned inward suggest an abstracted or trancelike state. The figures are probably shown during a drug–induced vision or introspection, and may represent shamans.

220
Female figure
Volcanic stone; h. 49 cm, w. 25.5 cm
Atlantic Watershed zone
Period VI, 1000–1550 A.D.
Banco Nacional de Costa Rica 979
See pl. 56
221
Female figure
Volcanic stone; h. 47 cm, w. 24.7 cm
Atlantic Watershed zone
Period VI, 1000–1550 A.D.
Banco Nacional de Costa Rica 974
See pl. 55
Female figures were apparently manufactured in some quantity during Period VI in the Central Highlands–Atlantic Watershed zone, although none (except those found in the Retes cache) has been recovered by archaeologists in controlled excavations. The static quality of these figures is also seen in the poses of contemporary freestanding statuary—seated shamans and warriors holding trophy heads and axes. All these poses seem stereotypic, as if role models or ritual behavior were strictly defined. The breast–holding posture may have conveyed the idea of fertility. Brief girdles and plastered–down coiffures are portrayed. Number 221 shows scarification.

222
Female figure holding objects
Volcanic stone; h. 11 cm, w. 5.5 cm
Atlantic Watershed zone
Period VI, 1000–1550 A.D.
Banco Nacional de Costa Rica 964

223
Figure holding objects
Volcanic stone; h. 12.6 cm, w. 6 cm
Atlantic Watershed zone
Period VI, 1000–1550 A.D.
Collection Alfonso Jiménez–Alvarado
Tiny human figures are shown grasping a
cylindrical or barbell–shaped object in each
hand. These objects have been called rattles
(Stone 1977: 200, 203); some contemporary
cast–gold figures have a similar pose, with
more realistically rendered maracas. Yet, on
some stone examples, the hand–held objects
have a slight relief, suggesting birds or perhaps
a fruit or tuber. The pose is repeated over and
over, as if part of a ritual. It is significant that
both males and females are portrayed in this
pose.

224
Figure with hands on chest
Volcanic stone; h. 18 cm, w. 8.5 cm
Atlantic Watershed zone
Period VI, 1000–1550 A.D.
Collection Alfonso Jiménez–Alvarado
Similar in style and proportions to the preceding
figures, this one seems to be in the often–seen
female pose of hands on breasts, although
neither breasts nor genitals are shown; perhaps
the posture was sufficient to characterize the
sculpture as female. Other small, carefully
worked figures show women braiding their
hair. The stylistic similarity of stone miniatures
like these suggests a single center of
manufacture.

225
Pedestal bowl
Volcanic stone; h. 10 cm, w. 14 cm
Atlantic Watershed zone
Period VI, 1000–1550 A.D.
Banco Nacional de Costa Rica 902
See pl. 31

226
Pedestal bowl
Volcanic stone; h. 11 cm, w. 21 cm
Atlantic Watershed zone
Period VI, 1000–1550 A.D.
Banco Nacional de Costa Rica 907

227
Pedestal bowl
Volcanic stone; h. 11.3 cm, w. 22 cm
Atlantic Watershed zone
Period VI, 1000–1550 A.D.
Collection Alfonso Jiménez–Alvarado
In all three of these delicately carved pedestal
bowls, Atlantean figures—monkeys in one
case, felines and men in the others—support a
shallow vessel. These are obviously special–
purpose or ceremonial vessels, too fragile for
ordinary use; they probably held potions,
foodstuffs, or drugs. The zoomorphic effigies
were most likely clan symbols.

228
Zoomorphic–effigy bowl
Volcanic stone; h. 9 cm, l. 27 cm
Atlantic Watershed zone
Period VI, 1000–1550 A.D.
Museo Nacional de Costa Rica 14934
See pl. 30

229
Jaguar metate
Volcanic stone; h. 19.5 cm, w. 25 cm, l. 56 cm
Reportedly from Finca La Colombiana, Línea
* Vieja, Atlantic Watershed*
Period VI, 1000–1550 A.D.
Banco Nacional de Costa Rica 909
See pl. 52

In these two objects, function almost becomes
secondary to form. Number 228 might be
from the same hand that produced the tiny,
finely finished human figures of this period
(nos. 222–224). Its animated sculptural line,
almost modern in its dynamism, is unlike that
of most other contemporary stone carving.
The animal that forms the bowl, supported by
felines, may be a turtle.

The jaguar–effigy metate, number 229,
shows an exceptional amount of sculptural
and incised detail; monkeys perch between the
legs, and a head appears at the end of the
jaguar tail, probably a reminder of the user's
power. Although this and others like it show
grinding use, this style of metate is the most
likely to have doubled as a seat.

231
Ocarina, seated figure
Ceramic; h. 21.2 cm, w. 8.5 cm
Reportedly from Carbonera vicinity, Osa
* Peninsula, Diquís*
Middle Period IV, c. 200–100 B.C.(?)
Collection Oduber
See pl. 38

Supposedly found in an isolated part of the
sparsely inhabited Osa Peninsula in Diquís,
these two effigy ocarinas (a few others are also
known) represent a style unique to that zone.
Their zoned–incised red–on–buff decoration,
combined with a resist–painted dot motif,
recalls pottery traditions from the area between
northern Peru (Gallinazo and Vicús styles) and
southern Colombia (Tumaco), including many
coastal Ecuadorian styles. That area, from c.
300–200 B.C. until several centuries after
Christ, produced quantities of similarly
resist–decorated pottery, often complemented
by red–on–buff zoning. This part of South
America is often said to show strong
Mesoamerican stylistic influences before and
during the time in question.

The figures shown here have a serene and
contemplative air; one holds a round tablet in
front of him, as if it were a mirror, a pose
repeated in other Carbonera–style figures.

233
Ceremonial metate
Volcanic stone; h. 25 cm, w. 87 cm, l. 112 cm
Reportedly from Atlantic Watershed
Early Period V, c. 500–800 A.D.
Banco Nacional de Costa Rica 994

Although this immense metate was ostensibly
found in the Atlantic Watershed, its style is
very close to those known from the Barriles
site in Panama (Linares and Ranere 1980: 50),
where they were excavated from shaft tombs.
Some metates from that site were even larger
than this example. Human trophy heads form
both leg supports and border on this piece and
Barriles examples. Because Period V marks
the appearance of many "southern" traits in
Atlantic Costa Rica, it would not be surprising
to see the dissemination of a sculptural style
associated with a major ceremonial center in
western Panama. Smaller oval metates—also
tetrapod, but with longer, undecorated legs—
began to appear in Atlantic and Central sites
sometime around 500 A.D.; all of these have
small relief decorations at the ends of the
metate plate.

DIQUÍS Nos. 230–293

230
Ocarina, seated figure
Ceramic; h. 13.2 cm, w. 5.5 cm
Reportedly from Carbonera vicinity, Osa
* Peninsula, Diquís*
Middle Period IV, c. 200–100 B.C.(?)
Collection Oduber

232
Annular base
Ceramic; h. 19.5 cm, w. 18.2 cm
Provenance unknown
Late Period IV, 1–500 A.D.
Museo Nacional de Costa Rica 12800
See pl. 36

Objects like this ceramic base were used as
stands for round–bottomed jars. The type of
incising on this one recalls Barriles–style
pottery from Chiriquí, Panama.

234
Metate seat
Stone; h. 43 cm, w. 58 cm, l. 110 cm
Reportedly from Bremen, Línea Vieja, Atlantic
* Watershed*
Late Period IV–Period V, c. 300–700 A.D.
Banco Nacional de Costa Rica 992

The function of objects like this is not
understood. The tetrapod, oval shape, with
carved projections on the upper surface, is
almost identical to that of artifacts from
Barriles, Panama, where the large size of the
objects virtually eliminates an everyday
functional role. Later ceramic sculptures show
human figures reclining on similar furniture.
Complicating the problem is the provenance of

this piece—reportedly the Atlantic Watershed. Fragments of similar objects, usually with grinding wear, have been found in El Bosque–phase contexts. Ceremonial metates may have been traded among elite groups, or this style may have been manufactured in the Atlantic zone under southern influence.

235
Sphere
Stone; diam. 95 cm
Diquís zone
Late Period IV–Period VI, c. 400–
*   1200 A.D.(?)*
Collection Alfonso Jiménez–Alvarado

The stone spheres of Diquís are probably the best known, but least understood, of Costa Rica's Precolumbian artifacts. They have been found in the vicinity of cemeteries, in lines, mounted on platforms of cobbles (Lothrop 1963). Sedimentary, as well as igneous, rock was used in their manufacture, obviating the hypothesis that they may have been natural volcanic ejects. They range in size from a few inches in diameter to over two meters, the best large examples varying only a few centimeters from the perfectly spherical. They were shaped by pecking and grinding, employing techniques well within the capacity of the prehistoric stonemason. A perfectly hemispherical wooden template (like the support frame around a model globe of the earth) could be obtained by using a string compass. This would then be applied to, and rotated around, a boulder of the desired size that was nearest to round; projecting areas would be pecked down. Other possible manufacturing techniques have also been described (Lothrop 1963).

Such spheres may be solar or lunar symbols, but this is not known for certain, and, until their symbolism is understood, we cannot say why they were produced. The largest of them are monumental stone sculptures, representing a great investment of time, labor, and skill. Possession of them, or control of their disposition, probably implied high politico–religious status.

236
Basket–handled jar
Ceramic; h. 18.5 cm, w. 17.5 cm
Diquís zone
Period VI, 1000–1550 A.D.
Collection Oduber

237
Jar
Ceramic; h. 19.5 cm, w. 23 cm
Diquís zone
Period VI, 1000–1550 A.D.
Museo Nacional de Costa Rica 23123
See pl. 37

238
Jar
Ceramic; h. 23.9 cm, w. 21.5 cm
Diquís zone
Period VI, 1000–1550 A.D.
Collection Molinos de Costa Rica

The so–called Tarragó *Galleta*, or Biscuit, pottery type is one of the hallmarks of Period VI in the Diquís zone. Its elegant and voluptuous shapes are usually accentuated by tiny appliqué adornos; the whole is very appealing to modern aesthetic sensibilities. This type represents the zenith of the potter's craft in Diquís; certain large globular jars may have walls less than two millimeters thick, a remarkable achievement without the use of a potter's wheel. Haberland (in press) has suggested that Tarragó Biscuit was made by specialized artisans; its limited distribution in Diquís sites points to a very limited number of centers of manufacture. A few trade sherds were found by Aguilar (1972) at the important Period VI Atlantic Watershed site of Guayabo de Turrialba.

239
Deer–effigy vessel
Ceramic; h. 17.7 cm, w. 20.2 cm
Diquís zone
Period VI, 1000–1550 A.D.
Collection Molinos de Costa Rica

240
Camelid–effigy vessel
Ceramic; h. 18.5 cm, w. 25.3 cm
Diquís zone
Period VI, 1000–1550 A.D.
Collection Molinos de Costa Rica
The finely crafted Tarragó Biscuit pottery includes many zoomorphic effigies, some quite realistic. Number 239 is a deer, complete with horns, in a naturalistic posture. Number 240 is, surprisingly, an American camelid (llama or guanaco), a faunal family whose native habitat is the Andes, extending perhaps as far north as southern Colombia. While the production of this camelid effigy in Diquís does not necessarily mean that such animals were brought as far north as Costa Rica, there is good evidence that lower Central American peoples were cognizant of the Andean culture area: the 16th–century Panamanian chief Tumaco surprised the Spaniard Vasco Nuñez and his men by modeling in clay a long–necked beast which they immediately recognized as a *camello*. Pointing south, Tumaco went on to tell the Spaniards that much gold was to be found there, and that the people of that region used such long–necked creatures as beasts of burden.

241
Tripod vessel
Ceramic; h. 30.6 cm, w. 8.1 cm
Diquís zone
Period VI, 1000–1500 A.D.
Instituto Nacional de Seguros 4913
See pl. 40
In Diquís, the tradition of long–legged tripod vessels appears later than in the rest of Costa Rica. Most examples have legs in the form of fish, as in number 241. A small feline adorno perches on the vessel shoulder; the punctate pattern on the collar probably symbolizes an alligator.

242
Cylindrical jar
Ceramic; h. 20.1 cm, w. 23 cm
Diquís zone
Late Period VI, 1200–1550 A.D.
Collection Alfonso Jiménez–Alvarado
243
Seated figure
Ceramic; h. 13 cm, w. 12 cm
Diquís zone
Late Period VI, 1200–1550 A.D.
Collection Alfonso Jiménez–Alvarado
See pl. 39
Early investigators called this pottery Alligator Ware, because motifs symbolic of that animal were repeated with great frequency. Number 242 is a highly stylized example. The alligator was perhaps the most important zoomorphic effigy for ceramics in all periods in Diquís.

For the most part, Diquís polychromes are inferior to those of Guanacaste–Nicoya; however, the sharing of some decorative modes in Period VI and the fact that Nicoya polychrome trade sherds have been found in Diquís suggest that there was communication between the two areas. The seated figurine (no. 243) shows the usual color scheme of red and black on cream. Polychrome of this type has been found with Spanish iron tools and glass (Stone 1977: 113).

244
Peg–base figure
Stone; h. 55 cm, w. 24 cm
Diquís zone
Period VI, 1000–1550 A.D.
Museo Nacional de Costa Rica 14582

245
Peg–base figure
Stone; h. 35.5 cm, w. 12.7 cm
Diquís zone
Period VI, 1000–1550 A.D.
Collection Alfonso Jiménez–Alvarado
The stone sculpture of Diquís is markedly
different from that of the rest of Precolumbian
Costa Rica. As these two peg–base figures
attest, it is highly stylized and virtually two–
dimensional. There is no question that it is
a South American–looking style; comparisons
can be drawn to Colombian gold work (Muisca)
and statuary. Number 244 is representative: a
stiff pose and only the slightest bow to realism
in body features result in a formality that
recalls architectural embellishment (which
peg–base figures may have been) rather than
individual sculpture. Number 245, which was
carved in a more appealing, full–round style,
makes it clear that these figures are probably
warriors; this one carries an inverted trophy
head in front of him. He may be wearing a
mask. An interesting detail is the serpent belt,
which is also seen on many gold figurines.

246
Feline
Stone; h. 18 cm, l. 31 cm
Diquís zone
Period VI, 1000–1550 A.D.
Museo Nacional de Costa Rica 14682
See pl. 64

247
Armadillo
Stone; h. 39 cm, w. 23 cm
Diquís zone
Period VI, 1000–1550 A.D.
Museo Nacional de Costa Rica 21276
See pl. 65
Not all Diquís stone sculpture is formalized
and rigid. These two animal figurines have
rounded shapes, which, although simplified,
lose none of their character in the translation
to stone. Less ferocious than Atlantic Watershed
examples, the feline (no. 246) is all curves
and swelling masses, almost Disneylike in
appearance. The armadillo (no. 247) shows
a characteristic shape with a minimum of
carving. The symbolic value of such statuary is
unknown.

248
Avian pendant
Gold; h. 9.6 cm, w. 10 cm
Reportedly from San Isidro del General
vicinity, Diquís
Late Period V–Period VI, c. 700–1550 A.D.
Banco Central de Costa Rica 265
249
Avian pendant
Gold; h. 10.9 cm, w. 12.8 cm
Reportedly from Sierpe vicinity, Diquís
Late Period V–Period VI, c. 700–1550 A.D.
Banco Central de Costa Rica 760
See pl. 42
Avian pendants of this general morphology,
found throughout the Greater Chiriquí subarea
(Diquís and Chiriquí, Panama), are perhaps its
most typical metal artifact. More than one kind
of bird may be represented, but the model
seems to have been carrion birds like the king
vulture; such pendants are usually called
"eagles." The composition emphasizes wings,
exaggerated tail, and often head tufts. Although
most avian pendants have nonrealistic features

or are in some way anthropomorphized,
the pose can be observed even today, when,
after a rain, certain soaring birds spread their
wings to dry in the sun while perched in trees.
These two pendants are the so–called Veraguas
type, known from central Panama and probably
deriving from a Colombian prototype. Although
both have bird feet, the first has spiral
elements not unlike ear spools; the second has
a filigree decoration along the lower edges
of the wings.

250
Avian pendant
Gold; h. 11.5 cm, w. 13.2 cm
Reportedly from Palmar Sur vicinity, Diquís
Late Period V–Period VI, c. 700–1550 A.D.
Banco Central de Costa Rica 1172

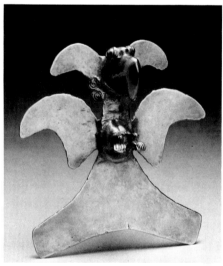

251
Avian pendant
Gold; h. 8.7 cm, w. 8.9 cm
Reportedly from Finca Jalaca, Diquís
Late Period V–Period VI, c. 700–1550 A.D.
Banco Central de Costa Rica 868
Aguilar (1972a) has published a stylistic analysis
of the gold collection of the Banco Central de

Costa Rica, incorporating some of Lothrop's (1950) nomenclature. According to Aguilar, the Jalaca type of avian pendant, closely related to the preceding Veraguas type, shows double ear spirals and bands around a drastically hooked beak. In number 250, the very narrow upper beak is joined to the lower, perhaps for hanging another ornament. Spiral ear spools and curved ear tufts are also evident.

254
Avian pendant
Gold; h. 5.8 cm, w. 5.3 cm
Reportedly from Palmar Norte vicinity, Diquís
Late Period V–Period VI, c. 700–1550 A.D.
Banco Central de Costa Rica 911
This group of avian pendants emphasizes the diagnostic spread wings and tail of this form. Number 252 is of the Chánguina type, with a head cast in elaborate detail, including two false–filigree alligator heads that project from either side of the main avian figure, probably emphasizing the symbolic union of the mythological traits of these two animals in the human wearer of this pendant. Number 253 is unusual in that it emphasizes grasping feet and alligator–head lateral projections at the expense of the central avian figure. This is even more apparent in number 254, where the avian aspect is almost entirely subjugated to the alligator effigies and the simpler, armlike projections suggestive of the human figure. It is known as the Guanacaste type, for many objects like this have supposedly been found in that northern zone (Aguilar 1972a: 30–31).

256
Spider ornament
Gold; h. 2.1 cm, w. 1.7 cm
Reportedly from San Isidro del General vicinity, Diquís
Late Period V–Period VI, c. 700–1550 A.D.
Museo Nacional de Costa Rica 14578

252
Avian pendant
Gold; h. 10.1 cm, w. 11.6 cm
Reportedly from Chirripo Sur, Diquís
Late Period V–Period VI, c. 700–1550 A.D.
Banco Central de Costa Rica 766

253
Avian pendant
Gold; h. 10.1 cm, w. 10.3 cm
Reportedly from Palmar Sur vicinity, Diquís
Late Period V–Period VI, c. 700–1550 A.D.
Banco Central de Costa Rica 928

255
Peccary ornaments
Gold; all l. 2–2.3 cm
Reportedly from Palmar Sur vicinity, Diquís
Period V–Period VI, 500–1550 A.D.
Banco Central de Costa Rica 495, 496, 497, 498, 499, 500, 501, 502
See pl. 88
Cast zoomorphs of many kinds are known from Diquís. This set of peccaries was made by the lost–wax process, with ring feet for stringing. The manufacture of a group of peccary effigies is of interest for these animals run in fairly large herds.

257
Scorpion pendant
Gold; h. 6.8 cm, w. 3.2 cm
Reportedly from San Isidro del General vicinity, Diquís
Late Period V–Period VI, c. 700–1550 A.D.
Museo Nacional de Costa Rica 14504
The variety of zoomorphic gold ornaments from Diquís is noteworthy. While birds, alligators, and felines are probably the most numerous, many other realistic sculptures are known. They include monkeys, deer, tapirs, armadillos, snakes, sharks, lobsters, shellfish, and even insects, like the pair shown here. Number 256 represents a spider not unlike the black widow, while number 257 portrays a scorpion poised to strike.

258
Crab bell pendant
Gold; h. 5.4 cm, w. 7.7 cm
Reportedly from Palmar Sur vicinity, Diquís
Period V–Period VI, c. 700–1550 A.D.
Banco Central de Costa Rica 534
Realistic gold castings like this one are much
more frequent than true–to–life carvings in
jade, undoubtedly reflecting the nature of the
gold–casting medium, in which the original
model from which the cast was made was
usually of wax, a forgiving and easily modified
material. Likewise, the metal itself could be
reused many times if the first casting went
awry; this was not so, of course, for jade or any
other stone.

259
Double–bell pendant with spider
Gold; h. 7.4 cm, w. 4.4 cm
Reportedly from Cabecera de Chánguina
  vicinity, Diquís
Late Period V–Period VI, c. 700–1550 A.D.
Banco Central de Costa Rica 1297
See pl. 90
A beautiful composition, perhaps inspired by
the image of a spider and egg case within a
web, this double–bell pendant incorporating a
realistic arachnid was probably achieved entirely
by lost–wax casting. This piece is not just a
vehicle for socio–mythological symbolism; it is
also accessible and appealing to the modern
eye.

260
Feline pendant
Gold; h. 4.9 cm, l. 12 cm
Reportedly from Puerto González Víquez
  vicinity, Diquís
Late Period V–Period VI, c. 700–1550 A.D.
Banco Central de Costa Rica 1251
See pl. 87
This admirably realistic jaguar was made to
hang head up on a cord or necklace strung
through the front paws.

261
Deer pendant
Gold; h. 5.1 cm, l. 11.3 cm
Reportedly from Buenos Aires vicinity, Diquís
Late Period V–Period VI, c. 700–1550 A.D.
Banco Central de Costa Rica 297

262
Alligator pendant
Gold; h. 5.5 cm, l. 15.8 cm
Reportedly from Cabagra vicinity, Diquís
Late Period V–Period VI, c. 700–1550 A.D.
Banco Central de Costa Rica 1245
See pl. 97
These two gold sculptures are technically
impressive and clearly permeated with
symbolism—if only it could be interpreted
properly. In number 261, a rather
fierce–looking deer with horns holds a maize
cob in its mouth and another in its tail; a tiny
feline perches on its back. Number 262 has
a similar pose, but it is an alligator or
crocodile with a human body in its mouth. It is
possible that, in the case of number 262, an
analogy was intended with the pan–American
Precolumbian myth of a giant saurian (alligator,
turtle) on whose back the world rests.

263
Bell pendant with bat effigy
Gold; h. 7.1 cm, w. 13 cm
Reportedly from Palmar Sur vicinity, Diquís
Late Period V–Period VI, c. 700–1550 A.D.
Banco Central de Costa Rica 975
See pl. 92
A wonderfully realistic bat graces this large
gold bell pendant.

264
Bat pendant
Gold; h. 5.2 cm, w. 6 cm
Reportedly from Palmar Sur vicinity, Diquís
Late Period V–Period VI, c. 700–
  1100 A.D. (?)
Banco Central de Costa Rica 684

265
Bat pendant
Gold; h. 7 cm, w. 8 cm
Reportedly from El General valley, Diquís
Late Period V–Period VI, c. 700–
  1100 A.D. (?)
Banco Central de Costa Rica 51
These two bat pendants reiterate the general
form of the avian varieties, even including a
nonrealistic bifurcated tail; they have batlike
wings, however, especially in the case of
number 265. With their bulbous eyes, spiral
ear spools, and visible masculine sex, they
recall the modeled human–bat figures on
Guanacaste–Nicoya ceramic types like Guinea
Incised and Tola and Carrillo Polychromes. The
impression of a costume is strengthened by the
alligator effigies visible at each wing tip.

266
Avian pendant
Gold; h. 4.8 cm, w. 5.2 cm
Diquís zone
Late Period V–Period VI, c. 700–1550 A.D.
Museo Nacional de Costa Rica 22898
This realistic bird pendant may actually represent an eagle, in this case the harpy eagle, because of the hornlike tufts on the head; it might also be an owl.

267
Monkey pendant
Gold; h. 9.5 cm, w. 7.5 cm
Reportedly from Palmar Sur vicinity, Diquís
Late Period V–Period VI, c. 700–1550 A.D.
Banco Central de Costa Rica 1174
See pl. 41
This pendant has a symmetrical, yet very dynamic design, in which a monkey figure is encircled by his own tail. The tail and ears are decorated with false filigree volutes. Two upward–looking alligator heads are attached to the knees and hips.

268
Pendant, framed figures
Gold; h. 6.3 cm, w. 7 cm
Reportedly from San Vito de Java vicinity,
  Diquís
Late Period V–Period VI, c. 700–1550 A.D.
Banco Central de Costa Rica 796

Pendants that display figures in a filigree frame along with other decorative elements, forming complex openwork compositions, are known as the Carbonera type (Aguilar 1972a: 46). Number 268 shows two men side by side playing conch–shell trumpets; the shells also have a masklike aspect. Of interest here is the abundance of serpent elements; braided, they form a belt for the two figures, and what look like bells on the toes are probably also stylized serpent heads. The sexual organs are replaced by serpents, too, although perhaps these are penis sheaths.

269
Bell pendant, framed jaguar–man figure
Gold; h. 8.7 cm, w. 8.1 cm
Reportedly from Farm 4, Palmar Sur, Diquís
Late Period V–Period VI, c. 700–1550 A.D.
Banco Central de Costa Rica 532
See pl. 98
This splendid pendant is a baroque composition with but a single theme: the jaguar. The central human figure wears a feline mask and is surrounded by four tiny feline figures. His hands are jaguar heads, and tiny quadrupeds with curling tails line the outside of the square frame. Only the figure's belt varies the theme; it is the typical two–headed serpent. The belly of the central figure is a bell.

270
Bell pendant with deer and snake motifs
Gold; h. 7.7 cm, w. 8.5 cm
Reportedly from Palmar Sur vicinity, Diquís
Late Period V–Period VI, c. 700–1550 A.D.
Banco Central de Costa Rica 964
See pl. 99
This elegant bell pendant may represent a ceremonial shield. Three deer heads are placed along a braided, circular element that turns up into two serpent heads at the bottom. Tiny bicephalic serpents also fill the space between the deer heads. Triangular feather symbols surround the whole composition, and a larger example serves as a base, just as it does in the avian pendants.

271
Masked figure pendant
Gold; h. 8.5 cm, w. 7.2 cm
Reportedly from Punta Burica, Diquís
Late Period V–Period VI, c. 700–1550 A.D.
Banco Central de Costa Rica 1226
This and the following group of pendants feature a costumed man situated between two long, curved plaques of sheet gold. The plaques have the obvious function of anchoring the plethora of elements fixed between them, but, since the dominant symbol in such compositions seems to be the alligator/crocodile, it might be suggested that the plaques themselves represent the jaws of that creature. Here, a man wearing an "eagle" mask has arms distorted to appear winglike.

272
Masked–figure pendant
Gold; h. 8.5 cm, w. 8.5 cm
Reportedly from Farm 4, Palmar Sur, Diquís
Late Period V–Period VI, c. 700–1550 A.D.
Banco Central de Costa Rica 593
See pl. 93
273
Masked–figure pendant
Gold; h. 6.6 cm, w. 7.6 cm
Reportedly from Buenos Aires, Diquís
Late Period V–Period VI, c. 700–1550 A.D.
Banco Central de Costa Rica 439
See pl. 94

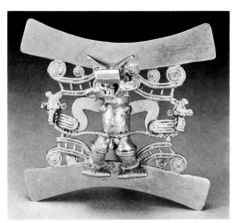

274
Masked–figure pendant
Gold; h. 8.1 cm, w. 7.5 cm
Reportedly from Palmar Sur vicinity, Diquís
Late Period V–Period VI, c. 700–1550 A.D.
Banco Central de Costa Rica 588
In number 272, the central figure wears a batlike mask and holds a small alligator in the mouth. Filigree alligator heads spring from ears and feet as well as from the upper tips of scalloped wings. Number 273 has most of the same alligator–head details, but here the mask itself is an alligator, and a twisted–wire, double–headed serpent is held in both hands, passing through the mouth. A waistband and ligatures on the legs are present. Number 274 is at once the finest and symbolically most complex of this group. The main mask combines elements of both alligator and bat effigies, bewilderingly overlaid. The embellished double–headed serpent serves as a belt, and the sexual organs are emphasized.

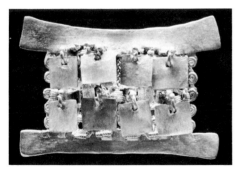

275
Pendant, two figures with danglers
Gold; h. 6.3 cm, w. 8.9 cm
Reportedly from Palmar Sur vicinity, Diquís
Late Period V–Period VI, c. 700–1550 A.D.
Banco Central de Costa Rica 597
Although related to the preceding pendants, this one has small square plaques of hammered gold hung from specially made hooks in front of the two main figures. The motifs are not unusual; they show one or two human males with zoomorphic (especially alligator/crocodile) attributes or adornment.

276
Bell pendant, two figures with danglers
Gold; h. 6.2 cm, w. 7 cm
Reportedly from Palmar Sur, Diquís
Late Period V–Period VI, c. 700–1550 A.D.
Banco Central de Costa Rica 589
See pl. 95

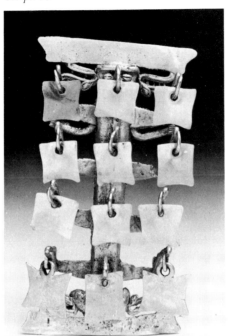

277
Pendant, figure with danglers
Gold; h. 12.8 cm, w. 7.2 cm
Reportedly from Carbonera vicinity, Osa
  Peninsula, Diquís
Late Period V–Period VI, c. 700–1550 A.D.
Banco Central de Costa Rica 455
Apart from making the pendants showier and more impressive, the occluding plaques may have symbolized the protean aspect of the shaman–*cacique*, who was probably thought to be able to assume animal shapes and attributes at will.

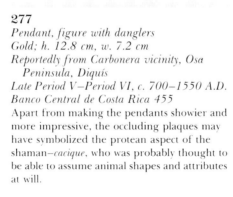

278
Two–headed avian pendant
Gold; h. 7.8 cm, w. 8.6 cm
Reportedly from Quepos vicinity, Diquís
Probably Period VI, 1000–1550 A.D.
Banco Central de Costa Rica 1
Pendants in this style seem to be purely avian, although highly modified. In this bicephalic example, the heads are copiously adorned, each sporting a double–alligator head plume. The dangling plaques were added after casting. The treatment of the wings is especially interesting, for they seem to read as the gaping mouths of snakes or sharks.

279
Disk
Gold; diam. 21 cm
Reportedly from Palmar Sur vicinity, Diquís
Late Period V–Period VI,
  c. 700–1550 A.D.
Banco Central de Costa Rica 516

280
Disk
Gold; diam. 18.5 cm
Reportedly from Farm 4, Palmar Sur, Diquís
Late Period V–Period VI,
*   c. 700–1550 A.D.*
Banco Central de Costa Rica 521
Gold disks like the pair illustrated here were probably worn as headdresses or caps. Some of the relief in the coiffures observed in stone sculptures may actually represent such disks. Other disks might have been worn as breastplates. Both of these have alligator motifs. Number 279 has an embossed realistic version, surrounded by four circles, while number 280 has only embossed triangles (alligator scutes).

281
Diadem
Gold; h. 3.9 cm, diam. 17.2 cm
Reportedly from Palmar Sur vicinity, Diquís
Period VI, 1000–1550 A.D.
Banco Central de Costa Rica 943

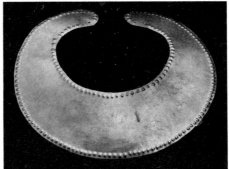

282
Collar
Gold; diam. 35.8 cm
Reportedly from Palmar Sur vicinity, Diquís
Period VI, 1000–1550 A.D.
Banco Central de Costa Rica 507
Spanish chroniclers described headbands, collars, and ornamental breastplates as among the gold ornaments of Indians in Panama and Costa Rica. These articles impressed the Spaniards greatly, feeding their already–burning desire for gold. This circlet and collar were hammered into shape, embossed along the edges with dots, and perforated.

283
Pendant, costumed figure
Gold; h. 10.8 cm, w. 8.2 cm
Reportedly from Palmar Sur vicinity, Diquís
Late Period V–Period VI, c. 700–1550 A.D.
Banco Central de Costa Rica 963
See back cover

284
Pendant, two–headed figure
Gold; h. 7.5 cm, w. 5.9 cm
Reportedly from Farm 4, Palmar Sur, Diquís
Late Period V–Period VI, c. 700–1500 A.D.
Banco Central de Costa Rica 531
See pl. 89
Pendants with human figures like these are often called musicians, for they seem to be playing flutes and/or drums. In number 283, the drum is clear, but the object in the figure's left hand is a snake, not a flute, with its tail in the figure's mouth. Number 284 may be interpreted in the same way, with each hand holding a snake with the heads doubled over. Flutes are not held obliquely from the body with one hand, and it is probable that a kind of ritual snake dance, where the performer holds the reptile in his mouth, is represented here; similar dances are known among the Hopi of the southwestern United States.

Number 283 is spectacularly adorned with three pairs of alligator heads. Note the inverted triangular elements on the headdress; they are like those used to represent tails in avian pendants (no. 266) and may thus be symbolic of feathers in this context. The bicephalic figure in number 284 is of unknown significance. The spiral, false–filigree headdress elements are reminiscent of Quimbaya gold figures from Colombia.

285
Alligator pendant
Gold; h. 5.1 cm, w. 4.2 cm
Diquís zone
Period VI, 1000–1550 A.D.
Museo Nacional de Costa Rica 22904
Number 285 is unusual in that it does not portray a man costumed as an alligator, but rather an alligator that has been anthropomorphized. The elements on the ends of the curving headdress, on the hands, and on the bifurcated tail seem to be serpents with bifid tongues. This and the split tail, stylistic traits known from many Colombian gold pieces, also appear in the stone sculpture of the San Agustin site in that country. A large petroglyph near the Guayabo de Turrialba site depicts a creature not unlike this one (Carlos Aguilar, personal communication).

286
Double aspect pendant
Gold; h. 8 cm, w. 7.5 cm
Reportedly from Punta Burica, Diquís
Late Period V–Period VI, c. 700–1550 A.D.
Banco Central de Costa Rica 1218

The protean quality of prehistoric symbolism in Costa Rica is apparent in this pendant, as it often is in other media, like jade carving or stone sculpture. A naturalistic frog or toad posture catches us off guard with what is probably a feline head turned back to front. It is almost as if the feline head were transposed from a different pendant. The twisted element over the mouth is of unknown significance.

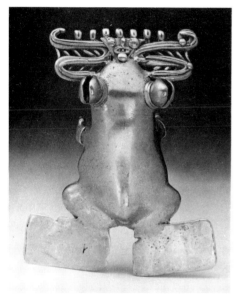

287
Frog pendant
Gold; h. 10.4 cm, w. 8.4 cm
Reportedly from Farm 4, Palmar Sur, Diquís
Period VI, 1000–1550 A.D.
Banco Central de Costa Rica 522

288
Frog pendant
Gold; h. 11.2 cm, w. 11 cm
Reportedly from Farm 4, Palmar Sur, Diquís
Period VI, 1000–1500 A.D.
Banco Central de Costa Rica 523
See pl. 96

Amphibian animals were favorite subjects of Diquís goldsmiths. Since they, like other animals often represented in Precolumbian art, were of a significance now mostly beyond our understanding, we cannot easily interpret their symbolic importance. Their mythic roles frequently involved supernatural or extraordinary traits, some of which are undoubtedly portrayed in the sculptures that have come down to us.

The filigree in front of the snout of number 287 is an example of a nonrealistic trait. In number 288, the same idea is carried further with a double–headed snake issuing, mustachelike, from the frog's mouth. Both examples were lost–wax cast.

289
Lobster pendant
Gold; h. 10.7 cm, w. 8.3 cm
Reportedly from Puerto González Viquez
*   vicinity, Diquís*
Probably Period VI, 1000–1550 A.D.
Banco Central de Costa Rica 1246
See pl. 91

A wide variety of realistically portrayed animals appears in Diquís gold pendants that are skillfully constructed by lost–wax casting and annealing. One of the most impressive is this superbly detailed lobster, locally known as a *langostina*. Only the tail has been symbolically modified, perhaps into stylized alligator heads.

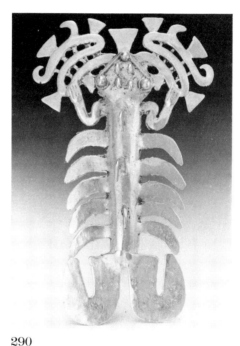

290
Crustacean pendant
Gold; h. 12.5 cm, w. 7.8 cm
Reportedly from Diquís coast
Probably Period VI, c. 1000–1550 A.D.
Banco Central de Costa Rica 423

The animal depicted here is not readily recognizable. It has fishlike elements, reminiscent of those on the tall tripod ceramic vessels from Diquís, but it also could be a salamander or crayfish. There is no doubt that it has been embellished with fantastic crests at the front of the head, in the style of the alligator *incensarios* (nos. 89–92) from Guanacaste–Nicoya.

291
Articulated pendant
Gold; h. 14.7 cm, w. 12 cm
Reportedly from Puerto González Viquez
*   vicinity, Diquís*
Late Period V–Period VI, c. 700–1550 A.D.
Banco Central de Costa Rica 1247

This interesting pendant was cast in three parts—head, middle body, and legs—which were then joined, perhaps using other materials, so as to be movable. The pendant represents a human figure with bird (vulture) costume. Both headdress and wings are decorated with filigree alligator heads; a two–headed serpent forms a belt.

292
Alligator–man pendant
Gold; h. 15 cm, w. 10.2 cm
Reportedly from Puerto González Viquez
*   vicinity, Diquís*
Late Period V–Period VI, c. 700–1550 A.D.
Banco Central de Costa Rica 1249
Not illustrated

293
Alligator–man pendant
Gold; h. 12.3 cm, w. 7.5 cm
Reportedly from Puerto González Viquez
*   vicinity, Diquís*
Late Period V–Period VI, c. 700–1550 A.D.
Banco Central de Costa Rica 1250
See pl. 100

Some of the most impressive gold figurines from Diquís are men costumed as alligators or crocodiles. In number 292, the headdress elements may also be alligators; the general shape of the headdress recalls certain figures from the Sinú region of Colombia. A two–headed serpent is held in both hands and the mouth. The sexual organ is replaced by a serpent head, which might represent a penis sheath.

Number 293 is at once dynamic and splendidly elaborate. Again, a double serpent hangs from the mouth of the alligator mask, and feather symbols outline the large raised arms. Tiny monkey or human figures perch along the top of the pendant.

BIBLIOGRAPHY

Abel–Vidor, Suzanne

1978   An Interpretation of Two Burnt Clay Features in an Early Central American Village: Vidor Site, Bay of Culebra, Guanacaste, Costa Rica. Unpub. M.A. thesis, Department of Anthropology, Brown University, Providence.

1980a   Dos Hornos Precolombinos en el Sitio Vidor, Bahía Culebra, Guanacaste. *Vínculos* 6 (2). San José.

1980b   The Historical Sources for the Greater Nicoya Archaeological Sub–Area. *Vínculos* 6 (2). San José.

Accola, Richard M.

1977   Análisis de la Difracción de Rayos X: su Aplicación Experimental en el Estudio de la Cerámica Policromada de Nicoya, Costa Rica. *Vínculos* 3 (1): 37–45. San José.

1978   Revisión de los Tipos de Cerámica del Periódo Policromo Medio en Guanacaste. *Vínculos* 4 (2): 80–105. San José.

1980   Sitio Nacascolo: Arqueología en un Sitio Saqueado. *In* Memoria del Congreso sobre el Mundo Centroamericano de su Tiempo: IV Centenario de Gonzalo Fernández de Oviedo: 167–174. Editorial Texto, San José.

Acosta, Ana Celia, and Roberto le Franc

1980   Breve Reseña Arqueológica y Etnológica de Costa Rica. Ministerio de Cultura, Juventud y Deportes, San José.

Aguilar Piedra, Carlos Humberto

1952   El complejo de las cabezas–trofeo en la etnología costarricense. *Revista de la Universidad de Costa Rica* 7: 39–63. San José.

1953   Retes: Un depósito arqueológico en las faldas del Irazú. Universidad de Costa Rica, San José.

1965   Religión y magia entre los indios de Costa Rica de origen sureño. *Publicaciones de la Universidad de Costa Rica, Serie Historia y Geografía* 6. San José.

1972a   Colección de Objetos Indígenas de Oro del Banco Central de Costa Rica. *Publicaciones de la Universidad de Costa Rica, Serie Historia y Geografía* 13. San José.

1972b   Guayabo de Turrialba. Editorial Costa Rica, San José.

1974   Asentamientos Indígenas en el Área Central de Costa Rica. *América Indígena* 34 (2): 311–317. Mexico City.

1975   El Molino: El Sitio de la Fase Pavas en Cartago. *Vínculos* 1 (1): 18–56. San José.

1976   Relaciones de las Culturas Precolombinas en el Intermontano Central de Costa Rica. *Vínculos* 2 (1): 75–86. San José.

Alfaro, Anastasio

1892   Arqueología Costarricense. *El Centenario* 4: 5–12. Madrid.

1935   Investigaciones Científicas. Editorial Trejos Hermanos, San José.

Allen, R.O., and S.E. Pennell

1977   Rare earth element distribution patterns to characterize soapstone artifacts. *In* G.F. Carter, ed., Archaeological Chemistry II: 230-257. *Advances in Chemistry Series* 171. American Chemical Society, Washington.

Andagoya, Pascual de

1865   Narrative of the Proceedings of Pedrarias Dávila in the Provinces of Tierra Firma.... The Hakluyt Society, London.

Angulo, José Antonio

1966   Informe sobre Matina, Moin, costa atlántica y Talamanca en 1862. *Revista de los Archivos Nacionales* 30: 217–243. San José.

Balser, Carlos

1966   Los objetos de oro de los estilos extranjeros de Costa Rica. *In* Actas y Memorias del XXXVI Congreso Internacional de Americanistas, Sevilla, 1964, 1: 391–398. Seville.

1968   Metal and Jade in Lower Central America. *In* Actas y Memorias del XXXVII Congreso Internacional de Americanistas, República Argentina, 1966, IV: 57–66. Buenos Aires.

1974   El Jade de Costa Rica. Librería Lehmann, San José.

1980   Jade Precolombino de Costa Rica. Instituto Nacional de Seguros, San José.

Bancroft, Hubert Howe

1886   History of Central America I. The Works of Hubert Howe Bancroft VI. The History Company, Publishers, San Francisco.

Barrantes Ferrero, Mario

1961   Primera expedición de Vásquez de Coronado al sur del país. Instituto Geográfico Nacional, San José.

Baudez, Claude F.

1959   Nuevos Aspectos de la Escultura Lítica en Territorio Chorotega. *In* Actas del XXXIII Congreso Internacional de Americanistas, San José, 1958, 2: 286–95. Librería Lehmann, San José.

1967   Recherches archéologiques dans la vallée du Tempisque, Guanacaste, Costa Rica. *Travaux et Mémoires de l'Institut des Hautes Études de l'Amérique Latine* 18. Paris.

1970   Central America. (Trans. by James Hogarth.) Barrie and Jenkins, London; Nagel Publishers, Geneva.

————, and Michael D. Coe

1962   Archaeological Sequences in Northwestern Costa Rica. *In* Akten des 34. Internationalen Amerikanistenkongresses, Wien, 1960: 366–373. Verlag Ferdinand Berger, Vienna.

Benzoni, Girolamo

1857   History of the New World, by Girolamo Benzoni. (Trans. and ed. by W.H. Smyth.) The Hakluyt Society, London.

1967   La Historia del Nuevo Mundo. Caracas.

Bernstein, D.

1980   El Valor del Análisis Lítico en la Reconstrucción de las Actividades Prehistóricas: Un Ejemplo de Guanacaste, Costa Rica. *In* Memoria del Congreso sobre el Mundo Centroamericano de su Tiempo: IV Centenario de Gonzalo Fernández de Oviedo: 185–191. Editorial Texto, San José.

Bishop, Ronald L., and Robert L. Rands

1980   Resource Procurement Zones and Patterns of Ceramic Exchange in the Palenque Region, Mexico. *In* R.E. Fry, ed., Models and Methods in Regional Exchange: 19-46. *Society for American Archaeology Papers* I. Washington.

Blanco V., A., and S. Salgado G.

1980   Rescate Arqueológico del Sitio 26–CN–Barrial de Heredia. *In* Memoria del Congreso sobre el Mundo Centroamericano de su Tiempo: IV Centenario de Gonzalo Fernández de Oviedo: 133–138. Editorial Texto, San José.

Blessing, Agustín

1900   Descubrimiento y catequización de los indios de las cabeceras del río Telire. *Mensajero del clero* 12 (143): 382–384. San José.

1921   Apuntes sobre los indios bribris de Costa Rica. *Revista de Costa Rica* 3: 99–101. San José.

Bovallius, Carl

1887   Resa i Central-Amerika 1881–1883, 1: 227–275. Almqvist & Wiksell's boktryckeri, Uppsala.

Bozzoli de Wille, María Eugenia

1975   Birth and Death in the Belief System of the Bribri Indians of Costa Rica.

           Unpub. Ph.D. diss., Department of Anthropology, University of Georgia, Athens.

1977   Narraciones bribris. *Vínculos* 2 (2): 165–199; 3 (1): 67–104. San José.

1979   El nacimiento y la muerte entre los bribris. Editorial Universidad de Costa Rica, San José.

Bray, Warwick

1977   Maya Metalwork and its External Connections. *In* Norman Hammond, ed., Social Process in Maya Prehistory: 365–403. Academic Press, London, New York, and San Francisco.

1978   The Gold of El Dorado. The Royal Academy, London.

Caldwell, Joseph R.

1964   Interaction Spheres in Prehistory. *Hopewellian Studies* 12: 133–143. Springfield.

Carneiro, Robert L.

1961   Slash–and–Burn Cultivation among the Kuikuru and its Implications for the Cultural Development in the Amazon Basin. *In* Johannes Wilbert, ed., The Evolution of Horticultural Systems in Native South America: Causes and Consequences: 47–67. Sociedad de Ciencias Naturales La Salle, Caracas.

1970   A Theory of the Origin of the State. *Science* 169 (3947): 733–738. Washington.

Casas, Fray Bartolome de las

1965   Historia de las Indias. 3 vols. Fondo de Cultura Económica, Mexico City.

1974   The Devastation of the Indies: A Brief Account. (Trans. by Herma Briffaut.) Seabury Press, New York.

Casimir de Brizuela, G.

1971   Informe Preliminar de las Excavaciones en el Sitio Arqueológico Las Huacas, Distrito de Soná, Veraguas. *In* Actas del II Symposium Nacional de Antropología, Arqueología y Etnohistoria de Panamá: 249–256. Panama.

Castro–Tossi, Norberto

1968   Caciques de Costa Rica bajo la monarquía española. *Ande* 49: 49–70. San José.

Chadwick, Robert

1965   Archaeological Synthesis of Michoacan and Adjacent Regions. *In* Robert Wauchope, ed., Handbook of Middle American Indians 11 (2): 657–693. University of Texas Press, Austin.

Chapman, Anne M.

1960   Los Nicarao y los Chorotega según las Fuentes Históricas. San José.

Ciudad Real, Fray Alonso de

1873   Relación breve y verdadera de algunas cosas de las muchas que sucedieron al Padre Fray Alonso Ponce en las provincias de la Nueva España. Madrid.

Coe, Michael D.

1962a   Costa Rican Archaeology and Mesoamerica. *Southwestern Journal of Anthropology* 18: 170–183. The University of New Mexico, Albuquerque.

1962b   Preliminary Report on Archaeological Investigations in Coastal Guanacaste, Costa Rica. *In* Akten der 34. Internationalen Amerikanistenkongresses, Wien, 1960: 358-365. Verlag Ferdinand Berger, Vienna.

————, and Claude F. Baudez

1961   The Zoned Bichrome Period in Northwest Costa Rica. *American Antiquity* 26 (4): 505–515. Salt Lake City.

————, and Richard A. Diehl

1980   In the Land of the Olmec. 2 vols. University of Texas Press, Austin and London.

Coe, William R.

1965   Artifacts of the Maya Lowlands. *In* Robert H. Wauchope, ed., Handbook of Middle American Indians 3 (2): 594–602. University of Texas Press, Austin.

Colección Somoza

1953–   Documentos para la historia de Nicaragua. Madrid.
57

Coleman, Robert

1980   The Natural Occurrence of Jade and its Bearing on the Sources of Mesoamerican Jade Artifacts. Paper delivered at Mesoamerican–Central American Jade Conference, Dumbarton Oaks, Washington.

Colón, Hernando

1947   Vida del Almirante don Cristóbal Colón. Editorial Fondo de Cultura Económica, Mexico City.

Conrad, Geoffrey W.

1974   Toward a Systemic View of Mesoamerican Prehistory: Inter-Site Sociopolitical Organization. *In* Jeremy A. Sabloff and C. C. Lamberg-Karlovsky, eds., The Rise and Fall of Civilization: 145–156. Cummings Publishing Co., Menlo Park.

Cook, Sherburne F., and Woodrow W. Borah

1960   The Indian Population of Central Mexico, 1531–1610. *Ibero-Americana* 44. University of California Press, Berkeley and Los Angeles.

Cooke, Richard G.

1976   Panamá: Región Central. *Vínculos* 2 (1): 122–140. San José.

Cortés, Hernán

1971   Hernán Cortés, Letters from Mexico. (Trans. and ed. by A. R. Pagden.) Grossman Publishers, New York.

Creamer, Winifred

1980   Evidence for Prehispanic Exchange Systems in the Gulf of Nicoya, Costa Rica. Paper presented at 45th Annual Meeting of Society for American Archaeology, Philadelphia.

Day, Jane S., and Suzanne Abel–Vidor

1980   The Late Polychrome Period: Guanacaste, Costa Rica. Paper presented at 79th Annual Meeting of American Anthropological Association, Washington.

Drucker, Philip

1952   La Venta, Tabasco: A Study of Olmec Ceramics and Art. *Bureau of American Ethnology Bulletin* 153. Smithsonian Institution, Washington.

1955   The Cerro de las Mesas Offering of Jade and Other Materials. *Bureau of American Ethnology Bulletin* 157, *Anthropological Papers* 44. Smithsonian Institution, Washington.

———, Robert F. Heizer, and Robert J. Squier

1959   Excavations at La Venta, Tabasco, 1955. *Bureau of American Ethnology Bulletin* 170. Smithsonian Institution, Washington.

Easby, Elizabeth K.

1963   Un "Dios Hacha" de las Tierras Altas Mayas. *Estudios de Cultura Maya* 3: 97–106. Universidad Nacional Autónoma de México, Mexico City.

1968   Pre–Columbian Jade from Costa Rica. André Emmerich, Inc., New York.

Falchetti de Sáenz, Ana María

1979   Colgantes "Darién:" Relaciones entre Áreas Orfebres del Occidente Colombiano y Centroamérica. *Boletín Museo del Oro* 2: 1–55. Bogotá.

Fernández, León, ed.

1881–   Colección de documentos para la historia de Costa Rica. 10 vols. San José, Paris,
1907   and Barcelona.

1976   Colección de documentos para la historia de Costa Rica. 10 vols. San José.

Fernández Guardia, Ricardo

1913   History of the Discovery and Conquest of Costa Rica. (Trans. by Harry Weston Van Dyke.) Thomas Y. Crowell Company, New York.

1918   Reseña histórica de Talamanca. Imprenta Alsina, San José.

Ferrero, Luis

1975   Costa Rica Precolombina. *Serie Biblioteca Patria* 6. San José.

1977a   Costa Rica Precolombina. 2nd ed. *Serie Biblioteca Patria* 6. Editorial Costa Rica, San José.

1977b   La representación de frutos en el arte precolombino costarricense. *Troquel* 1 (8): 15–27. San José.

1978   William M. Gabb y Talamanca: Introduction to William M. Gabb, Talamanca, el espacio y los hombres. *Serie Nos Ven* 7. Ministerio de Cultura, Joventud y Deportes, San José.

Findlow, Frank J., Michael J. Snarskis, and Phyllis Martin

1979   Un análisis de zonas de explotación relacionadas con algunos sitios prehistóricos de la Vertiente Atlántica de Costa Rica. *Vínculos* 5 (2): 53–71. San José.

Flannery, Kent

1972   The Cultural Evolution of Civilizations. *Annual Review of Ecology and Systemics* 3: 399–426. Palo Alto.

Fonseca Zamora, Oscar
    1979   Informe de la primera temporada de reexcavación de Guayabo de Turrialba. *Vínculos* 5 (2): 35–52. San José.

————, and James B. Richardson III
    1978   South American and Mayan Cultural Contacts at the Las Huacas Site, Costa Rica. *Annals of Carnegie Museum* 47 (13): 299–317. Pittsburgh.

————, and Richard Scaglion
    1978   Stylistic Analysis of Stone Pendants from Las Huacas Burial Ground, Northwestern Costa Rica. *Annals of Carnegie Museum* 47 (12): 281–298. Pittsburgh.

Foshag, W. F.
    1957   Mineralogical Studies on Guatemalan Jade. *Smithsonian Miscellaneous Collections* 145 (5). Washington.

Gabb, William M.
    1875   On the Indian Tribes and Languages of Costa Rica. *Proceedings of the American Philosophical Society* 14: 483–602. Philadelphia.

    1978   Talamanca, el espacio y los hombres. (Luis Ferrero, ed.) *Serie Nos Ven* 7. Ministerio de Cultura, Juventud y Deportes, San José.

Gage, Thomas
    1958   Thomas Gage's Travels in the New World. University of Oklahoma Press, Norman.

Gagini, Carlos
    1917   Los aborígenes de Costa Rica. Imprenta Trejos, San José.

Garber, J.
    1980   Patterns of Jade Consumption and Disposal at the Late Preclassic Center of Cerros, Northern Belize. Paper presented at Mesoamerican–Central American Jade Conference, Dumbarton Oaks, Washington.

Golliher, Jeffrey M.
    1977   Casas Comunales Autóctonas en Talamanca, Costa Rica: Análisis etnohistórico. *Vínculos* 2 (2): 145–163. San José.

Graham, Mark
    1979   Symbolic Agriculture: Utilitarian Sources of Elite Art in Guanacaste Province, Costa Rica. Paper presented at 44th Annual Meeting of Society for American Archaeology, Vancouver.

Guerrero M., J. V.
    1980   Problemática de la Investigación en la Arqueología de Rescate. *In* Memoria del Congreso sobre el Mundo Centroamericano de su Tiempo: IV Centenario de Gonzalo Fernández de Oviedo: 129–132. Editorial Texto, San José.

Haberland, Wolfgang
    1955   Preliminary Report on the Aguas Buenas Complex, Costa Rica. *Ethnos* 20 (4): 224–230. Stockholm.

    1959   Archäologische Untersuchungen in Südest–Costa Rica. *Acta Humboldtiana, Series Geographica et Ethnographica* 1. Wiesbaden.

    1960   Península de Osa: Anotaciones Geográficas y Arqueológicas. *Informe Semestral* (enero–junio): 75–86. Instituto Geográfico Nacional, San José.

    1961a   Arqueología del Valle del Río Ceiba, Buenos Aires. *Informe Semestral* (enero–junio): 31–62. Instituto Geográfico Nacional, San José.

    1961b   New Names for Chiriquian Pottery Types. *Panama Archaeologist* 4 (1): 56–60. Balboa.

    1969   Early Phases and their Relationship in Southern Central America. *In* Verhandlungen der XXXVIII Internationalen Amerikanistenkongresses, Stuttgart–München, 1968, 1: 229–242. Kommissionsverlag, Klaus Renner, Munich.

    1973   Stone Sculpture from Southern Central America. *In* The Iconography of Middle American Sculpture: 135–152. The Metropolitan Museum of Art, New York.

    1976   Gran Chiriquí. *Vínculos* 2 (1): 115–121. San José.

    In   The Archaeology of Greater Chiriquí. *In* Advanced Seminar on Central American Archaeology. School of American Research, Santa Fe.
    press

Hammond, Norman A., A. Spinall, S. Feather, J. Hazeldon, T. Gazard, and S. Agrell
    1977   Maya Jade: Source Location and Analysis. *In* Timothy K. Earle and J. E. Ericson, eds., Exchange Analysis Systems in Prehistory: 35–67. Academic Press, New York.

Hartman, Carl V.

1901   Archaeological Researches in Costa Rica. The Royal Ethnographical Museum, Stockholm.

1907a   Archaeological Researches on the Pacific Coast of Costa Rica. *Memoirs of the Carnegie Museum* 3 (1). Pittsburgh.

1907b   The Alligator as a Plastic Decorative Motif in Certain Costa Rican Pottery. *American Anthropologist*, n.s. 9 (2): 307–314. Lancaster.

Healy, P. F.

1974   Archaeological Survey of the Rivas Region, Nicaragua. Unpub. Ph.D. diss., Department of Anthropology, Harvard University, Cambridge.

Helms, Mary W.

1977   Iguanas and Crocodilians in Tropical American Mythology and Iconography with Special Reference to Panama. *Journal of Latin American Lore* 3 (1): 51–132. Los Angeles.

1979   Ancient Panama: Chiefs in Search of Power. University of Texas Press, Austin and London.

Hennessy, A.

1978   The Frontier in Latin American History. Albuquerque.

Herrera, Diego de

1875   Carta a Su Magestad del Licenciado Diego de Herrera, acerca de la Residencia tomada a Rodrigo de Contreras (1545). *In* Colección de Documentos Ineditos …de las Indias 24: 397ff. Madrid.

Herrera y Tordesillas, A. de

1934–   Historia General de los Hechos de los Castellanos en las Islas y Tierra Firma
57   del Mar Oceano. Madrid.

Hoffman, Carl

1976   Carl Hoffman; viajes por Costa Rica. (Carlos Meléndez Chaverri, ed.) *Serie Nos Ven* 6. Ministerio de Cultura, Juventud y Deportes, San José.

Holdridge, Leslie R.

1978   Ecología basada en zonas de vida. Instituto Interamericano de Ciencias Agrícolas, San José.

Holdridge, William

1947   Life Zone Ecology. Centro Científico Tropical, San José.

Holmes, William H.

1888   Ancient Art of the Province of Chiriquí, Colombia. *Sixth Annual Report of the Bureau of American Ethnology to the Secretary of the Smithsonian Institution 1884–85*: 3–187. Washington.

Ichon, Alain

1980   Archéologie du Sud de la Péninsule d'Azuero, Panama. *Études Mésoaméricaines, Série 2* (3). Mission Archéologique et Ethnologique Française au Méxique, Mexico City.

Johnson, Frederick

1948   The Caribbean Lowland Tribes: The Talamance Division. *In* Julian H. Steward, ed., Handbook of South American Indians: 231–251. *Bureau of American Ethnology Bulletin* 143. Smithsonian Institution, Washington.

Joralemon, Peter David

1976   The Olmec Dragon: A Study in Olmec Iconography. *In* Henry B. Nicholson, ed., Origins of Religious Art and Iconography in Preclassic Mesoamerica: 27–71. Los Angeles.

Kennedy, William H.

1968   Archeological Investigation in the Reventazón River Drainage Area, Costa Rica. Unpub. Ph.D. diss., Department of Anthropology, Tulane University, New Orleans.

1976   Prehistory of the Reventazón River Drainage Area, Costa Rica. *Vínculos* 2 (1): 87–100. San José.

Lange, Frederick W.

1971a   Culture History of the Sapoá River Valley, Costa Rica. *Logan Museum of Anthropology Occasional Papers in Anthropology* 4. Beloit.

1971b   Northwestern Costa Rica Pre–Columbian Circum–Caribbean Affiliations. *Folk* 13: 43–64. Copenhagen.

1975   Excavaciones de Salvamiento en un Cementerio del Período Bicromo en Zonas, Guanacaste, Costa Rica. *Vínculos* 1 (2): 92–98. San José.

1976   Bahías y Valles de la Costa de Guanacaste. *Vínculos* 2 (1): 45–66. San José.

1977   Estudios Arqueológicos en el Valle de Nosara, Guanacaste, Costa Rica. *Vínculos* 3 (1): 27–36. San José.

1978   Coastal Settlement in Northwestern Costa Rica. *In* Prehistoric Coastal Adaptations, B. Stark and B. Voorhies, eds.: 101–119. Academic Press, New York.

1979   Shells, Spoons, Maces and Stools: A Look at Social Organization in Pre–Columbian Costa Rica. Paper read at 78th Annual Meeting of American Anthropological Association, Cincinnati.

1980a   The Formative Zoned Bichrome Period in Northwestern Costa Rica (800 B.C.–A.D. 500), based on Excavations at the Vidor Site, Bay of Culebra. *Vínculos* 6 (2). San José.

1980b   La Presencia de Metates Precolombinos en Guanacaste. *In* Memoria del Congreso sobre el Mundo Centroamericano de su Tiempo: IV Centenario de Gonzalo Fernández de Oviedo: 149–156. Editorial Texto, San José.

In press   The Greater Nicoya Subarea. *In* Advanced Seminar on Lower Central American Archaeology. School of American Research, Santa Fe.

————, and Richard M. Accola

1979   Metallurgy in Costa Rica. *Archaeology* 32 (5): 26–33. New York.

————, and K. Scheidenhelm

1972   The Salvage Archaeology of a Zoned Bichrome Cemetery, Costa Rica. *American Antiquity* 37: 240–245. Washington.

Lathrap, Donald

1973   Gifts of the Cayman: Some Thoughts on the Subsistence Basis of Chavin. *In* D. W. Lathrap and Jody Douglas, eds., Variation in Anthropology: 91–107. Illinois Archaeological Survey, Urbana.

Laurencich de Minelli, L., and L. Minelli

1966   Informe preliminar sobre excavaciones alrededor de San Vito de Java. *In* Actas y Memorias del XXXVI Congreso Internacional de Americanistas, Sevilla, 1964, 1: 415–427. Seville.

1973   La Fase *Aguas Buenas* en la Región de San Vito de Java. *In* Atti del XL Congresso Internazionale degli Americanisti, Roma–Genova, 1972: 219–224. Casa Editrice Tilgher, Genoa.

Lee, Thomas A., Jr.

1969   The Artifacts of Chiapa de Corzo, Chiapas, Mexico. *Papers of the New World Archaeological Foundation 26*. Provo.

Lehmann, Walter

1920   Zentral Amerika 1: 178–356. Reimer, Berlin.

Linares, Olga F.

1976   Animals that were bad to eat were good to compete with: An analysis of the Conte style from ancient Panama. *In* P. Young and J. Howe, eds., Ritual and Symbol in Native Central America. *University of Oregon Anthropological Papers* 9: 3–20. Eugene.

1977   Ecology and the Arts in Ancient Panama. *Studies in Pre–Columbian Art and Archaeology* 17. Dumbarton Oaks, Trustees for Harvard University, Washington.

————, Payson D. Sheets, and E. Jane Rosenthal

1975   Prehistoric Agriculture in Tropical Highlands. *Science* 187 (4172): 137–145. Washington.

————, and Anthony J. Ranere, eds.

1980   Adaptive Radiations in Prehistoric Panama. *Peabody Museum Monographs* 5. Harvard University, Cambridge.

Linés Canalias, Jorge Antonio

1938   Sukia, Tsugur e Isogro. *Anales de la Sociedad de Geografía e Historia de Guatemala* 14 (4): 407–431. Guatemala.

1941   Cabezas retrato de los huetares. Imprenta Nacional, San José.

1942   Estatuaria huetar del sacrificio humano. *Revista Mexicana de Estudios Antropológicos* 6: 36–50. Mexico City.

Lockhart, J.

1968   Spanish Peru, 1532–1650: A colonial society. Madison.

Long, Stanley V.

    1966   Archaeology of the Municipio of Etzatlán, Jalisco. Unpub. Ph.D. diss., Department of Anthropology, University of California, Los Angeles.

López de Gómara, Francisco

    1954   La Historia General de las Indias. Barcelona.

López de Velasco, J.

    1894   Geografía e Descripción Universal de las Indias. Madrid.

Lothrop, Samuel K.

    1926   The Pottery of Costa Rica and Nicaragua. 2 vols. *Contributions from the Museum of the American Indian, Heye Foundation* 8. New York.

    1937–   Coclé: An Archaeological Study of Central Panama. 2 vols. *Memoirs of the*
      42   *Peabody Museum of Archaeology and Ethnology, Harvard University* 7, 8. Cambridge.

    1942   The Sigua: Southernmost Aztec Outpost. *Eighth American Scientific Congress Proceedings* 2: 109–116. Washington.

    1950   Archaeology of Southern Veraguas, Panama. *Memoirs of the Peabody Museum of Archaeology and Ethnology, Harvard University* 9 (3). Cambridge.

    1955   Jade and String Sawing in Northeastern Costa Rica. *American Antiquity* 21: 43–51. Salt Lake City.

    1963   Archaeology of the Diquís Delta, Costa Rica. *Papers of the Peabody Museum of Archaeology and Ethnology, Harvard University* 51. Cambridge.

MacCurdy, George G.

    1911   A Study of Chiriquian Antiquities. *Memoirs of the Connecticut Academy of Arts and Sciences* 3. Yale University Press, New Haven.

MacLeod, M. J.

    1973   Spanish Central America, A Socioeconomic History, 1520–1720. Berkeley.

Martír de Anglería, Pedro

    1964–   Décadas del Nuevo Mundo. (Edmundo O'Gorman, ed.) 2 vols. Editorial José
      65   Porrua, Mexico City.

Mason, J. Alden

    1945   Costa Rican Stonework: The Minor C. Keith Collection. *Anthropological Papers of the American Museum of Natural History* 39. New York.

Meggers, Betty J.

    1971   Amazonia: Man and Nature in a Counterfeit Paradise. Aldine Publishing Company, Chicago.

Meyers, P., Lambertus van Zelst and Edward V. Sayre

    1974   Major and Trace Elements in Sasanian Silver. *In* C.W. Beck, ed., Archaeological Chemistry: 22–33. *Advances in Chemistry Series* 138. *American Chemical Society, Washington.*

Mitchell, R. H.

    1961   Recent Discoveries in Northern Panama. *Archaeology* 14: 198–204. New York.

———, and Edward V. Sayre

    1965   New Developments in the Azuero Peninsula, Province of Los Santos. *Panama Archaeologist* 6: 13–26. Balboa.

Moreau, J.–F.

    1980   A Report on the Hunter–Robinson and Sardinal Sites. *Vínculos* 6 (2). San José.

Motolinia (Benavente), Fray Toribio de

    1970   Memoriales e Historia de los Indios de la Nueva España. Madrid.

Norman, V. Garth

    1976   Izapa Sculpture. *Papers of the New Archaeological Foundation* 30 (2). Provo.

Norr, L.

    1979   Stone Burial Mounds and Petroglyphs of the Zoned Bichrome Period. Paper presented at 44th Annual Meeting of Society for American Archaeology, Vancouver.

Norweb, Albert H.

    1964   Ceramic Stratigraphy in Southwestern Nicaragua. *In* Actas y Memorias del XXXV Congreso Internacional de Americanistas, México, 1962, 1: 551–561. Mexico City.

Oviedo y Valdés, Gonzalo Fernándo de

    1945   Historia General y Natural de las Indias, Islas y Tierra Firme del Mar Oceano. Madrid.

1976   Nicaragua en los Cronistas de Indias: Oviedo. Managua.

Parsons, Lee

1978   The Peripheral Coastal Lowlands and the Middle Classic Period. *In* Esther Pasztory, ed., Middle Classic Mesoamerica: A.D. 400–700: 25-34. Columbia University Press, New York.

Pasztory, Esther

1978   Artistic Traditions of the Middle Classic Period. *In* Esther Pasztory, ed., Middle Classic Mesoamerica: A.D. 400-700: 108–142. Columbia University Press, New York.

Paulsen, Allison C.

1977   Patterns in Maritime Trade between South Coastal Ecuador and Western Mesoamerica. *In* Elizabeth P. Benson, ed., The Sea in the Pre–Columbian World: 141–161. Dumbarton Oaks Research Library and Collections, Trustees for Harvard University, Washington.

Peralta, Manuel María de

1883   Costa Rica, Nicaragua y Panamá en el siglo 16. Librería de M. Murillo, Paris.

Pittier, Henri

1883   Nombres geográficos de Costa Rica, I: Talamanca (Primera contribución). *Anales del Instituto Físico–Geográfico de Costa Rica* 6: 93–101. San José.

1898   Die Sprache der Bribri–Indianer in Costa Rica. *Sitzungsberichte der Kaiserliche Akademie der Wissenschaften in Wien, Philologisch–historische Classe* 136 (6): 1–149. Vienna.

1903a   Folklore of the Bribri and Brunca Indians of Costa Rica. *Journal of American Folk–lore* 16 (60): 1–9. Boston.

1903b   Die Tírub: Térribes oder Térrabas, ein im Aussterben begriffener Stamm in Costa Rica. *Zeitschrift für Ethnologie* 35 (5): 702–708. Berlin.

1938   Apuntamientos etnológicos sobre los indios bribri. *Museo Nacional de Costa Rica, Serie etnológica* 1 (1): 11–28. San José.

Pohorilenko, Anatole

1981   The Olmec Style and Costa Rican Archaeology. *In* The Olmec and Their Neighbors, Essays in Memory of Matthew W. Stirling: 309–327. Dumbarton Oaks Research Library and Collections, Trustees for Harvard University, Washington.

Proskouriakoff, Tatiana

1974   Jades from the Cenote of Sacrifice, Chichen Itza, Yucatan. *Memoirs of the Peabody Museum of Archaeology and Ethnology, Harvard University* 10 (1). Cambridge.

Radell, D. R.

1976   The Indian Slave Trade and Population of Nicaragua during the 16th Century. *In* W. M. Denevan, ed., The Native Populations of the Americas in 1492: 67ff. Madison.

Rathje, William J.

1974   The Origin and Developments of Lowland Classic Maya Civilization. *In* Jeremy A. Sabloff and C. C. Lamberg–Karlovsky, eds., The Rise and Fall of Civilizations: 84–94. Cummings Publishing Co., Menlo Park.

Reichel–Dolmatoff, Gerardo

1954a   Investigaciones Arqueológicas en la Sierra Nevada de Santa Marta 1, 2. *Revista Colombiana de Antropología* 2 (2): 145–206. Bogotá.

1954b   Investigaciones Arqueológicas en la Sierra Nevada de Santa Marta 3. *Revista Colombiana de Antropología* 3: 139–170. Bogotá.

Rivas, Francisco

1979   Descubrimiento de Costa Rica. Unpublished *Licenciatura* thesis, Universidad de Costa Rica, San José.

Robicsek, Francis

1975   A Study in Maya Art and History: The Mat Symbol. Museum of the American Indian, Heye Foundation, New York.

Ryder, P.

1980   Informe de las Investigaciones Arqueológicas Preliminares de la Región de Guayabo de Bagaces, Guanacaste. *In* Memoria del Congreso sobre el Mundo Centroamericano de su Tiempo: IV Centenario de Gonzalo Fernández de Oviedo: 157–165. Editorial Texto, San José.

Sanders, William T., and Barbara J. Price
  1968   Mesoamerica: The Evolution of a Civilization. Random House, New York.
Sapper, Karl
  1900   Ein Besuch bei den Chirripe–und Talamanca–Indianer von Costa Rica. *Globus* 82: 1–8; 28–31. Brunswick.
  1902   Mittelamerikanische Reisen und Studien aus den Jahren 1888 bis 1900. Druck und Verlag von Friedrich Viehweg und Sohn, Brunswick.
Sayre, Edward V., and Robert W. Smith
  1974   Analytical Studies of Ancient Egyptian Glass. *In* A. Bishay, ed., Recent Advances in the Science and Technology of Materials: 47-70. New York.
Service, E. R.
  1975   Origins of the State and Civilization. W. W. Norton and Co., New York.
Sharer, Robert J.
  In   Lower Central America as seen from Mesoamerica. *In* Advanced Seminar on
  press   Central American Archaeology. School of American Research, Santa Fe.
Sharer, Robert J., ed.
  1978   The Prehistory of Chalchuapa, El Salvador. 3 vols. University of Pennsylvania Press, Philadelphia.
Sherman, William L.
  1971   Indian Slavery and the Cerrato Reforms. *Hispanic American Historical Review* 51 (1): 25–50. Durham.
  1979   Forced Native Labor in Sixteenth Century Central America. Lincoln.
Skinner, Alanson
  1920   Notes on the Bribri of Costa Rica. *Indian Notes and Monographs* 6 (3): 41–105. Museum of the American Indian, Heye Foundation, New York.
  1926   Notes on Las Mercedes, Costa Rica Farm, and Anita Grande. Appendix IV *in* Samuel K. Lothrop, Pottery of Costa Rica and Nicaragua 2: 451–467. Museum of the American Indian, Heye Foundation, New York.
Smith, M.E., and C.M. Heath-Smith
  In   Waves of Influence in Postclassic Mesoamerica?: A critique of the Mixteca-
  press   Puebla concept. *Anthropology* 4 (2). State University of New York, Stony Brook.
Snarskis, Michael J.
  1975   Excavaciones Estratigráficas en la Vertiente Atlántica de Costa Rica. *Vínculos* 1 (1): 2–17. San José.
  1976a   Stratigraphic Excavations in the Eastern Lowlands of Costa Rica. *American Antiquity* 41: 343–353. Washington.
  1976b   La Vertiente Atlántica de Costa Rica. *Vínculos* 2 (1): 101–114. San José.
  1977   Turrialba (9–FG–T), un Sitio Paleoindio en el Este de Costa Rica. *Vínculos* 3 (1): 13–26. San José.
  1978   The Archeology of the Central Atlantic Watershed of Costa Rica. Unpub. Ph.D. diss., Department of Anthropology, Columbia University, New York.
  1979a   El Jade de Talamanca de Tibás. *Vínculos* 5 (2): 89–107. San José.
  1979b   Turrialba: A Paleoindian Quarry and Workshop Site in Eastern Costa Rica. *American Antiquity* 44 (1): 125–138. Washington.
  In   Central America: The Lower Caribbean. *In* Advanced Seminar on Central
  press   American Archaeology. School of American Research, Santa Fe.
———, and Aida Blanco
  1978   Dato sobre Cerámica Policromada Guanacasteca Excavada en la Meseta Central. *Vínculos* 4 (2): 106–113. San José.
———, and C. E. Herra
  1980   La Cabaña: Arquitectura Mesoamericana en el Bosque Tropical. *In* Memoria del Congreso sobre el Mundo Centroamericano de su Tiempo: IV Centenario de Gonzalo Fernández de Oviedo: 139–147. Editorial Texto, San José.
Stevens, Rayfred L.
  1964   The Soils of Middle America and Their Relation to Indian Peoples and Cultures. *In* Robert Wauchope, ed., Handbook of Middle American Indians 1: 265–315. University of Texas Press, Austin.
Stirling, Matthew W.
  1950   Exploring Ancient Panama by Helicopter. *National Geographic Magazine* 97 (2): 227–246. Washington.